EVIDENCE, CRIME, AND FORENSICS IN THE EARLY MODERN MEDITERRANEAN

Recent historians have pinpointed the ways in which legal systems in early modern Europe were improvisational, flexible, and contingent rather than immovable, hierarchical, and gendered. *Evidence, Crime, and Forensics in the Early Modern Mediterranean* amplifies such findings by looking at law and its consumers in the Mediterranean, broadly imagined, between 1500 and 1750. The volume's essays enhance our awareness of how crimes were defined, evidence was offered, and forensic awareness appeared in secular, inquisitorial, and specially commissioned courts in Spain, Italy, and the Hapsburg Balkans.

This collection threads an important needle: our authors recognize formal chains of command and legal commonplaces but nonetheless emphasize how such factors could be challenged, manipulated, or ignored by illiterate and vulnerable populations. It turns out that ordinary individuals in the early modern Mediterranean did not find themselves limited in their legal options, and their degree of sophistication in court speaks volumes about networks of legal knowledge. Furthermore, in no way does the use of the courts between 1500 and 1750 imply more "rational" ways of seeking justice since emotions were always firmly on display, even if rage and regret were being deployed for performative reasons.

Evidence, Crime, and Forensics in the Early Modern Mediterranean illustrates the range of questions we can put to archival sources from the early modern Mediterranean, with plentiful insights as to how legal sources can illuminate history from below. This collection will be a welcome addition for undergraduate and graduate courses on European history, as well as a provocative resource for more general audiences.

Lu Ann Homza is a professor of history at William & Mary in Williamsburg, VA. Her books include *Religious Authority in the Spanish Renaissance* (2000), *The Spanish Inquisition, 1478–1614: an Anthology of Sources* (2006), *Village Infernos and Witches' Advocates: Witch-Hunting in Navarre, 1608–1614* (2022), and *The Child-Witches of Olague* (2024).

Amanda L. Scott is an associate professor of history and women, gender, and sexuality studies at Penn State University. She has published articles in, among others, *The Journal of Social History*, *Renaissance Quarterly*, *The Sixteenth Century Journal*, and *Church History*. Her previous publications include *The Basque* Seroras*: Local Religion, Gender, and Power in Northern Iberia, 1550–1800* (2020).

EVIDENCE, CRIME, AND FORENSICS IN THE EARLY MODERN MEDITERRANEAN

Edited by Lu Ann Homza and Amanda L. Scott

Routledge
Taylor & Francis Group
LONDON AND NEW YORK

Designed cover image: Murder in the House by Jakub Schikaneder (1890). © Impaint/Alamy Stock Photo 2WN606X.

First published 2026
by Routledge
4 Park Square, Milton Park, Abingdon, Oxon OX14 4RN

and by Routledge
605 Third Avenue, New York, NY 10158

Routledge is an imprint of the Taylor & Francis Group, an informa business

British Library Cataloguing-in-Publication Data
A catalogue record for this book is available from the British Library

ISBN: 978-1-032-78147-1 (hbk)
ISBN: 978-1-032-78146-4 (pbk)
ISBN: 978-1-003-48640-4 (ebk)

DOI: 10.4324/9781003486404

Typeset in Sabon
by Apex CoVantage, LLC

CONTENTS

CONTRIBUTORS

Edward Behrend-Martínez is a professor of history at Appalachian State University. He has published articles in *Gender and History* and *European Review of History/Revue européenne d'histoire* and has contributed multiple chapters to edited volumes. He published *Unfit for Marriage: Impotent Spouses on Trial in the Basque Region of Spain, 1650–1750* in 2007.

Bradford A. Bouley is an associate professor of history at the University of California, Santa Barbara. His articles have appeared in *Osiris*, *Sixteenth Century Journal*, *Rivista di Storia del Cristianesimo*, and *The Catholic Historical Review*. He published *Pious Postmortems: Anatomy and the Creation of Early Modern Saints* in 2017.

Jodi Campbell is a professor *emerita* of history at Texas Christian University. She has contributed multiple essays to edited volumes and has had an article appear in *Cuadernos Hispanoamericanos*. She co-edited *Women in Port: Gendering Communities, Economies, and Social Networks in Atlantic Port Cities, 1500–1800* in 2012. She published *Monarchy, Political Culture, and Drama in Seventeenth-Century Madrid: Theater of Negotiation* in 2006 and *At the First Table: Food and Social Identity in Early Modern Spain* in 2017.

Francesco Paolo de Ceglia is a professor of the history of science at the University of Bari in Italy. He has published or edited six books, among them *The Body of Evidence: Corpses and Proofs in Early Modern European Medicine* (2020), *Vampyr: Storia naturale della resurrezione* (2023), and *The Natural History of a Neapolitan Miracle: The Secret of San Gennaro's Blood* (2024).

John Christopoulos is an associate professor of history at the University of British Columbia. He has published articles in *Renaissance Quarterly* and *I Tatti Studies in the Italian Renaissance* and has co-authored another piece in *Past & Present*. He published *Abortion in Early Modern Italy* in 2021 and co-edited *Making Stories in Early Modern Italy and Beyond: Essays in Honour of Elizabeth S. Cohen and Thomas V. Cohen* in 2024.

Lu Ann Homza is a professor of history at William & Mary in Williamsburg, VA. She has published articles in *The Catholic Historical Review*, *The Journal of Modern History*, *Archiv für Reformationsgeschichte*, and *Renaissance Quarterly* and has contributed multiple chapters to edited volumes. Her books include *Religious Authority in the Spanish Renaissance* (2000), *The Spanish Inquisition, 1478–1614: An Anthology of Sources* (2006), *Village Infernos and Witches' Advocates: Witch-Hunting in Navarre, 1608–1614* (2022), and *The Child-Witches of Olague* (2024).

Vincenzo Lavenia is a professor of history at the University of Bologna, Italy. He is a co-editor of *Dizionario storico dell'Inquisizione* (4 vols., 2010), *Fruits of Migration: Heterodox Italian Migrants and Central European Culture, 1550–1620* (2018), and *Sacre metamorfosi: Roma e I racconti di conversone di infedel e pagani (secoli XVI–XVIII)* (2022). He published *L'infamia e il perdono: Tributi, pene e confessione nella teologia morale della prima età moderna* in 2004 and *Dio in uniforme: Cappellani, catechesi cattolica e soldati in età moderna* in 2017.

Blanca Llanes Parra has been a postdoctoral researcher at the University of Cantabria and the University of Valencia in Spain. She has recently been awarded a Marie Skłodowska-Curie Global Fellowship to carry out a three-year project (GENVIOMADRID) at Harvard University and the University of Cantabria. She has published articles in *Clio & Crimen: Revista del Centro de Historia de Crimen en Durango* and *Urban History* and has contributed multiple essays to edited volumes.

Celeste I. McNamara is a tenured assistant professor of history at Dublin City University in Ireland. She has published articles in *The Journal of Modern History*, *The History of the Family*, *Church History*, *Historični Seminar*, *The Catholic Historical Review*, and *Archiv für Reformationsgeschichte*. She has contributed multiple essays to edited volumes. She published *The Bishop's Burden: Reforming the Catholic Church in Early Modern Italy* in 2020.

Colin Rose is an associate professor of history at Brock University in Canada. He has published articles in *Urban History*, *Renaissance Quarterly*, *The Sixteenth Century Journal*, *Documenta*, and *Crime, History, Societies/Crime,*

Histoires, Sociétés. He has contributed multiple essays to edited volumes. He co-edited *Mapping Space, Sense, and Movement in Florence: Historical GIS and the Early Modern City* in 2016 and published *A Renaissance of Violence: Homicide in Early Modern Italy* in 2019.

Amanda L. Scott is an associate professor of history and women, gender, and sexuality studies at The Pennsylvania State University. She has published articles in *The Journal of Social History*, *The Journal of Jesuit Studies*, *Renaissance Quarterly*, *The Sixteenth Century Journal*, *The Bulletin of Spanish and Portuguese Historical Studies*, and *Church History*. She published *The Basque* Seroras*: Local Religion, Gender, and Power in Northern Iberia, 1550–1800* in 2020.

Gretchen D. Starr-LeBeau is the Jeanne and George Todd Professor of Religious Studies at Principia College in Illinois. She has contributed multiple essays to edited volumes. She is the co-editor of *Judging Faith, Punishing Sin: Inquisitions and Consistories in the Early Modern World* (2017). She published *In the Shadow of the Virgin: Inquisitors, Friars, and Conversos in Guadalupe, Spain* in 2003, and *Seven Myths of the Spanish Inquisition* in 2023.

Andrew Vidali is an assistant professor at the University of Pisa. He has published articles in *Acta Histriae*, *Journal of Early Modern History*, and *Le Carte e la Storia* and has contributed multiple essays to edited volumes. He published *Giustizia e violenza delle élites in una repubblica aristocratica: Politica del diritto, tribunali e patriziato nel Cinquecento veneziano* in 2024.

INTRODUCTION

Evidence, Crime, and Forensics in the Early Modern Mediterranean

The aim of this comparative volume is at once direct and intricate. We plan to illustrate the variety of questions that historians can put to the criminal justice systems of the Catholic Mediterranean, imagined as a flexible space, between 1500 and 1750. We intend to demonstrate how inclusive and flexible legal proceedings could be in terms of expertise and evidence, as well as contingent in terms of verdicts and punishments. We wish to highlight how specific historical settings affected the processes of criminal justice, from charges to depositions and arrests to convictions. Law courts can look like immovable structures, but they were not. Prosecutions can appear to tilt power and authority toward male elites, but they did not always or inevitably do so. On the surface, criminal courts might be expected to grant no ground whatsoever to the illiterate or disabled, but that conclusion could be mistaken. Given their particular queries and contexts, it is not surprising that our authors are not in agreement as to who benefitted from what, when, in the deployment of criminal justice in the early modern Mediterranean. But the variety of their conclusions confirms the dynamism of the field while also demonstrating how much more there is to investigate.

In many ways, we have been inspired by previous research. Historians before us posed large questions as to whether law courts should be thought of as a structure or a culture, or both.[1] They pondered the relationships and potential gaps between legal theory and legal practice. They wondered if court systems could increase the authority of monarchs; they asked whether a rise in the use of that system implied a growth in rationality on the part of the populace.

Recent answers to these queries have been nuanced. What we currently know is that law courts may have contained formal chains of command,

DOI: 10.4324/9781003486404-1

layers of hierarchy, and rhetorical commonplaces, but all three could be challenged, manipulated, or ignored.[2] Sometimes, published treatises on legal processes, decision-making, and forensic investigations had profound effects on the ways in which trials were conducted and decisions were reached, yet in other instances, legal personnel improvised or were operated upon by others.[3] At the same time, formal court systems in the early modern Mediterranean existed alongside communal, local modes of restorative and retributive justice, which is why, for example, disputes in early modern Spain and Italy could be settled via public apologies, notarized peace contracts, or communal outrage as well as lawsuits.[4] Nevertheless, in this volume, we emphasize that ordinary individuals in the early modern Mediterranean did not find themselves excluded from formal court proceedings or limited in their legal options: despite widespread illiteracy, they very often launched lawsuits or criminal complaints and won.[5] At the same time, only rarely would historians presently argue for a teleological interpretation of law courts as signs of increasing reason.[6] Emotions behind the use of the law seem all too obvious, even when the rage, fear, or sorrow on display had performative contexts or were being deployed at least in part out of cultural expectations about gender, profession, or socioeconomic status.[7]

Then too, there is the question of whether we should imagine early modern courts as tools that benefitted the "state" by expanding the powers of centralized authorities and their experts.[8] Some of the essays in this volume will agree; some will disagree; still others will emphasize that the people who were turning to the law for solutions did not care if they were amplifying the weight of the state by default. This particular query then raises one more conundrum, which is whether people who went to court can tell us anything about themselves, as well as larger environments and values. Should we think of people who filed lawsuits and complaints as agential? Can we recover their voices, or were their expressions of their worries and priorities confined to and smothered by legal formulas? We know that surviving court records should not be construed as "ego documents," not least because of the mediation that always occurred when oral testimony was written down.[9] Notions of honor, community loyalties, anxieties over family welfare and money, hunger, being jailed, and torture: such circumstances could materially affect what plaintiffs, defendants, or witnesses said in court under oath.

Still, many of us remain optimistic about the insights that court records can relay about early modern people who tried to deploy the law to their advantage, as well as the larger culture their legal maneuvers revealed. As readers will see, our confidence here rests upon the extraordinary character of the surviving legal records for early modern Spain and Italy. We have been amazed to see not only the extent to which men and women participated in the court systems in the early modern Mediterranean but also their degree of sophistication as they made their cases or testified. They knew how to complain and to whom; sometimes, they pooled their financial resources in quests for redress. They understood degrees of culpability as well as what details to offer if they sought conviction or exculpation.

Equally startling is the fact that legal awareness was not confined to a male, elite, and literate echelon. Basque-speaking children understood the importance of eyewitnessing; illiterate Italian women knew how to invoke cause and effect. Everyone realized that signs on bodies as well as the settings of crimes could heighten or diminish legal proof. As to how this kind of consciousness came about, no one was sworn to secrecy in criminal courts: deponents were free to say to others what they had reported while under oath. Some scholars recently have highlighted how the circulation of oral, non-written legal knowledge could take place in urban settings.[10] Essays in this volume demonstrate that such communication networks also spanned rural, village environments.

That being said, we and our contributors would be hesitant to argue that ordinary individuals and legal experts "co-created" the legal systems at work in Spain and Italy between 1500 and 1750.[11] What we can note instead is that the scope of crimes—how they were defined, what they entailed, and how they might be proven—entailed a set of commonly-held suppositions in the early modern Mediterranean, albeit one that was subject to interpretation, contestation, and change.

Of course, we and our contributors are guided by the nature of our sources: in contrast to Northern Europe and the British Isles, the Southern European and Mediterranean legal sphere shared certain commonalities in law, criminal procedure, and, importantly, the role of witnesses, notaries, and observation throughout investigation and trial. Above all, Mediterranean courts were prodigious record keepers throughout all stages of legal proceedings: scholars working in criminal archives in Spain, Italy, and Portugal have an abundance of sources to draw upon, allowing them to interpret those sources in creative and compelling ways. The sheer numbers of criminal complaints and investigations in Italian cities, for instance, allow for deep quantitative studies, and more recently, vibrant digital projects using methods like Geographic Information Systems.[12] Scholars working in Spain have also fruitfully applied computational methods at the regional, tribunal, and chancery levels, though certain entire collections of records were lost during the Napoleonic Wars. Thus, their accuracy rests more upon large sampling rather than comprehensive counting.[13]

Though much variation existed across local and regional court systems, particularly regarding what sections of criminal trials were saved following the conclusion of the case, courts in Spain and Italy also relied heavily on depositions via notaries, allowing us to "hear" the voices of not just victims and defendants but also a range of other people involved in the conflict. Character witnesses played a crucial role in these cases, and what communities thought about both victims and defendants was considered critical evidence. Hearsay also played an important role, providing us with tantalizing glimpses into the aural networks of early modern neighborhoods.[14] Expert witnesses like medics, surgeons, and occasionally architects and engineers provided critical information to early modern people on how to "read" the physical remains of a crime. Notaries, in particular, documented fundamental observations about the state of crime scenes, bodies, and objects at the time that criminal justice personnel arrived on site; in interviewing and deposing multiple witnesses, notaries were also critical players in constructing and normalizing reasonable timelines for crimes. Courts in Spain and Italy not only relied upon notaries for a wide variety of tasks regarding witnesses and evidence, but they also actively solicited their opinions and expertise.

More prosaically, we also see commonalities in our contributors' approaches to how they take seriously the voices recorded in early modern criminal trials. Each essay, in its own way, argues for a kind of victim justice while also empathizing with the circumstances and plight of the perpetrators; then, like today, crime was not clear-cut, and many "criminals" were victims themselves.[15] Equally importantly, each author views their criminal material as a window into the past, an otherwise missing echo of past desires, burdens, miseries, motivations, and lives.

As scholars of microhistory have reminded us in a variety of contexts, criminal and inquisitorial depositions are to historians what field interviews are to anthropologists: in the words of Carlo Ginzburg, "the elusive evidence that inquisitors were trying to elicit from defendants was not so different, after all, from our own objectives." Trials and investigations ultimately were dialogues among authorities and witnesses, and we are lucky to be able to listen in.[16] The criminal trials that we and our contributors confront in this volume are ultimately exercises in the search for proof and for truth. The questions authorities asked defendants and witnesses, the processes they undertook to capture and preserve physical evidence, and the autopsies and examinations they constructed were not futile motions: they were intended to provide answers to problems at the time. Yet in going through these motions, early modern authorities and witnesses recorded information that is equally useful to us.

The dialogic nature of these documents—and the reminder that they were produced in a context that had no notion that we would later be reading them and mining them in our own ways—is all the more important to keep in mind considering that many of our contributors are dealing with documents that lack final conclusions. It can be too easy to draw and then impose our own conclusions on these cases, especially in instances in which physical evidence and witness testimony are abundant and well-preserved.[17] Thus, these cases are a sharp reminder that we must be careful to silo our own notions about evidence and proof from those of the people of the past. The development of criminal procedure and forensic technologies was an ongoing process, one we are fortunate to be able to glimpse, even from a distance.

Of course, not all our contributors use criminal trials in the same way; some of our authors are more interested in the theory and erudition behind evidence collection and production, while others are more interested in how ordinary people became trapped in or even collaborated with the growing webs of complex forensic thinking. Yet on the whole, even when our contributors come to different conclusions about the importance of certain kinds of evidence or the role of certain kinds of experts, we see a common call to approach these cases with empathy. The events that they record mattered to the people of the past, and as much as we can mine these documents for information about forensic practice and criminal procedure, we must always remind ourselves that they speak of gruesome and cataclysmic events that disrupted people's lives, often leaving them broken and traumatized.

Divided into four parts, this volume addresses approaches to and applications of evidence within the context of crimes and the ways in which legal experts, court personnel, and ordinary people engaged in conversations about proof and cause. Collectively, but each arriving in their own way, all our authors come to the conclusion that the presentation of evidence, and particularly the collection of physical evidence, was highly contextual: communities were insistent that they be allowed to provide information about the circumstances of the crime, including the backgrounds and social histories of the people involved. For the most part, courts accommodated them. Placed together, our contributors argue in unison that the development of forensic technologies, socio-legal medicine, and the admission of evidence in legal settings was a collective project that involved many interested parties, was subject to contestation, and was anything but top-down.

Part I, *Legal and Intellectual Foundations*, examines the ways in which inquisition theory and practice, along with the burgeoning field of forensic medicine, established the categories and hierarchies of evidence that were supposed to imply that truth had been reached. Significantly, the watchword for the three chapters in Part I is ambiguity. As Gretchen D. Starr-LeBeau points out, the Spanish Inquisition in the early modern period existed in a profoundly oral as well as written culture, but its judges and officials paid attention to physical signs—facial expressions, noises, gestures—as well as the bodies of defendants. For both sorts of evidence, whether verbal or corporal, Spanish inquisitors inevitably had to engage in interpretation and act on their discretion. Spoken words and physical signs might seem to promise certainty in a legal setting, but they did not.

Vincenzo Lavenia dives equally into questions of uncertainty and evidence in his essay on the Roman Inquisition, also known as the Holy Office or the Congregation for the Doctrine of the Faith. Lavenia focuses on three categories of potential crime that Roman inquisitors found especially difficult in terms of proof: false sanctity, harmful magic and witchcraft, and sexual abuse by confessors against their penitents. In each, the Holy Office preferred to exercise a sort of spiritual discernment to ascertain the truth rather than relying upon physical evidence offered and interpreted by doctors. That emphasis came from its pastoral mission, which prompted its leadership to discount so-called physical signs of witchcraft and to accept the depositions of unique, female witnesses in clerical solicitation cases. The Roman Inquisition favored a paternalistic, pastoral approach to justice that relied on discretion.

The last essay in Part I is Bradford A. Bouley's treatment of forensic medical evidence, and here too, the topic is replete with nuance. As late as the fifteenth century, medical professionals were not at all sure that dead bodies could be read for causes of death; by the seventeenth century, forensic evidence had achieved so much credibility that physicians fused empirical investigations—autopsies—with textual evidence as they investigated crimes and reported results. Clear medical practices and guidelines came into focus via influential published texts, such as Paolo Zacchia's *Quaestiones medico-legales*. Still, medical investigations into violent murder and poisoning remained problematic and were recognized by everyone as liable to error. Physical evidence could be equivocal; often, the behavior of the deceased and their social relationships had to enter into the analysis. Nevertheless, judges and doctors insisted that medical testimony was useful, a finding that raises important contrasts with the Spanish and Roman Inquisitions' more erratic and guarded approach.

Part II, *Urban Violence*, turns to violent crime in urban contexts, with essays on homicide in Bologna, murder in Madrid, and vendettas in Venice. These essays address large questions about the ways in which courts, court officials, and bystanders intersected, often most willingly, in the pursuit of justice. For example, Colin Rose seeks to understand how, after 1509, newly papally controlled Bologna established respect for a centralized, institutional court, the *Tribunale del Torrone*, after eons of law only being administered by podestas and feudal tribunals. The secret to developing widespread admiration for the *Tribunale*'s legal processes lay in its enlistment of experts and "good men" [*buon uomini*] as assistants. Rose notes that this wider range of legal participants not only augmented the authority of the *Tribunale* but also deflected responsibility for its verdicts and decisions by placing the responsibility on members of the wider community. Here, expert medical testimony was again essential, but so were notarial recordings of events and statements, as well as character validations by victims' relatives.

Blanca Llanes Parra then turns to Madrid to ask how medical and forensic practices intersected with the highest criminal court there, the *Sala de Alcaldes de Casa y Corte*, when it came to spousal murder. Early modern Spaniards certainly were participating in the legal and scientific advances sweeping Europe, with Spanish royal surgeon and physician Juan Fragoso publishing his "Universal Surgery" [*Cirugía Universal*] in 1581, decades before volumes appeared by Paolo Zacchia. Combining judges' and prosecutors' memorials about their legal principles, along with evidence from actual cases, Llanes Parra illustrates the ways in which legal experts pursued forensic investigations, invoked medical opinions, and evaluated the moral character of husbands and wives. Her findings also confirm the intersection of law, medicine, and Catholicism.

Our last essay in Part II is Andrew Vidali's exploration of feuding, social status, and legal outcomes in sixteenth-century Venice. Paying special attention to peace agreements and requests for pardons, Vidali highlights the ways in which religious and political rhetoric and concepts were invoked by all sides, namely, defendants, plaintiffs, and the Council of Ten, which oversaw the investigations and prosecutions. Sometimes, the Council demanded proof that peace arrangements had been achieved before it would agree to a lesser penalty. In other instances, Venetian noble families proffered one narrative after another to explain away violence, which contained different details, often gendered, about the emotional states of the perpetrators. Making peace in early modern Venice was a highly complex phenomenon.

We and our contributors are careful to not necessarily portray violent crimes as categorically masculine nor to fall into traps that stereotype certain domestic crimes as female, so we follow this section with a third grouping of essays on gendered crimes. The essays in Part III investigate uxoricide (wife murder) in Spain, infanticide in Spain, and miscarriage by assault in Italy, though each is careful to place these topics into a broader European conversation. In Edward Behrend-Martínez's essay on uxoricide, we are confronted by the uncomfortable fact that spousal murders were not uncommon. To make sense of these killings, witnesses and courts paid close attention to forensic evidence regarding the scene of the crime, as well as contextual evidence about unhappy marriages and abuse. They deployed tropes with which they were already familiar, such as the cuckold, the adulteress, and the abusive or drunk husband. Yet these definitions were flexible: from the outset, prosecutors and other interested parties came to conclusions about culpability—including whether the wife "deserved" what she got—which helped shape pre-modern definitions of abuse. Questions over the morality and rationality of women's actions are picked up again by Jodi Campbell through a single case study in the small village of Loeches outside of Madrid. Here, Campbell evokes the pain and suffering by a wife and mother, whose depressive episodes led her to murder one of her own children. In this case, the mother was clearly guilty, but as Campbell explains, madness and infanticide lacked clear definitions in early modern Spanish law, meaning how exactly to handle her case remained unclear. Placing this episode in context with infanticide in the British Isles and Germany, Campbell makes the case that Spanish authorities were given wide discretion in handling and sentencing such crimes. In this case, they treated the mother as a person, paying close attention to the contextual evidence about her mental state that her neighbors provided. John Christopoulos continues with these themes of female culpability and the trauma of child loss with a sensitive treatment of several cases of miscarriage by assault in Rome and how, in this context, women's bodies themselves became objects of evidence in the pursuit of justice. Christopoulos considers how ordinary people (particularly midwives) contributed to medico-legal arguments relating to child loss, but almost more importantly, he uses these cases to shed light on the traumatic violence lower-class women experienced during the early modern period. As he argues, through the application of experience and expertise, many of these ordinary women contributed unwittingly to the development of forensic medicine and criminal justice.

Finally, Part IV riffs off the titles of some popular crime shows with four essays on "Special Victims." Of all the sections, readers may find this portion of the volume not only the most surprising but also the most triggering; readers should be prepared for content dealing directly with sexual assault as well as horrific violence inflicted upon children. Lu Ann Homza headlines this section with an essay on violent crimes and assaults against children in sixteenth- and seventeenth-century Navarre. As Homza shows, child victims appeared prominently in the legal record, and the kinds of evidence—on their physical bodies as well as through the testimony they could uniquely provide—formed a critical part of Navarrese forensic investigations. Communities were deeply invested in protecting local children, yet this also involved limits: cultural norms discouraged neighbors from involving themselves in the discipline and raising of other people's children. Still, when children were the victims of crimes, neighbors were well-equipped to provide contextualizing evidence and to read crime scenes for information on what had happened in order to communicate these things to authorities and seek resolution in these tragic events.

Celeste I. McNamara then brings us to eighteenth-century Italy, where she introduces us to another group of special victims whose crimes were likely underreported and often ignored by community members who, like today, were prone to disbelieve victims. Here, McNamara introduces us to a troubling database of sexual assaults and sex crimes in Venice. Surprisingly, despite the limited number of cases that actually made it before a tribunal, McNamara finds that justices were sympathetic to victims. Courts relied upon accounts from the victim, accounts from neighbors and friends, and physical evidence from women's and girls' bodies to determine if crimes had been committed. McNamara focuses on this last type of physical evidence to illustrate the difficulties regarding prosecution of sex crimes and to help explain why the criminal sentencing for heinous crimes like the rape of children was punished similarly to the (perceived) less serious crime of seduction of adult women.

With Amanda L. Scott's essay, we return to Northern Iberia, to a different kind of special victim, namely, disabled victims of violent crimes who could not testify about their experiences through standard legal procedures. Focusing primarily on the blind, but including disabled perpetrators as well, Scott argues that Navarrese courts were remarkably flexible in admitting non-standard evidence, particularly in cases in which blind victims were *told* about what had happened to them. As Scott shows, certain kinds of disability tended to surface more easily in the court records, but even still, court personnel were remarkably well-equipped at soliciting, weighing, and challenging evidence from people involved in crimes who also had disabilities. Framed in the context of disability studies, these cases emphasize how our modern understanding of ability/disability goes only so far to understand how premodern people constructed and navigated disability in a legal setting.

To conclude this section, Francesco Paolo de Ceglia leaves us questioning the fictionalization and reality of crime through a study on vampirism, medicine, and the law in the Balkans. What can we make of early modern peasant accusations that corpses were rising from cemeteries to prey upon the living and to infect other dead, especially when medical practitioners confirmed through autopsy that these things were indeed occurring? Through a close reading of events in Habsburg-controlled Serbia in the 1730s and 1740–50s, Ceglia argues that professional forensics created a feedback loop of information and confirmation, leading to a situation in which belief, superstition, science, and evidence worked together to support one another.

Although it is somewhat outside the geographic scope of our other contributors, Ceglia's chapter provides a powerful conclusion for this volume. Whose version of events matters more? Those of the illiterate lower classes or those of elite practitioners of the law and medicine? And how do we reconcile our modern beliefs about proof, evidence, and forensics with those of our early modern forebears? Ultimately, as Ceglia and the rest of our contributors argue, we must take our informants of the past seriously. We must trust what they tell us, however unlikely or contradictory it may seem. As victims and perpetrators, it was they who experienced crime, just as it was they who created the records. Early modern jurists, notaries, doctors, and witnesses helped interpret the physical nature of these crimes, thus communicating their collective experiences to us as readers and scholars hundreds of years later. Still, they did so for themselves and within their own legal and cultural contexts. Decisively, this is their world, and we can only observe the pieces of evidence they chose to leave us.

The material that informs the essays in this volume has intersected across various conferences and panels over the last few years. Several of us first came together to think about forensics and crime at the 2022 Renaissance Society of America meeting, which met that year in Dublin. Later, several of us reconvened with other material at the 2023 Toronto Worlds of Conflict conference. Finally, many of the contributors to this volume again reunited at the 2024 Sixteenth Century Society meeting in Toronto across several panels. We are grateful that we have had such consistent interest in this topic and would like to thank our engaged audiences and the many people who commented upon our work over these years. Finally, we also are indebted to our editors at Routledge and to the anonymous reviewers who helped guide the initial proposal for this volume.

Notes

1 For important comments on studying the law as an institution concerned with order vs. approaching the law as processual, see Simon Roberts, "The Study of Dispute: Anthropological Perspectives," in *Disputes and Settlements: Law and Human Relations in the West*, ed. John Bossy (The Past & Present Society, 1983), 1–24. For an overview of the "rule-centered" vs. "processual" paradigms, see Peter Just, "History, Power, Ideology, and Culture: Current Directions in the Anthropology of Law," *Law and Society Review* 66 (1992): 373–412.

2 Nevertheless, we cannot understand surviving court records without appreciating the legal norms and tropes that were supposed to govern their production and content. For an eloquent and still useful corrective on this point, see Thomas Kuehn, "Reading Microhistory: The Example of Giovanni and Lusanna," *The Journal of Modern History* 61 (1989): 512–34.

3 See the essays in this volume by Gretchen D. Starr-LeBeau, Bradford A. Bouley, Blanca Llanes Parra, and Francesco Paolo de Ceglia in particular. For legal improvisation with terrible consequences, see Lu Ann Homza, *Village Infernos and Witches' Advocates: Witch Hunting in Navarre, 1608–1614* (Penn State University Press, 2022), 162–72, 178–80.

4 See the essays in this volume by Colin Rose, Andrew Vidali, and Jodi Campbell, as well as Stephen Cummins, "Forgiving Crimes in Early Modern Naples," in *Cultures of Conflict Resolution in Early Modern Europe*, eds. Stephen Cummins and Laura Kounine (Ashgate, 2016), 255–79; Homza, *Village Infernos and Witches' Advocates*, 142–45; and Shona Kelly Wray, "Instruments of Concord: Making Peace and Settling Disputes through a Notary in the City and *Contado* of Late Medieval Bologna," *Journal of Social History* 42 (2009): 733–68.

5 Early modern criminal justice also could be affected by principles of Christian charity. See Scott Taylor, *Honor and Violence in Golden-Age Spain* (Yale University Press, 2007).

6 Bianca Premo, *The Enlightenment on Trial: Ordinary Litigants and Colonialism in the Spanish Empire* (Oxford University Press, 2017), makes an explicit connection between the use of the law courts in Spanish America in the eighteenth century and the concept of Enlightenment as incipient modernity. Her objective is inclusion rather than teleology.

7 Daniel Lord Smail, *The Consumption of Justice: Emotions, Publicity, and Legal Culture in Marseilles, 1264–1423* (Cornell University Press, 2003); Julie Stone Peters, *Law as Performance: Theatricality, Spectatorship, and the Making of Law in Ancient, Medieval, and Early Modern Europe* (Oxford University Press, 2022).

8 We will put aside for the moment the fact that Spain and Italy were not nation-states in the sixteenth and seventeenth centuries. For an argument that an increase in state power was an accidental effect of the court system, see Smail, *Consumption of Justice*, 16–17; for a more critical outlook, see Michelle McKinley, "Fractional Freedoms: Slavery, Legal Activism, and Ecclesiastical Courts in Colonial Lima, 1593–1689," *Law and History Review* 28 (2010): 758. Chloe L. Ireton, "Black

Africans' Freedom Litigation Suits to Define Just War and Just Slavery in the Early Spanish Empire," *Renaissance Quarterly* 73 (2020), notes that even successful slave litigants might not actually achieve freedom or escape the violence of their owners: 1308–11.

9 For an adamant rejection of a link between trial documents and the voices of defendants due to torture, Rita Voltmer, "The Witch in the Courtroom: Torture and the Representations of Emotions," in *Emotions in the History of Witchcraft*, eds. Laura Kounine and Michael Ostling (Palgrave Macmillan, 2016), 97–116.

10 Ireton, "Black Africans' Freedom Litigation Suits."

11 The notion of a co-created legal system is much easier to see and assert when inhabitants of the Spanish empire filed petitions with Spanish governing councils and then saw royal decrees and laws created or changed according to the petitions' requests, suggestions, and demands. This is an energetic research field. See Nancy E. van Deusen, *Global Indios: The Indigenous Struggle for Justice in Sixteenth-Century Spain* (Duke University Press, 2015); José Carlos de la Puente Luna, *Andean Cosmopolitans: Seeking Justice and Reward at the Spanish Royal Court* (University of Texas Press, 2018); Adrian Masters, *We, the King: Creating Royal Legislation in the Sixteenth-Century Spanish New World* (Cambridge University Press, 2023).

12 See in particular the work of the Decima Project at https://decima-map.net/. Amanda Madden also reviews a number of new initiatives in mapping, transcription crowdsourcing, and other digital projects in "Introduction: Renaissance Italy and the Digital Humanities," *Early Modern Digital Review* 5, (2022). https://doi.org/10.33137/rr.v45i2.39765.

13 Much of the Spanish work is older, but it sheds important insights into the scope and limitation of the Inquisition. See, among others, Jaime Contreras and Gustav Henningsen, "Forty-Four Thousand Cases of the Spanish Inquisition (1540–1700): An Analysis of a Historical Data Bank," in *The Inquisition in Early Modern Europe: Studies on Sources and Methods*, eds. Gustav Henningsen, John Tedeschi, and Charles Amiel (Northern Illinois University Press, 1986).

14 In particular, see the essays in this volume by Colin Rose, Andrew Vidali, John Christopoulos, and Amanda L. Scott.

15 See Jodi Campbell's essay in this volume.

16 Carlo Ginzburg, "The Inquisitor as Anthropologist," in *Clues, Myths, and the Historical Method*, trans. John Tedeschi and Anne C. Tedeschi (The Johns Hopkins University Press, 1986), 158.

17 Carlo Ginzburg also warns against "ventriloquizing" through our subjects. "A Reflection on the Historian's Craft, Today," in *Our Words and Theirs*, ed. Giovanni Tarantino (Cromohs, 2013), 109.

Select Bibliography

Contreras, Jaime, and Gustav Henningsen. "Forty-Four Thousand Cases of the Spanish Inquisition (1540–1700): An Analysis of a Historical Data Bank." In *The Inquisition in Early Modern Europe: Studies on Sources and Methods*, edited by Gustav Henningsen, John Tedeschi, and Charles Amiel. Northern Illinois University Press, 1986.

Cummins, Stephen. "Forgiving Crimes in Early Modern Naples." In *Cultures of Conflict Resolution in Early Modern Europe*, edited by Stephen Cummins and Laura Kounine. Ashgate, 2016.

Ginzburg, Carlo. "The Inquisitor as Anthropologist." In *Clues, Myths, and the Historical Method*, translated by John Tedeschi and Anne C. Tedeschi. The Johns Hopkins University Press, 1989.

Ginzburg, Carlo. "A Reflection on the Historian's Craft, Today." In *Our Words and Theirs*, edited by Giovanni Tarantino. Cromohs, 2013.

Homza, Lu Ann. *Village Infernos and Witches' Advocates: Witch Hunting in Navarre, 1608–1614*. Penn State University Press, 2022.
Ireton, Chloe L. "Black Africans' Freedom Litigation Suits to Define Just War and Just Slavery in the Early Spanish Empire." *Renaissance Quarterly* 73 (2020): 1277–319.
Just, Peter. "History, Power, Ideology, and Culture: Current Directions in the Anthropology of Law." *Law and Society Review* 66 (1992): 373–412.
Kuehn, Thomas. "Reading Microhistory: The Example of Giovanni and Lusanna." *The Journal of Modern History* 61 (1989): 512–34.
Madden, Amanda. "Introduction: Renaissance Italy and the Digital Humanities." *Early Modern Digital Review* 5 (2022). https://doi.org/10.33137/rr.v45i2.39765.
Masters, Adrian. *We, the King: Creating Royal Legislation in the Sixteenth-Century Spanish New World*. Cambridge University Press, 2023.
McKinley, Michelle. "Fractional Freedoms: Slavery, Legal Activism, and Ecclesiastical Courts in Colonial Lima, 1593–1689." *Law and History Review* 28 (2010): 749–90.
Peters, Julie Stone. *Law as Performance: Theatricality, Spectatorship, and the Making of Law in Ancient, Medieval, and Early Modern Europe*. Oxford University Press, 2022.
Premo, Bianca. *The Enlightenment on Trial: Ordinary Litigants and Colonialism in the Spanish Empire*. Oxford University Press, 2017.
Puente Luna, Jose Carlos de la. *Andean Cosmopolitans: Seeking Justice and Reward at the Spanish Royal Court*. University of Texas Press, 2018.
Roberts, Simon. "The Study of Dispute: Anthropological Perspectives." In *Disputes and Settlements: Law and Human Relations in the West*, edited by John Bossy. The Past & Present Society, 1983.
Smail, Daniel Lord. *The Consumption of Justice: Emotions, Publicity, and Legal Culture in Marseilles, 1264–1423*. Cornell University Press, 2003.
Taylor, Scott. *Honor and Violence in Golden-Age Spain*. Yale University Press, 2007.
van Deusen, Nancy E. *Global Indios: The Indigenous Struggle for Justice in Sixteenth-Century Spain*. Duke University Press, 2015.
Voltmer, Rita. "The Witch in the Courtroom: Torture and the Representations of Emotions." In *Emotions in the History of Witchcraft*, edited by Laura Kounine and Michael Ostling. Palgrave Macmillan, 2016.
Wray, Shona Kelly. "Instruments of Concord: Making Peace and Settling Disputes through a Notary in the City and *Contado* of Late Medieval Bologna." *Journal of Social History* 42 (2009): 733–68.

PART I

Legal and Intellectual Foundations

1

ON THE INQUISITION IN SPAIN

Gretchen D. Starr-LeBeau

In 1653, a young married woman named María de Albín was arrested by the inquisitors in Madrid. The Portuguese immigrant was charged with baking matzah at Easter, that is, with practicing Judaism in secret. This charge is unsurprising; the mid-seventeenth century was a period of increased inquisitorial investigation of Portuguese immigrants for suspected Judaizing heresy. Furthermore, the ongoing Portuguese war for independence from Spain added to the hostility toward the expatriate Portuguese community in Spain. Unlike many people arrested and imprisoned by the Spanish Inquisition, however, María did not confess; in fact, she strongly asserted her innocence. The initial evidence for and against María was typical of what inquisitors, prosecutors, and defense attorneys collected. Some defense witnesses spoke admiringly of María's Christian devotion, but an accuser claimed to have seen María making matzah and to have heard her discussing her devotion to Judaism.[1] In other words, the evidence for and against María was oral testimony—words.

Inquisitors, theologians, and legal scholars who considered the prosecution of heresy assumed that evidence of heresy would be primarily oral, but this was not always the case. In practice, evidence brought forward by both the prosecution and the defense included a range of oral statements, physical artifacts, and bodily evidence. Furthermore, inquisitors had a certain amount of latitude when it came to defining and interpreting evidence regarding heresy. Shifting attitudes across the centuries and the preferences of particular inquisitors all influenced the interpretation of evidence. In short, the collection and evaluation of evidence in the Spanish Inquisition followed some general patterns but was not as rigidly consistent

DOI: 10.4324/9781003486404-3

as inquisitorial manuals might suggest. In this regard, as in many others, the Spanish Inquisition mirrored other early modern tribunals. In a predominantly oral culture, words—and an accurate recollection of them—mattered. Yet in prosecutions as varied as blasphemy, witchcraft, accusations related to sex and marriage, or even murder, it was the interpretation of those words and their physical, forensic, and narrative context that decided cases. The range of evidence was wide, and in most cases—even with physical evidence—it was not self-explanatory; it needed to be interpreted for its significance to the charge of heresy. The evidentiary environment of the Spanish Inquisition was the product of the ambiguous nature of much evidence regarding heresy; the procedural flexibility of the Spanish Inquisition; the differing needs and expectations of inquisitors, defendants, accusers, and witnesses; and the inquisitors' own uneasiness with the epistemological value of the testimony their tribunals generated.

Inquisitorial tribunals sometimes struggled with the challenges of proving legally that someone was a heretic. This was not a problem exclusive to the Spanish Inquisition or to heresy prosecution. "Speech crimes," such as slander, or even crimes that left physical evidence, such as assault, could be difficult to prove. But inquisitorial prosecution also wrestled with problems caused by the technical definition of heresy, which has two components. First, it must be an incorrect theological belief that the heretic knows is incorrect. An incorrect belief held in ignorance of the church's teachings is not heresy. Second, a heretic must share heretical beliefs with others. Heresy, which is held privately in the mind of the heretic, also does not fit the definition of heresy. In theory, any evidence used in a heresy trial needed to demonstrate that the accused knowingly believed heretical ideas or that the accused shared ideas that they knew to be contrary to church teaching. As a result, inquisitors faced the task of identifying the accused's beliefs through that person's words or actions. This also required discerning the accused's intentions. Did a particular action indicate heretical intent, and if so, did the accused understand that this intention was heretical? In other words, interpretation was fundamental to identifying heresy and to a forensic analysis of evidence brought before the Spanish Inquisition. Furthermore, the underlying assumption of inquisitorial juridical texts was that the evidence inquisitors interpreted would be primarily, if not exclusively, verbal. Witnesses would report to the inquisitors what they had seen and heard, and this would result in a finding of guilt (or, less commonly, innocence).

The inquisitors' expectation of verbal evidence reflected the nature of proof as it developed in Roman and later inquisitorial law (i.e., the investigative legal procedure that emerged around the turn of the thirteenth century and was used in many different tribunals in Europe, both secular and religious). Two eyewitnesses or a confession was necessary in Roman law to prove a person's guilt. Hearsay evidence on its own was insufficient to convict someone, as was any kind of circumstantial evidence. As John Langbein explains,

> [it] does not matter, for example, that the suspect is seen running away from the murdered man's house and that the bloody dagger and the stolen loot are found in his possession. The court cannot convict him of the crime.[2]

Instead, circumstantial evidence (which is how physical evidence was defined) received a value as a "partial proof." In the earlier example, inquisitorial (i.e., investigative) legal procedure assigned the dagger and the stolen money each a quarter of a proof. Eyewitness testimony, and especially confession from the accused, was the preferred form of evidence in inquisitorial tribunals.

Yet legal procedures in the Spanish Inquisition did not exclusively follow theoretical inquisitorial law. There was no single manual that directed the practice of the tribunals of the Spanish Inquisition, and inquisitorial procedure throughout its history was notably *ad hoc*. Successive Inquisitors General contributed to a brief series of basic procedural guidelines, which were compiled and known as the *Old Instructions* (1484) and the *New Instructions* (1561).[3] In addition, the *Suprema*, or Supreme Inquisitorial Council, wrote edicts providing guidance on specific questions or circumstances. The *Suprema* might also issue guidelines to particular regional tribunals. The letters (*cartas acordadas*) containing these guidelines might be shared beyond the jurisdiction for which they were originally written and then adopted elsewhere. In addition, some inquisitors wrote compilations and abbreviations of the *Instructions* and *cartas acordadas*, and these also seem to have been used extensively.[4] All of these were reprinted numerous times, but inquisitors were not provided with any of these resources upon assuming their roles. Rather, inquisitors were dependent upon what was left for them at the tribunal or what they could find. Extant copies show much wear and tear and can include additional notes from multiple hands, further emphasizing the difficulty inquisitors had in acquiring these books. As a result, inquisitors might develop individual libraries and individual preferences in procedure, and they might refer to disparate sources or even medieval inquisitorial manuals.[5]

These various procedural sources were not identical, but they did share some common assumptions about the kinds of evidence an inquisitor would expect to see in his tribunal. Most importantly, the *Instructions* and compilations were written with the expectation that evidence would come either from the testimony of witnesses or from a confession by the accused. The *New Instructions*, for example, describe questions that inquisitors must ask the accused; and they instruct inquisitors to provide warnings to the accused to speak, even as they warn inquisitors to be suspicious of anything that the accused might say. The scope of trial testimony was also generally limited to initial sworn statements from prosecution and defense witnesses. The 1624 compilation of instructions and guidelines confirms this expectation, providing prewritten forms for notaries and inquisitors to use with defendants and witnesses. For example, the compilation, *Orden que comunmente, . . .* includes all the questions to ask a defendant in their initial hearing, and even details how to ask for an accused person's genealogy—a central element in tracking individuals who might have learned from (or taught) baptized family members to practice Judaism or Islam in secret.[6]

Two other principles helped form expectations for evidence in the Spanish Inquisition. The first was the concept of *fama*, or reputation, a legal concept with specific implications in the medieval and early modern period. Because there was no aggrieved individual to initiate heresy trials, a person's reputation served as the accuser. This meant that *fama* needed to be proven in order to begin a trial, and as a result, a significant amount of investigative work usually preceded a formal trial.[7] This emphasis on establishing the reputation of a potential accused person also indirectly reinforced the inquisitorial presumption of verbal evidence. Reputation was more a matter of the words spoken about a person than it was the acts others described that person committing, and demonstrating a person's bad reputation (*mala fama*) required that inquisitors hear what others were saying about the potential defendant.

The second organizing principle was the central role of secrecy, which was an unusual feature of the Spanish Inquisition. The emphasis on secrecy dated to the founding of the institution under the Catholic Monarchs, Isabella and Ferdinand, in 1478. The joint monarchs hoped to reform the beliefs and behavior of their heretical subjects, and to punish heretics; specifically, they were concerned with a growing number of converts from Judaism to Christianity and their descendants, who collectively have become known as *conversos*, or New Christians. There was a suspicion, partly justified, that at least some of these converts and their descendants continued to practice Judaism in secret (a charge known as Judaizing). This threatened the collective salvation of their joint kingdoms; it also had political implications in kingdoms still reeling from civil war and unrest. Isabella, in particular, worried that any *conversos* who came before the Spanish Inquisition would exact retribution against their accusers, and so as part of the establishment of the Inquisition as an office of the state, she required that denunciations and prosecution testimony be given anonymously. The accused could not know who spoke against them.

The principles of *fama* and secrecy affected oral testimony for both the prosecuting attorney (*promotor fiscal*) and the defense attorney (*procurador*). People who made denunciations or provided evidence for the prosecution had the freedom to speak at length about whatever they had seen or heard, or any hearsay that they might know. Inquisition officials asked prosecution witnesses to respond to questions on the basis of the initial charges, and they also could add new denunciations. There were few limitations on what an accuser might say and few limitations on who might testify for the prosecution. Even individuals whose testimony was not legally acceptable in other contexts, such as minors and heretics, could testify before the inquisitors. In some cases, accusers were themselves imprisoned by the Spanish Inquisition, and their testimony undoubtedly reflected the emotional and physical coercion experienced in their own interrogations and ongoing trials. Furthermore, damaging information about individuals mentioned in passing in other trials was cross-referenced by name and kept on file. If additional denunciations appeared, individuals would be charged on the basis of that collective evidence. The Portuguese Inquisition (a separate institution, even when Spain and Portugal were united from 1580 to 1640) was particularly aggressive about asking its victims to name other people who engaged in heresy, and some Portuguese tribunals in the seventeenth century routinely sent copies of prosecution testimony regarding Spanish residents to the relevant local Spanish inquisitorial tribunal. For example, testimony collected by the Portuguese Inquisition in 1619 and 1636 was used when Mencía de Almeida was charged with heresy in Spain in 1654. The inquisitorial tribunal in Toledo also wrote to the Spanish Inquisition tribunal in Cuenca, asking them to check their records for information about Mencía's potential heresy.[8] In other cases, individuals voluntarily came before the Spanish Inquisition to denounce neighbors, acquaintances, and even family members. Their motivations for these denunciations are difficult to ascertain today, but local rivalries, resentments, and religious concerns might all play a role. Some people also chose to turn themselves in to the inquisitors. Again, the motivations of self-accusers varied from apparently genuine remorse to attempts to curtail more serious investigations initiated by others.

Witnesses for the defense did not have the same latitude that prosecution witnesses did, though accused people from all levels of Spanish and colonial society demonstrated some understanding of their legal rights. Well-educated and wealthy defendants often had more capability of launching a successful defense, but in all cases, the statements of defense witnesses were central to a defense case. Witnesses answered questions posed by the defense attorney with an eye toward the three modes of defense permitted in the Spanish Inquisition. *Indirectas* were direct contradictions of prosecution testimony. *Abonos* were character references for the accused. And the third legal defense strategy, called *tachas*, was to disqualify a prosecution witness for holding enmity against the accused. The first two legal techniques in effect meant that defense witnesses responded to specific questions from the defendant's attorney regarding the defendant's character and the specific charge brought by the prosecution; they could not speak in an open-ended fashion, as prosecution witnesses did. The third mode of defense, *tachas*, was difficult to carry out, given the anonymity of prosecution witnesses, although some defendants did make the attempt. They generated a list of accusers with capital enmity against them. If any prosecution witness appeared on the list, the inquisitors launched a subsidiary investigation to evaluate the validity of this claim for that witness. If enmity was proven, that witness' testimony was stricken from the record. For example, when Ana Gómez of Madrid was accused of Judaizing in 1631, she immediately named her former servant as a malicious accuser. Gómez's servant had been fired for stealing and had brought a civil suit against her former employer. After the civil suit was dismissed, the servant accused her former mistress of Judaizing and asked her friends to repeat her accusation. Ana Gómez successfully identified her primary accuser, and since all the other prosecution witnesses had only indirect (hearsay) information from the primary accuser, the case against Ana Gómez was suspended.[9]

In the first few decades of the Spanish Inquisition, tribunals almost exclusively investigated Judaizing, and eyewitness testimony for the prosecution was abundant. Since virtually entire communities faced investigation and punishment at the same time, it was easy to find neighbors and family members willing to testify or to compel people to speak for the prosecution. After those first few decades, however, the pattern of inquisitorial investigation changed. The kinds of heresies investigated in inquisitorial tribunals expanded to include the practice of Islam by baptized Christians, Protestantism, blasphemy, bigamy, and other minor heresies. The pace of investigations slowed, and trials usually had many fewer witnesses. Instead, inquisitors shifted their focus to gaining confessions from the accused. Some of the methods they employed were an accepted element of inquisitorial procedure. For example, after the accused was imprisoned but before they were charged formally, inquisitors issued multiple warnings to the accused to confess to anything that they might have done wrong. Extended imprisonment—before and after being charged—created immense physical and emotional hardship for the accused, and that experience could also lead demoralized and broken prisoners to confess. Other methods of gaining confessions used by the Spanish Inquisition pushed the limits of legality, as Francisco Bethencourt discusses in his recent book.[10] And in some places and times, the rules were completely ignored. Lu Ann Homza has recently expanded our understanding of the relationship between inquisitorial officials, ecclesiastical officials, state officials, and local residents in prosecuting heresy, sometimes through violent means. Her analysis of the Navarrese witchcraft trials of the early seventeenth century demonstrates that local vigilantes relied on brutal torments and physical and mental abuse to generate confessions, which they shared with complicit, local, and unpaid assistants to the Inquisition.[11]

Yet the shift to relying on confessions, even those obtained correctly, was problematic. The *New Instructions* of Inquisitor General Fernando de Valdés, promulgated in 1561, included numerous guidelines that cast suspicion on the reliability of statements made by the accused. For example, in order to "justly judge, [inquisitors] should always be suspicious that they are being tricked, either in the testimony against the prisoner or in the confessions."[12] Also,

> [I]t is necessary to advise that when during the course of his trial a prisoner should mention the names of many persons and afterward he wishes to recant them under the pretense of forgetfulness, such testimony should not be placed into the publication [of testimony provided to the defense], because the prisoner can easily trick them by not testifying to anything more than that which was declared.[13]

The confessions of prisoners who were reconciled on the scaffold also merited suspicion.

The confessions that most worried inquisitors were those gained through torture. When there was a strong disconnect between the prosecution's accusations and the defense witnesses' testimony, or if there was circumstantial evidence totaling at least a half proof, then inquisitors could use torture to gain a confession that would secure a conviction. The *New Instructions* of 1561 mandated that all Spanish Inquisition cases be recommended for torture, but in practice the use of torture was inconsistent. The relative lack of documentation for the first few decades of the Spanish Inquisition makes estimates of the frequency of torture impressionistic. In later periods, we have more records, which show significant variation in the use of torture at different times and places. For example, as many as 33% of trials for heresy in the tribunal of Toledo between 1575 and 1610 included torture, but in other periods it dropped to 11% and 7%.[14] By contrast, the Spanish Inquisition tribunal in Mexico City tortured around 5% of those accused of major heresies such as Judaizing or Protestantism, and only 3% of those accused of minor heresies, such as blasphemy.[15]

Complicating the use of torture was the recognition by many legal scholars at the time that a person undergoing torture might say anything—true or false—to bring the torture to a close.[16] To mitigate against the possibility of people speaking falsely to end the torture, the Spanish Inquisition developed an elaborate process around the administration of torture.[17] Once the inquisitors had permission to begin the torture, the procedure was designed to convince the accused person to confess without being tortured. First, the prisoner was brought to the door of the torture chamber and asked to confess. If the accused did not confess at that time, they were brought into the torture chamber, shown the torture instruments, and asked again to confess. The prisoner was subjected to a medical examination to ensure that they could survive the torture session, and in at least some tribunals the medical officer also examined the prisoner to make sure that they did not have any narcotics to mitigate the pain of the torture session. If the accused did not confess, then they were stripped of their outer garments and tied to the torture instrument, which itself was humiliating and painful. Only then, if the accused still had not confessed, did the inquisitors authorize torture to begin.

Even after the torture session, procedures existed to increase the likelihood that torture victims had spoken the truth. Most importantly, inquisitors required torture victims to ratify what they had said during the torture session at least one day after the torture occurred. This replicated the ratification of other kinds of witnesses' statements but gained additional importance due to concerns about the reliability of testimony gained under torture. Some torture victims did change their statements during ratification, despite the implicit risk of being tortured again (technically, in the Spanish Inquisition a single "suspended" torture session could be resumed). For example, inquisitors tied Juana González to a torture instrument on November 10, 1485, in Guadalupe, Spain, at which point she confessed to several heretical beliefs and acts. Almost a week later, on November 16, Juana was brought to the hall where the inquisitors heard trials and stood before the inquisitor primarily responsible for her case. Point by point, she confirmed some of the statements she had made while tied to the torture instrument (such as her nonstandard prayer in Spanish and the fact that someone had shown her husband Hebrew prayers) while denying others (such as doubting the perpetual virginity of the Virgin Mary).[18]

Torture also blurred the boundary between oral and physical testimony, because the early modern judicial logic behind the use of torture saw truth as physically embedded in the body. Lisa Silverman has argued that French judges believed that humans were fundamentally flawed by original sin and would not voluntarily speak the truth. Torture created a means of spontaneous truth-telling because (she argues) for early modern judges, truth was located physically in the body.[19] Silverman's argument not only holds as an early modern justification for torture; it also explains a number of less coercive epistemological strategies employed by inquisitors. This was important as inquisitors grew more suspicious of the usefulness of torture, particularly as a result of the coerced confessions for witchcraft mentioned earlier. The resulting inquisitorial trials, countersuits in secular courts, and overturning of coerced confessions, in Homza's words, "destabilized the link between confessions and proof."[20] After certain Navarrese witch trials, inquisitors made a ruling in 1625 that all decisions to torture an accused person be appealed to the Suprema.

Despite the epistemological ambivalence about torture and despite the assumed primacy of oral testimony, bodies were essential sites of evidence for heresy. Inquisitors applied ideas already available in their judicial and religious experience, both of which suggested that the body of the accused could itself provide reliable evidence about internal states of mind. In her recent book, Abigail Shinn argues that religious conversion narratives emphasized bodily evidence of internal conversion experiences, both for Protestants and for Catholics. Shinn notes that bodily religious phenomena allow the reader to " 'see' the work of God upon the soul of the believer via the outward display of corporeal signs." And Shinn points out that corporeal evidence itself borrows from legal concepts of proof.[21] In short, we can see evidence of a kind of "embodied epistemology" at work in Spanish Inquisition trials, in that at least some inquisitors acted as if they believed that truth was embodied in the accused themselves, beyond the use of torture. This embodied truth appears through gestures, expressions, and exclamations, as well as from the physical appearance of the body itself.

The most common kind of physical or bodily evidence came from gestures. It had been customary from the sixteenth century, for example, to ask the accused to say standard Catholic prayers and to show that they knew how to cross themselves. *Morisca* María Hernández (whose family converted from Islam to Christianity) came from a village near Daimiel, but she could not recite the Our Father or the Creed, and she did not know how to cross herself, for example.[22] On the other hand, Juan Bacín from Daimiel, who converted to Islam but then returned to Spain and Christianity, demonstrated his renewed knowledge and commitment to Christianity through his ability to cross himself and say his prayers well.[23] Similarly, inquisitors understood that insincere Christians or heretics might have parallel gestures that aligned with their divergent practices and beliefs. Bartolomé Alfonso López was denounced to the Inquisition for the way in which he did penance. His unconventional approach to the altar during the main Mass of the day created so much gossipy chatter (*murmuración*) that his neighbor reported him.[24] *Ensalmadores* (spellcasters or healers), who spoke unique ritual prayers and called on divine powers for healing, often had distinctive gestures that accompanied their prayers. Francisco Díaz, a resident of Tembleque, voluntarily demonstrated for the inquisitors the gestures he used in his healing work.[25] When a fruit seller in Madrid named Francisco Gutiérrez was suspected of secretly being a Muslim, the local inquisition prosecutor asked Francisco's fellow prisoners to report if Francisco prayed like a Muslim, either by moving his arms or by making sounds in his throat.[26]

Facial expressions and noises could also indicate the truth of one's statements about correct or incorrect belief. During torture sessions, and sometimes even during other interrogations, notaries made a careful record of facial expressions, blushing, and exclamations for the information that they might provide inquisitors. In 1634, for example, inquisitors arrested María de Acosta of Ciudad Real on the basis of testimony sent from the Portuguese Inquisition tribunal of Coimbra. During her torture session, the notary carefully recorded her inarticulate cries of pain ("ay ay ay") as well as the fact that in her distress she called upon the Virgin of the Prado to save her from the agony of the rack.[27]

In some cases, the body could provide outward evidence of a person's inner beliefs. A familiar (unpaid) assistant to the Inquisition who was resident in Ocaña, Luis de Pesquera, came before the inquisitors in Toledo in 1654 to denounce a tapestry worker and native of Salonika named Domingo de Guzman, or Isaac Benzamerro. Benzamerro had deprecated Christianity, according to the familiar's informant (who helpfully accompanied the familiar to the Holy Office). Benzamerro may have converted to avoid harassment; he at least started the process. Yet he spoke disparagingly of inquisitors and claimed that he continued to observe the Jewish Sabbath and Yom Kippur. The familiar's informant (like Benzamerro, a recent convert from Judaism to Christianity) also claimed that Benzamerro had said that "he would give his right arm not to be among these Christian dogs" and that he had even bought a knife so that he could wreak vengeance against the inquisitor. None of this evidence was corroborated and theoretically should not have been sufficient to convict, but there was another piece of evidence lodged against Benzamerro. His former coreligionist said that Benzamerro was "a Hebrew priest" and that the proof of this was visible in his thumbnails. His thumbnails were trimmed to make three points—one in the middle and one at each corner—and his accuser claimed that this was because that was how Jewish priests (mohels) circumcised infant boys. The notary even went so far as to draw a picture in the clean copy of the trial record showing what the thumbnails looked like. The legitimacy of this claim is irrelevant to the larger point that the inquisitors thought his nails could have been a physical manifestation of an inward commitment to Judaism—and particularly to performing Jewish rituals that were especially significant as a physical embodiment of male Jewish identity.[28]

Indeed, the part of the body most associated with physical proof of practicing Judaism or Islam after conversion to Christianity was male genitalia. Circumcision in normative Judaism and Islam is evidence of commitment to an ongoing covenant, but for people who were baptized as Christians, circumcision was a defiant statement of practicing Judaism or Islam. Furthermore, inquisitors associated circumcision with Christian baptism; that is, they saw it as an indelible mark on the soul that permanently changed an individual's identity.[29] And some conversos described it the same way. As Miriam Bodian notes, by calling circumcision an eternal sacrament, Mexican Judaizer Francisco de Carvajal reinforced the Christian linkage of an internal religious state and an external religious truth.[30] In the most intimate and powerful way, circumcision emphasized how truth could be read on the body of the accused.

Yet gestures and other bodily evidence were not the only kinds of physical evidence accepted by inquisitors despite the lack of support for physical evidence in inquisitorial procedural documents. For example, written texts appeared often in inquisition trials. In 1572, a 16-year-old in Madrid named Miguel de Vargas turned himself in to the Inquisitors. He had fallen in love with an older woman and had written her a long letter, but his mother had forbidden him from leaving the house to deliver his message. As a last resort, Miguel called upon the devil for help in trying to convince a woman to fall in love with him. When he denounced himself to the Spanish Inquisition, the young man handed over the folded scraps of paper where he had written out his petitions, and those scraps of paper were included as evidence in his trial folder.[31] Magic books of spells also made an appearance as evidence of sorcery or witchcraft. In one instance, Pedro Ruiz Calderón was charged by the Inquisition tribunal in Mexico City with practicing black arts and necromancy in 1540; books with "strange characters" were discovered in his possession, confirming the accusation and sealing his fate.[32] In other cases, texts were a means of preserving heretical knowledge. In 1485, for example, inquisitors arrested Manuel González in Guadalupe for Judaizing. One key piece of evidence against the innkeeper was a booklet, which was included in his trial dossier. In it, he recorded prayers that he and the inquisitors identified as Jewish. The prayers appear in different hands and inks, confirming the accusation that González had asked visiting Jews and Jewish converts at his inn to add to his limited store of knowledge about Judaism.[33]

Over a century and a half later, in 1662, debates about the doctrine of the Immaculate Conception of the Virgin Mary spilled into the tribunals of the Spanish Inquisition when a series of drawings and verses posted at a Franciscan friary in Reus caused an uproar. The friary of St. Francis planned to celebrate the feast of the Immaculate Conception, a doctrine rejected by the rival Dominican order. As part of their celebration, biblical citations and images were posted around the friary challenging the Dominicans' position. Apparently, at least some people found the challenges to the Dominicans offensive; furthermore, the inclusion of biblical quotations contravened the uses of scripture permitted by the Council of Trent. Ultimately, the guardian and the lector of the friary were charged before the Inquisition, and some examples of the texts and images were included in their trials as evidence of their misdeeds.[34]

Letters written by the accused could also serve as incriminating evidence. One of the most notable examples of this occurred in the trial of Francisco Maldonado de Silva, a crypto-Jewish martyr tried in seventeenth-century Peru. Maldonado's mother was a devout Christian, but his father considered himself Jewish, despite his baptism, and eventually he included his son Francisco in his secret Judaizing activities. Over time, Francisco Maldonado became deeply committed to Judaism, renamed himself Eli Nazareus, and circumcised himself. The inquisitors in Lima arrested Maldonado/Nazareus, and he spent the years of his trial writing copious letters and statements about his beliefs.

He also insisted on debating the inquisitors until they eventually lost interest in their prisoner. They did, however, keep some examples of his writing, including two letters Maldonado/Nazareus wrote to the synagogue in Rome, and sent them to the Suprema as evidence of his beliefs. The inquisitors also hung some of his notebooks around his neck when Maldonado/Nazareus was burned at the stake, suggesting that the mere existence of the texts had an importance for inquisitors beyond the significance of the words written in the texts.[35] Other correspondence might also cause suspicion, as when the fruit seller mentioned earlier, who was raised in a religiously diverse environment, wrote his brother and signed his name using Arabic letters.[36] In addition, some writing was important, not simply for its content, but for its physical presence in charms or amulets. Miguel de Vargas' ineffective incantations are just one example.

Other objects also played a role in inquisitorial investigations. In a witchcraft trial held in a tribunal in Aragon in 1640, one witness provided evidence to the inquisitors by bringing in the physical elements of a spell: a braided lock of hair, three metal nails, and some twine. A notary carefully wrapped the objects into a folded piece of paper, labeled it "charm," and included it in the trial dossier; later, the inquisitors sent it along to the Suprema.[37] Even congealed blood could indicate heretical intentions, as was the case with Fray Francisco García Calderón, who was tried in Madrid as an *alumbrado* (an early modern Spanish heresy) and sentenced to perpetual prison in 1628.[38] As late as 1777, the inquisitorial tribunal in Seville began proceedings against the Russian Vice Consul Jorge Birlendín for Masonic activity. In his possession were a number of Masonic materials that served as evidence against him, including a pair of white suede gloves, which were seized and preserved with his file.[39]

Physical evidence showed up more often in prosecution testimony, possibly because defense witnesses had much more limited opportunities to present evidence to defend the accused, let alone introduce physical evidence. Still, there were a few instances when physical evidence could support a defendant's claims to innocence. María de Albín, whose trial began this chapter, provides a particularly notable example of how an object—in this case, her apartment—could prove critical as evidence for the defense. In 1653, Portugal had been in open rebellion for over a decade, and Portuguese *conversos* had been investigated *en masse* on four continents. Little wonder, then, that María's Portuguese speech and Portuguese ancestry raised suspicion. She testified eloquently in her own handwriting (in Portuguese) to her devotion to Christianity and her observance of Christian fasts and feasts. But most striking was the way that a former servant defended María. The servant testified that it was "impossible" for the witness to have seen and heard María de Albín make matzah and talk about Judaism for two reasons. First, the servant never saw María and her husband engage in any Jewish ceremonies, though she did see them observe the rites of Christianity. Second, the servant insisted that no one in the main room of the house could see or hear into the kitchen. María and Bernando's home was on a small alleyway that included a set of six stairs at one end. The principal room of the house was on the right-hand side of the street, but the kitchen was up the stairs of the alley and located on the left-hand side of the street. Faced with this stark contradiction in the testimony of the prosecution and defense witnesses, the inquisitors sent a *comisario* (an unpaid assistant to the inquisitors) and his assistant to María and Bernardo's apartment. They reported that they could hear each other well in a normal tone of voice when the door was open. But when the door was closed, one could hear sounds but not intelligible words. Moreover, with the door closed, nothing could be seen between the two rooms. The physical evidence of María's home provided tangible support of the narrative of piety crafted by María and her servant and decisively countered the accusation raised by María's accuser. As a result, the inquisitors suspended her case.[40] Scholars have long recognized the importance of narratives in early modern legal proceedings, but María de Albín's case underscores how witnesses, prosecutors, and defendants in early modern European tribunals crafted persuasive narratives and verbal testimony in part through reference to physical evidence.

Nonverbal evidence might clearly support the accusations of the prosecutor or the statements of the accused; yet just as often, physical evidence became another site of contestation between the prosecution and defense. In practice, inquisitors placed significant value on physical evidence and the body as a site of external evidence about internal mental states, but they also recognized the limitations of physical evidence for proving heresy. Physical evidence, whether an object or bodily evidence, suggested the possibility of a self-evident truth, but often that evidence still needed to be interpreted, underscoring the uncertainty in Roman law regarding physical evidence. The case of Isaac Benzamerro, discussed earlier, presents one example. His thumbnails had attracted attention for their apparently intentional difference, but inquisitors couldn't read the intent behind that difference without an interpreter. For that, they relied upon the statement of their sole eyewitness, who still left inquisitors without the certainty they desired. Ultimately, the inquisitors rendered an ambiguous sentence: Benzamerro was assigned penance, catechized for six months, and then exiled for four years at a distance of ten leagues from the many Spanish cities with which he'd been associated, namely, Toledo, Madrid, Ocaña, and Cuenca. It was a harsh sentence but did not include flogging or more serious punishments. Similarly, María de Acosta, whose testimony under torture included cries of pain and appeals to the Virgin of the Prado, left inquisitors uncertain about her status as a heretic. She made conflicting statements, did not provide an unambiguous statement, and did not provide additional names of other Judaizers. Her testimony under torture provided only limited, indeterminate knowledge. The inquisitors' sentence reflected their uncertainty. They found the accusations against her "partially proven" and sentenced her to a one-year prison term, the seizure of all her possessions, and a requirement to dress in non-elite clothing—a relatively moderate sentence.[41]

Circumcision seems as though it should have been unproblematic and self-evident, but here, too, bodily evidence needed to be interpreted. Sometimes men admitted to being circumcised; crypto-Jewish martyrs like Francisco de Carvajal and Francisco Maldonado de Silva/Eli Nazareus celebrated their adult circumcisions as an essential part of their religious journey and self-definition. They interpreted their bodies for the inquisitors, or at least did not challenge inquisitorial suspicions. But in a few cases, men did challenge the reading of their own genitalia. In 1485, Manuel González, the innkeeper who kept the small prayer book mentioned earlier, denied that he had been circumcised. There was no medical investigation, but after returning to the cell he shared with his father, he asked what the truth was regarding his own body. His father informed Manuel that he had been circumcised and that his grandfather was to blame—a conversation Manuel told the inquisitors during torture.[42] By 1635, inquisitors' attitudes had changed. After this date, inquisitorial policy required all men accused of Judaizing to submit to an examination to determine whether the accused was circumcised. The evidence could be ambiguous, and physicians sometimes disagreed in their assessment as to whether the accused's foreskin appeared normal, "naturally" atypical, somewhat trimmed, or fully removed in circumcision.[43] Again, bodily evidence promised certainty but provided uncertainty, and inquisitors were forced to rely on the testimony of experts to make a final ruling.

Everyone involved in the Spanish Inquisition—inquisitors, prosecutors, defense attorneys, defendants, and witnesses—was vitally concerned with evidence. Indeed, the most common way that laypeople interacted with the Inquisition was as witnesses—a role exclusively related to providing, confirming, or challenging evidence. Defendants, too, strived to provide evidence that could save their lives or minimize their punishment. Yet that keen search to acquire and present evidence was structured by the legal framework of the Spanish Inquisition and the staff who recorded and helped shape that evidence. Procedural manuals and *cartas acordadas* limited when and how evidence could be obtained, how it could be used, and what was necessary to prove a case. They also limited the types of evidence permitted in inquisitorial tribunals. Specifically, they implicitly focused almost exclusively on spoken evidence, particularly confessions. Both inquisitorial professionals and laypeople seem to have understood these constraints to some extent. But these constraints also revealed a fissure in the legal foundation of the Spanish Inquisition. The rules were designed at least in part to provide certainty about what inquisitors concluded, yet oral testimony could be tricky and unreliable. In working to build certainty, witnesses, lawyers, and inquisitors turned to other forms of evidence with less legal standing. Embodied evidence, whether gestures, facial expressions, physical appearance, or words forced from a defendant during torture, pushed against procedural limitations. Physical evidence did as well. But in some cases, the underlying uncertainty remained. The fates of María de Albín and others tried by the Spanish Inquisition and elsewhere were as much bound up in the collection and interpretation of ambiguous evidence as they were in the verbal and nonverbal signs that the inquisitors heard and saw in their tribunals.

Notes

1 Archivo Histórico Nacional [AHN], Inquisition section [Inqu.], Legajo 131, expediente (exp.) 13.
2 John Langbein, *Torture and the Law of Proof: Europe and England in the Ancien Régime* (University of Chicago Press, 1977), 4.
3 Lu Ann Homza includes selections from the *Old* and *New Instructions* in *The Spanish Inquisition, 1484–1614: An Anthology of Sources* (Hackett, 2006). John F. Chuchiak IV translates the *New Instructions* in his *The Inquisition in New Spain, 1536–1820. A Documentary History* (Johns Hopkins University Press, 2012). He also includes some additional guidelines for the Mexican tribunal.
4 See Francisco Portero de la Vega et al., *Orden que comunmente se guarda en el Santo Oficio de la Inquisicion, acerca del processar en las causas que en el se tratan . . .* (n.p. circa 1624). https://inquisition.library.nd.edu/item/INQ-132
5 See Robin Vose, "I. Inquisitorial Manuals," *Hesburgh Libraries of Notre Dame, Department of Rare Books and Special Collections* (University of Notre Dame, 2010). https://inquisition.library.nd.edu/genre-inquisition-manuals-introduction and Kimberly Lynn, *Between Court and Confessional: The Politics of Spanish Inquisitors* (Cambridge University Press, 2013).
6 Portero, *Orden*, 9–11.
7 Thelma S. Fenster and Daniel Lord Smail, eds., *Fama: The Politics of Talk and Reputation in Medieval Europe* (Cornell University Press, 2003).
8 AHN, Inqu., Legajo 132, exp. 16.
9 Lu Ann Homza, "How to Harass an Inquisitor-General: The Polyphonic Law of Friar Francisco Ortíz," in *A Renaissance of Conflicts: Visions and Revisions of Law and Society in Italy and Spain*, eds. John A. Marino and Thomas Kuehn (Centre for Reformation and Renaissance Studies, 2004), 299–336; and Gretchen D. Starr-LeBeau, *Seven Myths of the Spanish Inquisition* (Hackett, 2023), 107–11.
10 Francisco Bethencourt, *Strangers Within: The Rise and Fall of the New Christian Trading Elite* (Princeton University Press, 2024).
11 Lu Ann Homza, *Village Infernos and Witches' Advocates: Witch-Hunting in Navarre, 1608–1614* (Penn State University Press, 2022).
12 Chuchiak, *The Inquisition in New Spain*, 63.
13 Chuchiak, *The Inquisition in New Spain*, 67.
14 Henry Kamen, *The Spanish Inquisition: A Historical Revision*, 4th ed. (Yale University Press, 2014), 239.
15 Chuchiak, *The Inquisition in New Spain*, 44.
16 Edward Peters, *Torture,* expanded ed. (University of Pennsylvania Press, 1996), 70–71.
17 A more complete description of torture practices in the Spanish Inquisition is available in Starr-LeBeau, *Seven Myths*, 100–5.

18 Gretchen D. Starr-LeBeau, *In the Shadow of the Virgin: Inquisitors, Friars, and* Conversos *in Guadalupe, Spain* (Princeton University Press, 2003), 273–75.
19 Lisa Silverman, *Tortured Subjects: Pain, Truth, and the Body in Early Modern France* (University of Chicago Press, 2001). When moral arguments against the use of torture, which had long existed, became stronger and more widespread, they drew on new concepts like natural law and the natural dignity of humans, which torture denied. French *philosophes* argued, moreover, that truth rested in the mind, not the body, and that therefore torture could only produce lies rather than truth. See Silverman, *Tortured Subjects*, 159–62.
20 Lu Ann Homza, "When Witches Litigate: New Sources from Early Modern Navarre," *The Journal of Modern History* 91 (2019): 250.
21 Abigail Shinn, *Conversion Narratives in Early Modern England: Tales of Turning* (Palgrave Macmillan, 2018), 169.
22 AHN Inqu., Legajo 88, part 1, exp. 7. The trial ran from 1544–1545.
23 AHN Inqu., Legajo 101, part 2, exp. 16.
24 AHN Inqu., Legajo 234, exp 28.
25 AHN Inqu., Legajo 85, part 1, exp. 6, regarding "Francisco Díaz, vecino de Tembleque, 1549."
26 AHN Inqu., Legajo 156, exp. 4, regarding "Francisco Gutiérrez, frutero, 1614–1616."
27 AHN Inqu., Legajo 131, exp. 4.
28 AHN Inqu., Legajo 156, exp. 15.
29 See for example Romans 2: 28–29, "For a person is not a Jew who is one outwardly, nor is circumcision something external and physical. Rather a person is a Jew who is one inwardly, and circumcision is a matter of the heart, by the Spirit, not the written code."
30 Miriam Bodian, *Dying in the Law of Moses: Crypto-Jewish Martyrdom in the Iberian World* (Indiana University Press, 2007), 75.
31 AHN Inqu., Legajo 97 (1), exp. 5.
32 Chuchiak, *The Inquisition in New Spain*, 301.
33 Starr-LeBeau, *In the Shadow*, 85.
34 AHN Inqu., MPD (Mapas, Planos, Dibujos), 182 and 193. The images and texts originally accompanied [AHN] Inqu., 4454, exp. 2. The Immaculate Conception, that Jesus' mother was born without original sin, did not become an official doctrine of the Catholic Church until the nineteenth century.
35 AHN Inqu., MPD 18, 20, 29. The letters were originally kept in the book that includes the summary of his trial, *Relaciones de causas de fe desde el año de 1639 hasta el año de 1666*, [AHN] Inqu., Libro 1031. For a description of Maldonado's execution, see Bodian, *Dying in the Law of Moses*, 140–44.
36 AHN Inqu., Legajo 156, exp 4.
37 AHN Inqu., MPD 6; it accompanied "Libro diez y seis de cartas de la Inquisición de Aragón al Consejo de Inquisición del año mil y seiscientos y treinta y siete hasta el de mil y seiscientos y cuarenta" [AHN] Inqu., Libro 976, between folios 303v and 304r.
38 AHN Inqu., MPD 7; a summary of his trial appears in [AHN] Inqu., Libro 3691.
39 The gloves are in [AHN] Inqu., MPD 3; his trial is available at [AHN] Inqu., 2073, exp. 1.
40 AHN Inqu., Legajo 131, exp. 13.
41 Starr-LeBeau, *Seven Myths*, 104–5.
42 Starr-LeBeau, *In the Shadow,* 191–92.
43 José Pardo Tomás, "Physicians' and Inquisitors' Stories? Circumcision and Crypto-Judaism in Sixteenth-Eighteenth-Century Spain," in *Bodily Extremities: Preoccupations with the Human Body in Early Modern European Culture*, eds. Florike Egmond and Robert Zwijnenberg (Routledge, 2003), 168–94, especially 184.

Select Bibliography

Bethencourt, Francisco. *Strangers Within: The Rise and Fall of the New Christian Trading Elite.* Princeton University Press, 2024.

Bodian, Miriam. *Dying in the Law of Moses: Crypto-Jewish Martyrdom in the Iberian World.* Indiana University Press, 2007.

Chuchiak, John F., ed. and trans. *The Inquisition in New Spain, 1536–1820. A Documentary History.* Johns Hopkins University Press, 2012.

García, Pablo. *Orden que comunmente se guarda en el Santo Oficio de la Inquisicion, acerca del processar en las causas que en el se tratan*, 1622

Homza, Lu Ann. *The Spanish Inquisition, 1484–1614: An Anthology of Sources.* Hackett, 2006.

Homza, Lu Ann. *Village Infernos and Witches' Advocates: Witch-Hunting in Navarre, 1608–1614.* Penn State University Press, 2022.

Shinn, Abigail. *Conversion Narratives in Early Modern England: Tales of Turning.* Palgrave Macmillan, 2018.

Silverman, Lisa. *Tortured Subjects: Pain, Truth, and the Body in Early Modern France.* University of Chicago Press, 2001.

Starr-LeBeau, Gretchen. *In the Shadow of the Virgin: Inquisitors, Friars, and* Conversos *in Guadalupe, Spain.* Princeton University Press, 2003.

Starr-LeBeau, Gretchen. *Seven Myths of the Spanish Inquisition.* Indianapolis: Hackett, 2023.

Vose, Robin. "I. Inquisitorial Manuals." In *Hesburgh Libraries of Notre Dame, Department of Rare Books and Special Collections.* University of Notre Dame, 2010. https://inquisition.library.nd.edu/genre-inquisition-manuals-introduction

2

ON THE ROMAN INQUISITION

Uncertainty and Discretion

Vincenzo Lavenia

Introduction: Uncertainty and Evidence

Recent scholarship has dealt with the historical relationships between truth and demonstration, and faith and empirical proof after the Reformation. While pagan thinkers may have disparaged credulity, the Augustinian-Thomistic tradition embraced a different view. According to late antique and medieval Christian thinkers, reason alone cannot fully support faith; instead, *credulitas*—understood as the willingness to believe even without seeing or having tangible evidence—holds intrinsic value.

In canon law, credulity occupied a position between ignorance and direct knowledge of a fact. Canon law allowed depositions from individuals who were not eyewitnesses when trials involved rites of purgation; it even recognized "witnesses and oaths" of credulity in matrimonial cases. Yet, to what extent could uncertainty be tolerated when adjudicating heresy? How much belief was permissible without direct evidence, and was space indeed given for *credulitas*? These problems became more pressing in the sixteenth century, when humanists, Protestants, and unbelievers began challenging the authority of the Catholic Church.

Following the repression of religious dissent in Italy (c. 1542–80), the Roman Inquisition, also known as the Holy Office, was mainly concerned with resolving doctrinal and procedural uncertainties. It refined its style and developed a capacity to admit diverse forms of evidence and points of view before issuing a verdict. While probabilism gained prominence in casuistry, and uncertainty dominated the fields of legal, medical, and theological knowledge, the Roman Inquisition became accustomed to deliberating on the basis

DOI: 10.4324/9781003486404-4

of the often-divergent opinions of theologians and jurists.[1] When overseeing local trials, it demanded a strict scrutiny of evidence from its magistrates.

Yet questions of superstition, harmful magic, and witchcraft involved problems with gauging the reliability of evidence, as did sex crimes committed by confessors against their penitents. The challenges here were manifold. Catholic authorities wanted to control popular devotion in cases of miraculous images, diabolical possession, and purported saints, but they faced competing priorities. They had to decide how to ascertain the authenticity of such extraordinary phenomena without fueling widespread skepticism toward divine prodigies; they also had to decide how to punish imposters.

Then there was the potential weight given to verbal and physical evidence and how to interpret it. Like their Iberian counterpart, the Holy Office tended to dismiss accounts of demonic Sabbath gatherings and refused to admit accusations made by alleged participants in such rites. Doctors in early modern Italy were eager to suppress popular medicine, and they too were often enlisted by inquisitors to offer expert opinions in cases of harmful magic.[2] Still, such advice seeking did not presage a modern system of "tangible" proof. Rather, doctors often sought to justify their failed medical treatments by agreeing with exorcists that the failure was due to the devil's occupation of sick or possessed bodies. The Holy Office was aware of this problem, and while it mandated expert examination of the *corpus delicti*, it remained skeptical of physical evidence for witchcraft, even when corroborated by doctors. Roman inquisitors preferred to decide on a case-by-case basis and promoted the discernment of spirits as a more appropriate framework for adjudicating cases of diabolic crimes. The Roman Inquisition's leadership favored a paternalistic, pastoral approach to justice that relied on discretion. Notably, the same priorities held when Roman inquisitors had to address sex crimes committed by priests and friars during the sacrament of penance. Here too, contradictory objectives were in play: the Holy Office had to investigate and confront clergy accused of abuse, but they also preferred to keep such offenses and punishments secret, for fear publicity about them would diminish the faith of Catholics at large. Remarkably, in these instances, the Holy Office would accept the sole testimony of a seduced woman as evidence.

The legal justification for these preferences lay in the inquisitorial courts' claim that they were tempering justice with mercy and hence operating according to canon law, even as the very concept of a single and binding canon law, or a unified legal system, the *ius commune*, was under attack, thanks to the Protestant Reformation. Inquisitors in both Spain and Italy were willing to condemn the relapsed but pardon a repentant heretic's first descent into error; they wished to push offenders to convert and reconcile with the church by abjuring their wrong or evil convictions. The penitential character of Italy's Holy Office became more evident after the harsh repressive period of the sixteenth century. Trials were often shortened and limited to gathering information; the scope for judicial discretion was expanded in the sifting of evidence. Significantly, the experts who drafted manuals on evidence, proof, and legal judgment wrote that the judges of faith could be satisfied by semi-full evidence or *semiplenae probationes*. They believed that inquisitors could base their inquiries and verdicts on a series of clues rather than waiting for two identical eyewitnesses and the "spontaneous" confession of the alleged offender. In such cases, magistrates were not to impose capital penalties but only certain minor punishments, especially in cases difficult to prove, such as heresy and witchcraft.[3]

Sight, Simulation, and Holiness

After the Sacred Congregation of Rites was established in 1588, the papacy, with the involvement of the Holy Office, increasingly asserted exclusive authority in the recognition of Catholic cults.[4] Yet the Holy See faced persistent demands from religious orders, cardinals, bishops, cities, princes, and nobles who sought to increase their prestige as patrons by promoting the recognition of saints. In response, a decree from the Holy Office on March 13, 1625, prohibited the faithful from offering any form of worship to men and women who might have died in the "odor of sanctity" but who had not received Rome's approval. No one could be depicted with a halo before the canonical process was concluded, nor could biographies of charismatic figures be published without the endorsement of the Apostolic See. These rules were relaxed in a subsequent decree on October 2, 1625, which permitted certain forms of veneration before a case of sanctity had reached Rome, as long as they were not sensational. On January 15, 1628, a third inquisitorial decree forbade the Sacred Congregation of Rites to label a deceased man or woman blessed, a martyr, or a saint until 50 years had passed since their death. Finally, with the brief *Caelestis Hierusalem cives* of 1634, Urban VIII formalized the canonization process and instituted control over it by the Holy Office.

To understand how the Roman Inquisition approached the question of sanctity, we shall cite just one document, which exemplifies efforts to police men and women who fell into a special form of heresy known as "the pretense of holiness." In 1636, one of the most influential members of the Holy Office, Desiderio Scaglia, drew up a handbook for local inquisitors, which circulated widely in manuscript. In it, he devoted a section to disordered devotions. He wrote that the following should not be trusted: those who practiced extreme fasts and dressed like hermits, those who sought to attract crowds by simulating ecstasies and inventing prophecies, and those who claimed to have received the stigmata or been visited by the Virgin. These individuals were mainly women, and they should be chastised for pretending to be living saints while disregarding ecclesiastical authority. But how could they be discovered? According to Scaglia, their behavior had to be carefully observed, outward signs of piety ignored, writings seized, and a reliable confessor consulted. Above all, the discernment of spirits should be practiced, following the teachings of authorities such as Jean Gerson.[5]

Yet discretion and the careful sorting of evidence still ruled the day. As the Dominican counselor Domenico Gravina wrote after a case of feigned sanctity that occurred in Naples between 1606 and 1615 (that of Giulia Di Marco), it was the *magisterium*, or teaching authority, of the church that declared what was authentic and divine vs. what was false and demonic.[6] Gravina pointed out that mystical episodes not only depended on physical conditions, such as uterine diseases, but also depended on psychic afflictions, such as *philautia,* or self-love. To distinguish the true from the false, moral judgment was essential, which required analyzing the status of the person who had the vision. Furthermore, the judge had to exclude the possibility that the person's mental and visual faculties were weakened. While the judgment of doctors and naturalists had to be taken into account, Gravina emphasized that the best remedy against simulation and illusions was the discernment of spirits [*discretio spirituum*], which prevented imposture from triumphing over truth.[7] That discernment came from experience as well as written texts. It allowed one to assess the character of an extraordinary case, beyond the material evidence.[8]

"Experientia Rerum Magistra": Evil Spells and Witchcraft

As scholar John Tedeschi established decades ago, understanding the pastoral objectives and judicial practices of the Holy Office requires attention to its rules. Ultimately, those rules sought to curb the fear of witches and to guide local inquisition judges; in the end, their goal was to eradicate superstition rather than lending credence to tales of witches' flights or evil spells.[9] Still, consensus was not immediate. One of the earliest serious cases of witchcraft addressed by the Roman Inquisition occurred in 1559, during the pontificate of Pope Paul IV. In Bologna, the bishop's episcopal court had prosecuted four women for witchcraft and issued four death sentences, although the accused were repentant and had not relapsed. The Holy Office's debate about the case revealed different opinions. For example, Pietro Belo drew up a juridical consultation that urged the cardinals to approach the alleged events in Bologna with skepticism. Had the witches truly attended a Sabbath, or had they only imagined it? Although the theologians adjudicating the case were inclined to believe in the reality of witches' ability to fly, Belo argued the opposite, suggesting it was more likely that the women had imagined the event.[10] It is not clear whether Belo's position was unique. Nonetheless, between the 1560s and 1570s, debates on witchcraft grew particularly heated. This is evident from the manuals for inquisitors circulating in Italy at the time, many of which were written or updated by Spanish authors such as Arnau Albert, Diego de Simancas, and Francisco Peña.

Notably, judicial caution toward witchcraft became the order of the day during the years when Giulio Antonio Santoro, Cardinal of Santa Severina, dominated the Roman Inquisition (1587–1602). Santoro endorsed important measures. He limited the involvement of secular magistrates in prosecuting witches. And in 1588, the Holy Office prohibited using the simple accusation of someone as an accomplice as sufficient evidence in trials involving purported flights to the Sabbath. Although witchcraft investigations were proliferating in northern Italy at the time, particularly in Liguria, Piedmont, and Lombardy, the Holy Office sought to ensure that the fight against superstition did not spiral into mass trials against alleged nocturnal followers of the devil.

A pivotal case in southern Italy that began in 1592 allowed the inquisition leadership to adopt an even clearer line. In the diocese of Bitonto, in Apulia, a woman named Laura Stella suffered convulsions that an archdeacon exploited to initiate a series of witchcraft trials against his enemies. An array of exorcists interrogated the possessed woman and other supposed demoniacs, transcribing the alleged words of devils and leveling accusations of witchcraft against men and women from all social classes. One young man preferred to commit suicide rather than suffer the shame of a trial; two women died of torture. By 1594, a local cleric informed the Holy Office of the abuses taking place in Apulia. In response, the Inquisition sent its own emissary, the Bolognese jurist Giulio Monterenzi, to Bitonto to investigate. Monterenzi concluded that confessions of witchcraft were false and had been extracted through torture. He had the judges responsible for the affair arrested, halted the trials, and sent two of the possessed women to Rome. After some initial hesitation, Santoro supported Monterenzi's decisions, and the trials were annulled.

Between 1594 and 1605, during Monterenzi's tenure as leading prosecutor of the Holy Office, a handbook for witch trials was drawn up, which later was entitled *Instructio pro formandis processibus in causis strigum, sortilegiorum et maleficiorum*. The *Instructio* circulated in manuscript form in Italy and beyond the Alps; it was partially edited in the vernacular in 1625 and later, in Latin. It circulated in an ad hoc way among local judges who were coping with serious allegations about witchcraft. It advised moderation in the use of torture, discouraged leading questions in interrogations, and rejected co-conspirators' accusations as evidence of participation in the Sabbath. The *Instructio* advised skepticism toward statements supposedly made by possessing demons and ordered the strict oversight of exorcists. It told judges to consult medical experts to decide whether an illness or death had a natural cause before attributing it to an evil spell. Experience suggested that more often than not, cases of harmful magic or demonic possession were nothing more than inventions or illusions of the devil.

Though unofficial, the *Instructio* was of undeniable importance. As figures such as Andrea Cesalpino and Giovan Battista Codronchi argued at the end of the sixteenth century, diabolic plagues might have existed, but they could be difficult to identify because of the occult and often indecipherable signs of harmful magic: pallor, sudden changes in temperature, vomiting, and contortions. In humans as well as animals, such physical alterations could arise from natural causes or from the direct intervention of the devil, who was adept at confusing the imagination and altering the balance between black bile and other humors, thus deceiving even the most skilled doctors and exorcists.

In ancient times, Galen had denied the existence of diabolic illnesses, attributing his disbelief to his rejection of both God and the soul's immortality. Similarly, early modern Averroist physicians and naturalists—influenced by the likes of Pietro Pomponazzi, the author of *De incantationibus* (1520), who had taught in Padua and Bologna—fostered skepticism regarding miracles, evil spells, and diabolic possessions.[11] Like other doctors of their generation, Cesalpino and Codronchi had also subscribed to Averroistic doctrines, but after the Council of Trent, they abandoned their previous positions, whether out of genuine conviction or out of fear of heresy charges. Declaring one's belief in evil spells perhaps served to demonstrate full adherence to Catholic orthodoxy or to provide an explanation when a learned physician failed to cure an illness or prevent a patient's death. Attributing an illness to a spell or a curse offered medical experts a means of shielding their professional credibility.

Exorcists, too, were far from inclined to favor the moderate strategy of the Holy Office. The most prominent author of texts for exorcists, Girolamo Menghi, openly challenged unbelieving physicians (such as Johannes Wier), Averroist philosophers (such as Pomponazzi), and those who did not believe in night flights, Sabbaths, and evil spells. Menghi argued that devils could hide in the humors and obstruct the healing process. As for possessed bodies, Menghi cautioned against relying too heavily on metaphysical signs of the devil's presence, such as the possessed being able to speak in unknown languages. Instead, he advised focusing on whether the alteration of the humors depended on supernatural causes, in collaboration with licensed doctors. Exorcists, like doctors, should challenge magicians, witches, and charlatans who falsely claimed to dispel evil spells and cure illnesses.[12]

Examination of inquisitorial witchcraft trials, which increased in number between the late sixteenth and early seventeenth centuries, reveals that the medical expertise of doctors prescribed by the *Instructio* to curb hasty accusations of witchcraft was often counterproductive. Doctors summoned to testify before local Holy Office tribunals often upheld widespread beliefs about diabolic diseases and rarely offered natural explanations for contentious phenomena. The evidence they relied upon mirrored that used by exorcists and demonologists.[13] Ultimately, then, the practice of calling upon doctors in cases of *maleficia*, as sanctioned by the Holy Office, did not have a "disenchanting" effect. The verification of the *corpus delicti* in cases of witchcraft and evil spells remained controversial, as did the regulation of exorcists. As the seventeenth century advanced, a cautious skepticism prevailed among the cardinals of the Holy Office and local inquisitors, who in Italy were predominantly Dominican or Franciscan friars with theological training. This skepticism stemmed more from a commitment to spiritual discernment than a desire to uncover physical proof of the devil's presence. In northern Europe, the fixation with finding physical proof of witchcraft prompted ordeal-like practices, such as immersing the alleged perpetrators in cold water. In Italy, pastoral discernment prevailed over the idea that evil spells and devils left physical traces to be brought to light.[14]

Against the "Tangible" Proof of the Devil Mark

The belief that the devil imprinted his followers with a mark was based on a passage in the New Testament (*Revelations* 13:16): "And he [the Antichrist] causeth all . . . to receive a mark in their right hand, or in their foreheads." When the idea took hold that physical evidence could give judges the ability to recognize witches, the mark came to be seen as a counter-baptism, as a false stigma of holiness, or as a sign of enslavement and beastliness. It was believed that when an individual sealed a pact with the devil, the latter imprinted upon that person's body a mark that could vary in shape and size and that lacked sensation and did not bleed, as if it were dead flesh. To search for the *punctum diabolicum*, the bodies of those supposedly guilty of demonic crimes were subjected to harrowing ordeals that, in many cases, were voluntarily accepted by the accused as the only way to prove their innocence. Surgeons collaborated with physicians in shaving the accused in search of an insensible spot. It was thought that the mark was often hidden in the most intimate areas, such as breasts, anus, armpits, or genitals. Scars, moles, and birthmarks were probed with needles driven into the flesh, which produced atrocious suffering. The reaction of the accused was regarded as evidence.[15]

Nevertheless, Catholic Inquisition leadership generally spurned the devil's mark as evidence in the early modern period. For instance, though one of Navarre's local inquisitors actively looked for the mark when he went on visitation in 1609, the Spanish Inquisition's new instructions on witchcraft in 1614 did not mention the mark at all.[16] A similar line was taken by the Roman Holy Office, whose *Instructio* recommended its exclusion, though in the 1630s, Cesare Carena still argued that the mark constituted credible evidence.[17] In contrast, French, Scottish, English, Swiss, and German courts accepted the mark as proof, as demonstrated not only by witchcraft trials but also by treatises published after the second half of the sixteenth century.

In 1609, a heated debate on the mark was sparked by an episode of demonic possession in Aix-en-Provence. There, two young Ursuline nuns, Madeleine Demandolx de la Palud and Louise Capeau, suffered spectacular convulsions and seemed to channel the devil's voice. Their possession was corroborated by several Dominican exorcists, which led the case to involve inquisitors in Avignon, who were under the authority of the Roman Holy Office. The judges identified the nuns' confessor, Louis de Gaufridy—a priest prone to lust—as the source of the curse that was tormenting the two women. In 1611, Gaufridy was burned at the stake by the Parliament of Aix after his body was subjected to terrible torture in search of the devil's mark.[18] After such marks were found, they were regarded by the exorcists—theologian François Domptius and vice-inquisitor of Avignon Sébastien Michaëlis—as proof of Gaufridy's guilt. In 1613, Michaëlis also published a *Histoire admirable* of the events of Aix, which became the model for all tales of collective demonic possession in Europe; so dangerous was this narrative that the Roman Inquisition immediately sought to prevent its circulation in the Italian peninsula.[19] For Michaëlis, the mark was a tangible sign of the offender's demonic affiliation, a symbol of having undergone a sort of black baptism to enter Satan's anti-Christian religion.

Support for Michaëlis' position came from one of the most influential professors at the Faculty of Medicine in Aix, Jacques Fontaine. Fontaine became Louis XIII's personal physician; his discourse on demonic marks was dedicated to Marie de' Medici and appeared in Paris and Lyon in two separate editions. He supported the notion of demonic possession and referred to the sentence against Gaufridy.[20] He also claimed to have participated in the search for Gaufridy's mark and noted that he had found around 30 suspicious signs on the priest's body, including a very large one near the man's kidneys, an allusion to the priest's lust.[21] The mark had been pierced with a three-finger-long needle without the defendant feeling any pain or emitting any blood.

Fontaine insisted that the mark was not only a symbol of demonic allegiance, like badges worn by soldiers of different regiments, but also prevented the devil's followers from abandoning their satanic loyalties. To those at the University of Aix who questioned whether the mark depended on the apostate's voluntary consent, Fontaine replied that God would not allow a priest to be accused unless he had willingly accepted a pact with the devil. The mark constituted incontrovertible proof precisely because it was tangible, immutable, and could be found on any part of the body. Those who suggested that the mark could be mistaken for other natural signs showed their ignorance. A skilled doctor could distinguish a wart from a mark and would also verify that a mole did not emit blood to establish that it was a diabolical mark.[22] This example once again shows how the involvement of doctors in witchcraft trials often reinforced the fear of evil as well as judicial persecution, especially since cases such as the one in Aix served to bolster the prestige of university professors and to cement the alliance between exorcists, doctors, and theologians in similar cases of possession and witchcraft.

Fontaine's text triggered a debate among European jurists, physicians, and theologians alike. When Peter Ostermann, a former Calvinist and consultant to the archbishop of Mainz, offered a *Commentarius juridicus* on marks in 1629, he quoted abundantly from accounts of demonologists such as Pierre de Lancre.[23] Ostermann's commentary in turn provoked a reaction from Johann Jordanaeus, a theologian from Nijmegen who was shocked by the witchcraft investigations carried out in the duchy of Kleve, where the mark test was used extensively by judge Franz Buirmann. In his *Disputatio brevis et categorica de proba stigmatica* (1630), Jordanaeus did not question the truth of the Sabbath myth, but attacked the inspection of marks, arguing that evidence in criminal trials must be clearer than the "light of a sundial." According to Jordanaeus, stigmatic evidence had no foundation in canon law and risked leading to the condemnation of many innocent people who unknowingly had been marked by the devil, the father of lies.[24]

After the events in Aix, the debate over the use of stigmatic evidence also affected the Italian peninsula, albeit to a lesser extent. For instance, theologians who taught in Rome, beginning with the Spanish Jesuit Juan Azor in the Collegio Romano, manifested a strong skepticism about witch trials and rarely addressed the diabolical mark, in line with the positions of Spanish and Italian inquisitors.[25] Then there was Paolo Zacchia, who would later become a papal chief physician. Zacchia established forensic medicine a century before it became a formal discipline taught in all European universities. A student of the Jesuits, a consulter of the Rota, and a member of the Sacred Congregation of Rites, Zacchia dealt with witchcraft in several sections of his monumental *Quaestiones medico-legales*, a work that developed in a gradual and layered manner.[26] Zacchia scattered skeptical critiques of diabolism throughout his volumes. For example, he interpreted sexual abnormalities as pathologies stemming from frigidity or impotence rather than as consequences of supposed evil spells.[27] He expressed distrust about extraordinary events in a section of Book III that dealt with the simulation of diseases; he also questioned the reality of demonic sex with incubi and succubi, alluding several times to the work of Johannes Wier.[28]

Notably, unlike his peers, Zacchia spoke at length about the demonic mark, and his prime polemical targets were French demonologists Jean Bodin and Father Michaëlis. Zacchia believed that the devil could deceive doctors and judges, leading them to overlook blood flow and sensitivity in marks such as moles. The devil created delusions that led people to believe in marks, which he invented as false proof of the imaginary crime of witchcraft. After all, the Holy Office had already disavowed the use of the mark as evidence, and it was thus not permissible to take up an opposite stance. Zacchia even asked why it was necessary to apprehend witches and sorcerers in the first place: was it not better to acquit a guilty person than to condemn the innocent on the basis of visible but dubious evidence? According to Zacchia, even the most absurd confessions of witches could be explained in more rational terms, such as demonic illusion, hysteria, or melancholic self-suggestion, all of which he considered natural, though occult, causes.[29]

In this regard, Zacchia reflected the views of the Roman Inquisition, which refused to consider physical and tangible evidence of witchcraft and diabolic possession as reliable. Italian inquisitors preferred instead to continue to practice a judicial style on the basis of the cautious discernment of spirits, a task assigned to theologians and spiritual directors rather than doctors and exorcists. The stories about witches in demonological treatises did not offer a valid way to determine the truth, as these stories could be the result of manipulation, illusions, or imbalances of the black bile. Cases of witchcraft might have been possible, but they were not certain. The opinions of jurists and doctors held less weight than the decisions of the Roman courts, which were the proper forum for sifting doctrinal and judicial truth. In this domain, as in the determination of miracles, visions, ecstasies, and apparitions, a sophisticated medico-legal language developed, but so too was the Curia's pastoral control reinforced when it came to female charisma and the clergy.

Scandal and the Testimony of Women: Evidence of Solicitation

If, as male experts agreed, women's bodies were unstable, affected by uterine diseases and an excess of black bile, could manifestations of female charisma—such as ecstasies, anorexia, and visions—be trusted? Could the tales of women accused of witchcraft be believed, and could a woman's testimony against a member of the clergy be taken as reliable evidence? The question of whether a woman's word was trustworthy became more urgent once incitement to commit impure acts in specific circumstances became a heretical crime. In 1559, Pope Paul IV issued a brief (*Cum sicut nuper*) in which he gave inquisitors in the Spanish city of Granada the power to initiate trials against priests who abused their role as confessors. The measure was requested by Granadan Archbishop Pedro Guerrero, who had sought papal guidance on how to intervene when it became known that a priest had tricked one or more women, whether religious or lay, into committing sexual offenses during confession. Such confessors exploited the trust that the flock placed in their shepherds. How could the wall of silence surrounding the sins of the clergy be broken, and how could this crime be proven? The solution was to entrust the investigations to the Inquisition, which was capable of correcting priests who had abused auricular confession by persuading penitents that the pleasures of the flesh were minor sins or even acts pleasing to God.

Of course, such abuses were by no means limited to Granada. In 1561, Pope Pius IV, in agreement with Spanish Inquisitor-General Fernando de Valdés, extended jurisdiction over clerical solicitation to all the inquisition tribunals of Castile and Aragon, along with their dependencies outside Spain. Scholars have emphasized the official repression of this clerical abuse as an important turning point. From that moment on, inquisition courts were transformed from an anti-heretical magistracy into a moral police force, tasked with identifying hidden offenders. A new type of heresy was thus born: the crime of *sollicitatio ad turpia*, which targeted not so much the abuse of power against a victim but the sacrilege committed against the sacrament of penance, a sacrament that became increasingly relevant after the Council of Trent.[30]

In Italy, a decree of the Holy Office in 1614 attributed jurisdiction over clerical solicitation to the pope's judges. Later, with the constitution *Universi Dominici gregis* (1622), which applied to the entire Catholic world, Pope Gregory XV established that solicitation by confessors was a heresy, punishable by bishops or inquisitors on the basis of a single witness, even if the solicitation occurred before or after the confession or if the perpetrator was impersonating a confessor.[31] In the eighteenth century, with the constitution *Sacramentum Poenitentiae* (1741), Benedict XIV allowed ecclesiastical courts to accept complaints even years after the act in question.[32] The regulations on solicitation in the confessional were later incorporated into the *Codex Iuris Canonici* (1917).[33]

Inquisition trials reveal that a large share of the complaints did not involve actual sexual intercourse in sacred spaces, but rather insinuating words, caresses, kisses, voyeurism, exhibitionism, masturbation, or sadomasochism. Not surprisingly, it was not easy to obtain information or evidence about the abuses of confessors. Penitent women—especially those who were young, psychologically fragile, or of high rank—were often reluctant to report illicit relationships with their confessors to the authorities. Such relationships could jeopardize a woman's honor and social capital, which were crucial for her marital prospects. As a result, the Spanish as well as Italian Inquisitions devised an indirect way to break this wall of silence. If a priest stumbled upon an instance of sexual grooming while listening to a penitent's recitation of sins, he had to refuse absolution without violating the confession's seal of secrecy; instead, he had to encourage the penitent to report the incident to inquisitors. Before taking such steps, the confessor was expected to evaluate the reputation and credibility of the penitent, as women were often considered prone to suggestion, or worse, tools of the devil. However, if the information seemed plausible to him, and if a repenting woman refused to testify in court (perhaps due to pressure from family members or the solicitor), the confessor had to endeavor to persuade her that she would not suffer any consequences as a result of the sacrilegious priest's conviction because that conviction would remain secret.

The ecclesiastical hierarchy thus decided to punish abusive confessors but have them abjure their sins in private in order to avoid scandal. Some clergy found even this privilege too much to bear: they petitioned the Apostolic See, demanding that penitent women who had accepted sexual offers or advances be prosecuted as well. The Holy Office, however, did not follow up on the proposal, deeming it untenable in 1635.[34] Moreover, the heresy of clerical solicitation in Spain always concerned heterosexual relations, rather than the abuse of young men, by both regular and secular clergy. The Spanish Inquisition dealt with the abuse of young men under the category of sodomy and involved the clergy as little as possible. In contrast, the Roman Inquisition only punished homosexual acts when they were linked to heretical beliefs, for instance, when the accused downplayed sodomy as a sin.

Treatises on the crime of solicitation became especially prevalent in the first 30 years of the seventeenth century, and they addressed a key question: could the sworn word of a single woman constitute sufficient evidence against a member of the clergy? In Italy, this issue was tackled by two Jesuit theologians, Giovan Battista Scorza and Antonio Santarelli. Scorza argued that the testimony of the *testis singularis* (the woman) must be accompanied by additional evidence proving the priest's guilt. Santarelli, on the other hand, insisted that this heresy was so hidden that there was no alternative but to accept the word of a single witness, even if they were women and thus by nature liars. Still, their testimony was not to be overly trusted, even if multiple women came forward, as women were often considered prone to false accusations. It was, therefore, the responsibility of the inquisitors to carefully evaluate the credibility of the accuser and the alleged offender.[35]

More nuances in terms of proof were proposed by Sicilian friar Girolamo Trimarchi in 1636, who directed his treatise to both Spanish and Roman inquisitors. Like other canonists, Trimarchi sought to soften the impact of the 1622 papal constitution on clerical lives. In his view, fraternal correction should be reinforced within the monastic orders so as to avoid the scandal of turning to the Holy Office. Trimarchi argued that often women urged confessors into sexual or romantic acts, not the reverse; if a priest had been led into temptation, he deserved lesser penalties.

The most pressing issue, however, was how to prove the crime had occurred. If a priest learned of clerical solicitation through a woman's confession, he had to examine the circumstances of the sin, the acts involved, and the nature of the physical contact. The responsibility, therefore, fell once again on a priest—not on the woman—to assess the seriousness of the offense and determine whether the abuse was severe enough to warrant a report to inquisitors. If the abuse warranted that report, the priest's role was to urge the penitent to denounce the crime. Trimarchi offered conflicting counsel on women as witnesses. On the one hand, they were never fully reliable, even if they belonged to the highest social ranks, and the word of two women was worth less than that of two men. Still, women who had been abused at different times could have their depositions combined, whereupon their statements could carry enough weight to convict a priest of "vehement suspicion" of heresy. In the end, Trimarchi urged inquisitors to respect the power of a woman's legal deposition while also warning them against too easily trusting a woman's word.[36]

We do not possess comprehensive data on the solicitation cases prosecuted by Italian inquisitors after 1622.[37] But the offense was frequent and came up often in investigations of alleged saints, demoniacs, and disturbances in convents. Only a fraction of solicitation allegations were pursued resolutely, and even then, investigators often hesitated to take women's accounts at face value. After the 1740s, the Roman Holy Office softened its disciplinary strategy and adopted a more lenient approach toward solicitation than the Spanish Inquisition. Nevertheless, the category of clerical sexual abuse continued to exist, and it should have allowed ecclesiastical courts to probe sexual offenses, whether in the context of auricular confession or beyond.[38] Today, we know that in Italy, as elsewhere, the legal system's willingness to punish failed to protect abuse victims, though eventually, outrage over pedophilia finally overwhelmed fears over scandal. As the Catholic Church was engulfed by disgrace, longstanding assumptions about clerical impunity were profoundly and rightly unsettled.

Notes

1 Stefania Tutino, *Uncertainty in Post-Reformation Catholicism: A History of Probabilism* (Oxford University Press, 2018), and especially Barbara Fuchs and Mercedes García-Arenal, eds., *The Quest for Certainty in Early Modern Europe: From Inquisition to Inquiry, 1550–1700* (University of Toronto Press-UCLA, 2020).

2 Maria Pia Donato, ed., *Medicine and the Inquisition in the Early Modern World* (Brill, 2019).

3 Giuseppe Mascardi, *Conclusiones probationum*, 3 vols. (Zenarius, 1583–88); Giacomo Menochio, *De praesumptionibus, coniecturis, signis, & indicijs*, 2 vols. (Ziletti, 1587–90); Sigismondo Scaccia, *Tractatus de iudiciis causarum ciuilium, criminalium, et haereticalium* (Sessa, 1596); Prospero Farinacci, *Praxis et theoricae criminalis*, 2 vols. (Variscus, 1595). This last work was updated and supplemented several times up to 1616, with a final part dedicated to evidence and heretical crimes.

4 Miguel Gotor, *I beati del papa. Santità, Inquisizione e obbedienza in età moderna* (Olschki, 2002).

5 The text of the *Prattica per procedere nelle cause del Sant'Officio* is partially published in Albano Biondi, "'L'inordinata devotione' nella 'Prattica' del cardinale Scaglia (ca. 1635)," in *Finzione e santità tra medioevo* ed *età moderna*, ed. Gabriella Zarri (Rosenberg & Sellier, 1991), 306–25: 316–23.

6 Domenico Gravina, *Ad discernendas veras a falsis visionibus et revelationibus Basanites, hoc est lapis Lydius, theoricam et praxim complectens ad directionem*

confessariorum et qualificatorum S. Inquisitionis (Bonini, 1638), part II, 2. See Paola Zito, *Giulia e l'inquisitore. Simulazione di santità e misticismo nella Napoli di primo Seicento* (Esi, 2000).

7 On *discretio*, see Moshe Sluhovsky, *Believe Not Every Spirit: Possession, Mysticism, and Discernment in Early Modern Catholicism* (University of Chicago Press, 2007); Clare Copeland and Jan Machielsen, eds., *Angels of Light? Sanctity and the Discernment of Spirits in the Early Modern Period* (Brill, 2013).

8 See "Introduction," in *Historia: Empiricism and Erudition in Early Modern Europe*, eds. Gianna Pomata and Nancy G. Siraisi (Harvard University Press, 2005).

9 John Tedeschi, *The Prosecution of Heresy. Collected Studies on the Inquisition in Early Modern Italy* (Medieval & Renaissance Texts & Studies, 1991), 205–27. Subsequent studies have affirmed and expanded Tedeschi's conclusions: Giovanni Romeo, *Inquisitori, esorcisti e streghe nell'Italia della Controriforma* (Sansoni, 1990); Oscar Di Simplicio, *Autunno della stregoneria. Maleficio e magia nell'Italia moderna* (Il Mulino, 2005); Matteo Duni, *Witchcraft and Witch Hunting in Late Medieval and Early Modern Italy* (Routledge, 2020); Michaela Valente, "Witch Hunting and Prosecuting in Early Modern Italy. A Historiographical Survey," *Religions* 14 (2023), https://doi.org/10.3390/rel14050610.

10 Vatican City, Biblioteca Apostolica Vaticana, *Vat. Lat.* 5468, *Responsa Petri Beli*, 136v–139r.

11 Andrea Cesalpinus, *Quaestionum peripateticarum libri V. . . . Daemonum investigatio peripatetica. . . . secunda editio* (apud Iuntas, 1593, first edition 1580), 145v, 153r, 164r-166v. Cf. Giovan Battista Codronchi, *De morbis veneficis ac veneficiis libri IV* (apud Franciscum de Franciscis, 1595). For the history of this debate, see Vincenzo Lavenia, "La medicina dei diavoli: il caso italiano, secoli XVI-XVII," in *Médicine et religion. Collaborations, compétitions, conflits (XIIe-XXe siècle)*, eds. Maria P. Donato et al. (École Française de Rome, 2013), 163–94.

12 Girolamo Menghi, *Compendio dell'arte essorcistica* (Rossi, 1576); Hieronymus Menghi, *Flagellum daemonum* (Rubeis, 1577).

13 See Federico Barbierato, "Il medico e l'inquisitore. Note su medici e perizie mediche nel tribunale del Sant'Uffizio veneziano fra Sei e Settecento," in *Paolo Zacchia. Alle origini della medicina legale, 1584–1659*, eds. Alessandro Pastore and Giovanni Rossi (FrancoAngeli, 2008), 266–85; Jonathan Seitz, *Witchcraft and Inquisition in Early Modern Venice* (Cambridge University Press, 2011).

14 Marco Cavina, "La prova mistica dell'acqua fredda. Diritto tradizionale, diritto dotto e stregoneria (secc. XVI-XVII)," *Historia et Ius* 21 (2021): 1–26.

15 Heikki Pihlajamäki, "'Swimming the Witch, Pricking for the Devil's Mark': Ordeals in the Early Modern Witchcraft Trials," *Journal of Legal History* 21 (2000): 35–58; Martine Ostorero, "Les marques du diable sur le corps des sorcières (XIVe-XVIIe siècles)," *Micrologus* 13 (2005): 359–88; Orna Alyagon Darr, *Marks of an Absolute Witch: Evidentiary Dilemmas in Early Modern England* (Routledge, 2011).

16 The instructions issued by the Spanish *Suprema* to prevent new waves of panic (1614) did not mention this evidence. For the role played by the mark in the massive witch hunt in the Basque Country, see Lu Ann Homza, *Village Infernos and Witches' Advocates: Witch-Hunting in Navarre, 1608–1614* (The Pennsylvania State University Press, 2022), 38, 105, 159.

17 Cesare Carena, *Tractatus de modo procedendi in causis Sancti Officii* (apud Marc'Antonium Belpierum, 1636), 263–64.

18 Sarah Ferber, *Demonic Possession and Exorcism in Early Modern France* (Routledge, 2004), 70–87; Sluhovsky, *Believe not Every Spirit*, 244–49; Brian Levack, *The Devil Within: Possession and Exorcism in the Christian West* (Yale University Press, 2013); Joris Astier, *L'affaire Gaufridy. L'imaginaire du mal dans la France moderne* (Presses Universitaires de Franche-Comté, 2021).

19 Sébastien Michaëlis, *Histoire admirable de la possession et conversion d'une pénitente, séduite par un magicien la faisant Sorcière et Princesse des sorciers au pays de Provence* (chez Charles Chastelain, 1613).
20 Jacques Fontaine, *Des marques des sorciers et de la reelle possession que le diable prend sur le corps des hommes. Sur le subiect du proces de l'abominable & detestable sorcier Louys Gaufridy* (par Claude Larjot, 1611), 37–45.
21 Fontaine, *Des marques*, 7: "Un marque de luxure."
22 Fontaine, *Des marques*, 15.
23 Wilhelm Beemelsmans, "Die Kölner Professor Peter Ostermann und seine Schicksale," *Jahrbuch des Kölnischen Geschichsvereins* 19 (1937): 1–88. Petrus Ostermannus, *Commentarius juridicus ad L. Stigmata C. de Fabricensibus . . . in quo de variis speciebus signaturarum characterum et stigmatum tam supernaturalium quam naturalium, imprimis vero Antichristi, et de illorum, quae sagis inusta deprehenduntur . . . breviter tractantur* (apud Petrum Metternich, 1629). The text mentions the case of Aix (47–49), citing Michaëlis but not Fontaine.
24 Johannes Jordanaeus, *Disputatio brevis et categorica de proba stigmatica, utrum scilicet ea licita sit, necne. In qua pars negativa propugnatur* (in Officina Egmondana, 1630), 50.
25 Johannes Azor, *Institutionum moralium . . . pars prima* (apud Aloysium Zanettum, 1600), *liber* IX, chap. XXV–XXVI, 1120–29.
26 Paulus Zacchia, *Alle origini della medicina legale* (1621–61), in nine volumes.
27 Paulus Zacchia, *Quaestiones medico-legales, Liber tertius* (apud Guilelmum Facciottum, 1628), 34–39.
28 Paulus Zacchia, *Quaestiones medico-legales, Liber septimus & postremus* (ex typographia Manelphi Manelphij, 1635), 63–74.
29 Zacchia, *Quaestiones medico-legales, Liber septimus & postremus*, 279–317.
30 Adelina Sarrión Mora, *Sexualidad y confesión: la solicitación ante el Tribunal del Santo Oficio (siglos XVI-XIX)* (Alianza, 1994); Stephen Haliczer, *Sexuality in the Confessional: A Sacrament Profaned* (Oxford University Press, 1996).
31 The text of the constitution is also found in Girolamo Trimarchi, *De confessario abutente sacramento poenitentiae* (ex typographia Calenzani et Farroni, 1636), 12–14.
32 The document is published in *Bullarium Benedicti Papae XIV editio recentior*, vol. 1 (sumptibus Bartholomaei Occhi, 1777), 43–45.
33 Benedetto Fassanelli, *Il corpo nemico. Organizzazione, prassi e potere del Sant'Ufficio nel primo Novecento* (Edizioni di Storia e Letteratura 2017).
34 Trimarchi, *De confessario abutente*, preface for the reader.
35 Giovan Battista Scorza, *In selectas Summorum Pontificum constitutiones epitome ac theoremata* (Ludovici Prost, 1625), 280–81; Antonio Santarelli, *Tractatus de haeresi, schismate, apostasia, sollicitatione in sacramento poenitentiae, et de potestate Romani Pontificis in his delictis puniendis* (apud haeredem Bartholomaei Zannetti, 1625), 448–50.
36 Trimarchi, *De confessario abutente*, 188–91, 290–98.
37 Marie Lezowski, "Sollicitation en confession et dénonciation de violences sexuelles devant le Saint-Office (Sienne, 1589–1730)," *Revue de l'Histoire des Religions* 3 (2024): 427–76.
38 Fassanelli, *Il corpo nemico*; Francesco Benigno and Vincenzo Lavenia, *Peccato o crimine. La Chiesa di fronte alla pedofilia* (Laterza, 2021); Agnès Desmazières, "Le Saint-Office face aux crimes sexuels des clercs (1916–1939)," *Archives de sciences sociales des religions* 193 (2021): 177–98.

Select Bibliography

Alessi, Giorgia. *Prova legale e pena. La crisi del sistema tra evo medio e moderno.* Jovene, 1979.

Badea, Andreea, Bruno Boute, Carco Cavarzere, Steven Vanden Broecke. *Making Truth in Early Modern Catholicism*, edited by Andreea Badea, Bruno Boute, Marco Cavarzere, and Steven Vanden Broecke. Amsterdam University Press, 2021.

Bouley, Bradford A. *Pious Postmortems: Anatomy, Sanctity, and the Catholic Church in Early Modern Europe.* University of Pennsylvania Press, 2017.

Ceglia, Francesco Paolo de. *The Body of Evidence: Corpses and Proofs in Early Modern European Medicine.* Brill, 2020.

Donato, Maria Pia, ed. *Medicine and the Inquisition in the Early Modern World.* Brill, 2019.

Fuchs, Barbara, and Mercedes García-Arenal, eds. *The Quest for Certainty in Early Modern Europe: From Inquisition to Inquiry, 1550–1700.* University of Toronto Press-UCLA, 2020.

Kelly, Henry Ansgar. *Inquisitions and Other Trial Procedures in the Medieval West.* Ashgate, 2001.

Lavenia, Vincenzo. "La medicina dei diavoli: il caso italiano, secoli XVI-XVII." In *Médecine et Religion. Collaborations, Compétitions, Conflits (XIIe-XXe siècle)*, edited by Maria P. Donato, Luc Berlivet, Sara Cabibbo, Raimondo Michetti, and Marilyn Nicoud. École Française de Rome, 2013.

Lemesles, Bruno, ed. *La Preuve en Justice. De l'Antiquité à nos jours.* Presses Universitaires de Rennes, 2003.

Lezowski, Marie. "Sollicitation en confession et dénonciation de violences sexuelles devant le Saint-Office (Sienne, 1589–1730)," *Revue de l'Histoire des Religions* 3 (2024): 427–76.

Pastore, Alessandro, and Giovanni Rossi, eds. *Paolo Zacchia. Alle origini della medicina legale, 1584–1659.* FrancoAngeli, 2008.

Romeo, Giovanni, *Inquisitori, esorcisti e streghe nell'Italia della Controriforma.* Sansoni, 1990.

Schutte, Anne Jacobson. *Aspiring Saints: Pretense of Holiness, Inquisition and Gender in the Republic of Venice, 1618–1750.* The Johns Hopkins University Press, 2001.

Sluhovsky, Moshe. *Believe not Every Spirit: Possession, Mysticism and Discernment in Early Modern Catholicism.* University of Chicago Press, 2007.

Tedeschi, John. *The Prosecution of Heresy: Collected Studies on the Inquisition in Early Modern Italy.* Medieval & Renaissance Texts & Studies, 1991.

3

ON FORENSIC MEDICAL EVIDENCE

Bradford A. Bouley

In about 1630, a fight broke out in Rome between two men named Silvio and Ansovino. The altercation ended when Silvio struck Ansovino on the head, causing "a wound of considerable size," but which did not appear to fracture the skull.[1] After the fight, a surgeon inspected Ansovino's wound and declared that it was not life-threatening, sending the injured man home to recuperate. However, three days later, Ansovino was in a high fever and suffering severe head pain. More manifestations of illness, including vomiting, vertigo, and dark sores covering his body, came in successive days, until Ansovino died on the sixth day after the fight. Everyone, including the judges for the Governor's Tribunal, which likely had tried the case, concluded that Ansovino's death was caused by the infection from the wound. Silvio was charged with murder, and it appeared likely he would be found guilty.[2]

However, the presumptive verdict was challenged when an expert witness, Paolo Zacchia (1584–1659), was brought to testify. Zacchia, a papal physician and a medical expert, had testified extensively in Rome in the 1620s and 1630s before various legal tribunals.[3] In this case, Zacchia argued that both the jurists and witnesses failed to take proper account of the nature of Ansovino's wound, the progression of sickness after such an injury, and the signs similar to those caused by plague. Plague had been raging in Rome at the time of Ansovino's death, and Zacchia claimed that the symptoms of Ansovino's illness were more typical of plague than infection due to a wound. Furthermore, Zacchia went back through witness testimonies and found that one of the friends who had attended Ansovino after his injury had contracted plague and died before Ansovino. This detail strongly suggested that the friend was already sick and capable of spreading the disease when he visited Ansovino.[4] Although a recorded verdict of this trial has been lost, that Zacchia included

DOI: 10.4324/9781003486404-5

it in a list of his 100 most important expert decisions in legal cases strongly suggests that his testimony had a profound influence on the case—including, no doubt, a not-guilty verdict in favor of Silvio.

That Zacchia could present evidence capable of overturning other considerable testimony illustrates the prominence that forensic evidence had achieved in Europe by the seventeenth century. Indeed, Zacchia himself testified in hundreds of cases and even published a popular book—*Quaestiones Medico-Legales*—which guided other medical practitioners in how to testify before legal tribunals.[5] But how did medicine, which even a hundred years previously had been considered insecure in its conclusions, come to have such an important role in legal proceedings?[6] This chapter will lay out the legal and intellectual foundations of early forensic medicine in Europe, up until the 1600s. It begins with a consideration of the medieval context, during which there had been some precedent set for asking for medical opinions in murder cases. This cooperation between physicians and jurists expanded during the fifteenth and sixteenth centuries, especially as medical practitioners began to assert their role as experts in anatomy after the important medical discoveries that occurred during those centuries. Finally, a few case studies will be considered—especially those related to poisoning and violent murder—which demonstrate the role that autopsy and anatomy now could have in forensics.

Early Medical Testimony in Legal Trials

The origins of medical testimony in legal trials come from the medieval rather than the ancient period in Europe. Ancient Roman law, on which so much European jurisprudence was based, did not assign any role to medical testimony in trials and does not seem to have advocated for the use of this sort of expertise.[7] There are some signs that Germanic tribes in the early medieval context may have occasionally consulted healers in settling judicial affairs. A common punishment for personal injury—including murder—among Germanic tribes was the *Weregild,* in which the offender paid the victim or his family a specific price on the basis of the nature of the wound and the status of the victim. Among the surviving legal sources for some tribes (e.g., the Alemanni, Lombards, and Franks), it is evident that an official inspection of any wound was required before the *Weregild* could be paid. Although it is not entirely clear who performed the inspection, historian Katherine Watson suggests that it was likely a person with some medical training who could professionally evaluate the extent of the damage.[8] Watson also suggests that medical professionals may have had some role in evaluating injuries caused by judicial ordeals in the same period.[9]

The first certain, recorded evidence of medical testimony being used in legal proceedings in Western Europe comes from cases put before the

Catholic Church. In 1209 AD, Pope Innocent III (r. 1198–1216) considered in his decretals two important cases in which a church official might have been responsible for murder. In the first, a chaplain struck a thief with a heavy farm implement when he caught the latter stealing from his abbey. The thief managed to escape but was subsequently killed by parishioners. A question arose as to whether the chaplain's blow had been the decisive one in the thief's death. If so, it would have been a violation of his religious vows. Hence, a medical expert was deputized to determine the cause of death and whether the chaplain was culpable.[10] In another, similar case, the Bishop of Sigüenza in Spain had used a cane to drive back a rowdy crowd from his church. A scuffle developed between the bishop's attendants and the masses. During the skirmish, a young man received a hard blow to the head. About a month later, the injured man underwent an operation on the wound and died shortly thereafter. Many in Sigüenza claimed that the man had died from the wound inflicted by the bishop or his attendants. The case was enough of a scandal that it was brought to the attention of the pope in Rome. Pope Innocent III ordered two surgeons and one physician to investigate. These medical practitioners asserted that it was the botched surgery, rather than the bishop's cane, that had caused the death.[11] Although these two cases are our earliest examples, they are not cited in the record as novelties or innovations. Indeed, that Innocent was ready and able to call medical professionals and those professionals were willing to take part in these cases suggests that cooperation between medicine and law had already been taking place.

The use of medical professionals in criminal trials expanded in the thirteenth century, especially in southern Europe. The pioneering city in this regard seems to have been Bologna, which possessed a university renowned both for its medical and legal faculties. Not coincidentally, Pope Innocent III had received his legal training in Bologna. There is strong evidence that this might have been the first city to mandate medical investigation in the case of murder: that legal requirement appeared in Bologna's legislation by 1265 but was employed in practice at least a decade earlier.[12] The statutes required that in the case of a murder, two medical professionals and a notary must be chosen to inspect the cadaver. The law further stipulated requirements that these medical men had to have been residents in Bologna for at least ten years, no younger than 40 years of age, and in possession of enough wealth to not be suspected of corruption.[13] Later statutes from the fifteenth century would alter these requirements, such as stating that at times the testimony of only one medical professional was mandated. They also broadened the range of cases that required medical investigation. The statutes specifically mentioned incidents in which the suspicion of suffocation, strangulation, or suspected murder required medical testimony.[14]

Other cities in Italy and southern Europe quickly followed Bologna's lead in embracing forensics and requiring medical investigation in cases of murder. Manosque in Southern France began to require such posthumous investigation in 1262; the Kingdom of Aragon did so in 1275, with Venice following suit in 1281 and Paris by 1311.[15] In Venice, the cooperation between medical professionals and the judiciary was such that all wounds that appeared to be caused by violence were to be reported to the authorities.[16] By the fourteenth century, this law was so well known—and perhaps common in other places— that even medical practitioners who were new to the city were aware of the obligation to report unusual injuries.[17] Thus, if not the custom everywhere, it was nevertheless a fairly widespread practice by 1300 to consult medical professionals in cases involving murder.

Despite the requirement of posthumous evaluation of corpses in murder trials in many cities beginning in the mid-thirteenth century, it was not until the early 1300s that there is evidence of an autopsy being performed in furtherance of a forensic examination. That is, up until this moment, bodies had been examined without any opening of the cadaver. The first recorded forensic autopsy dates from 1302 in Bologna. In February of that year, the records state that one Azzolino degli Onesti died under suspicious conditions. He had been ill for a few days and had sought a doctor the day before his death. The doctor thought Azzolino had intestinal worms but was not in any immediate danger of dying. When Azzolino suddenly died in his bed the next day, the death was therefore determined to be suspicious and led some to conclude that he might have been poisoned. The Bolognese judge for criminal injury, or *iudex ad maleficia*, therefore ordered that two physicians and three surgeons perform a postmortem autopsy to determine what had in fact killed Azzolino. This expert panel concluded that Azzolino was not poisoned; rather, he had died from a coagulation of blood in his vena cava and near his liver.[18]

The examination of Azzolino occurred at a moment in central Italy during which corpses were beginning to be opened for a variety of reasons. Although some human dissections were conducted in the ancient world, that had ended by the Hellenistic period. During the thirteenth century, corpses once again began to be opened for public health autopsies to ascertain whether a series of deaths were related and hence the beginning of an epidemic, as well as for embalming the bodies of elites. During the early fourteenth century, the bodies of saints came to be opened occasionally as needed for verification of sanctity. Finally, it was at about this moment that several medical schools, particularly in Bologna and Padua, began to have anatomical instruction for students that might include dissection.[19] The birth of forensic autopsy, therefore, occurred just as medical practitioners were beginning to explore the anatomical interior of the human body. This interest in anatomy and conviction of the utility of autopsy would have profound consequences for the development of forensic medicine.

Growing Anatomical Knowledge in the Early Modern Period

A prerequisite for the growth of forensic medicine was a conviction on the part of both medical professionals and jurists that physicians well understood human anatomy and could read a dead body to determine cause of death. That medical professionals had such certainty about the human body or, indeed, that the dead body was even a sufficient reflection of the living to make claims was not at all clear even as late as the fifteenth century.[20] Much of the understanding of the natural world in Europe into the Middle Ages relied on Aristotle, who argued that there was a profound difference between the living and dead bodies of animals and humans. Though the configuration of the parts might remain as they were in life, in Aristotle's view, this might not be enough to understand how the organism worked.[21] Even if there were those who disagreed with Aristotle in antiquity, his views were authoritative for many European scholars and were only overcome slowly. The conviction that medical professionals could use autopsy to understand the life and death of a corpse evolved over the course of the fourteenth through sixteenth centuries as autopsy became more common and more generally used to demonstrate medical facts.[22]

The university was a primary site where ideas about the human body as an object of knowledge developed in the early modern period. Mondino de' Liuzzi (1270–1326), a professor of surgery in Bologna, was the first instructor who was recorded to have used a human cadaver to illustrate anatomy as described in medical texts. He was soon followed by other physicians in Bologna and Padua, who used dissections to illustrate the principles observed in the canonical treatises of Galen, Aristotle, and Hippocrates.[23] By the fifteenth century, several universities had regular, annual dissections for their students. Official statutes seem to have been slow in representing this change, though, as the practice had long been established by the time they appear in the statutes of the University of Bologna (1405) and those of the University of Padua (1465).[24]

Despite having annual dissections, medical students officially had few first-hand opportunities to explore human anatomy. In these dissections, students generally did not touch the body, and the cadaver was more of a visual aid to the text rather than a source of knowledge in itself. Although there is some evidence that, beginning in the later sixteenth century, students were encouraged to interact more with the body, public autopsies were certainly not opportunities for students to explore human anatomy for themselves.[25] Rather, in the words of historian of medicine Andrea Carlino, the anatomy lesson was frequently "little more than a ritual to celebrate the ancient classical authorities on the subject through a reading of their texts and the *disputatio*."[26]

Nevertheless, by the early sixteenth century, there were a number of indicators of real change when it came to the understanding of human anatomy by medical professionals. One of the factors in this development was the role of doctors in testifying during forensic trials. In many city-states in the Italian peninsula, the law codes began to stipulate that the medical team examining a corpse needed to be skilled in dissecting bodies themselves so that they could capably perform the autopsy.[27] Likewise, individual physicians such as Alessandro Benedetti (1450–1512), Jacopo Berengario da Carpi (1460–1530), and Niccolò Massa (1485–1569) insisted on dissecting bodies with their own hands as a way of gaining knowledge.[28] These two trends seemed to fuse by the 1530s, by which point a number of anatomical texts included clear instructions on how to open bodies for autopsy or dissection.[29] Similarly, the Florentine physician Antonio Benivieni (1443–1502) included in his work, *On the Hidden Causes of Disease,* reports on at least 15 autopsies conducted to determine the cause of death.[30] This work clearly served a didactic purpose for the forensic field as well as furthering the claims of medical professionals who argued that they well understood human anatomy.

By the middle of the sixteenth century, a real change in attitudes toward anatomy among both medical professionals and a more general learned public had become clear. Physicians such as Charles Estienne, Realdo Colombo, and especially Andreas Vesalius produced highly detailed and richly illustrated works of human anatomy. In these publications, they claimed not only to have understood the interior of the human body but also to have mastered it far more than the ancients. Indeed, Vesalius cited at least 200 errors in Galen's account of anatomy in his 1543 *On the Fabric of the Human Body.*[31] Vesalius represented a fusion of knowledge-making techniques since he employed the empirical methods characteristic of surgeons and apothecaries as well as the use of classical texts as sources with which to make knowledge about the human body.[32]

By the seventeenth century, Vesalian methods of dissection, according to historian Roy Porter, "had become the golden method for anatomical investigation."[33] The utility and confidence of these new methods were demonstrated to contemporaries by a number of landmark anatomical studies that were produced around the year 1600. Such publications documented for the first time the valves in human veins, the mechanisms of digestion, the structure of female reproductive anatomy, and, finally, the circulation of blood.[34] Many physicians had now embraced an epistemology that fused empirical investigation with textual evidence as a way to understand the human body.

This confidence would also extend to the realm of forensic anatomy, which, at the end of the sixteenth century and the beginning of the seventeenth century, resulted in the first medical works dedicated to a forensic understanding of the human body. The French surgeon Ambroise Paré (1510–90) has been cited as the first medical professional to write a forensic guide, as he commented extensively on his work with tribunals and provided case studies.[35] However, that guide was more a recounting of what Paré had done rather than any advice for other anatomists. It would be the Italians, such as Giovanni Filippo Ingrassia (1510–80), Fortunato Fedele (1550–1630), and Giovanni Battista Codronchi (1547–1628), who would write treatises that gave specific advice to medical professionals on what the relationship between law and medicine should be, what sort of evidence one should give while testifying, and what signs to look for.[36] Although these scholars could be seen as creating the field of forensic medicine, it was really Paolo Zacchia—the physician who opened this chapter—who brought it to full maturity.[37] His *Quaestiones Medico-Legales,* which was published over the course of years and which clearly drew on extensive experience with legal tribunals, treated almost every possible scenario in which a physician might be called upon to testify in a legal case. This advice proffered by Zacchia was further supported by discussion of a hundred different case studies that Zacchia had overseen himself.

Forensic Medicine in the Early Modern Period

In the seventeenth century, then, medical and legal practices had developed to such an extent that forensic medicine was its own field with recognized texts. But what did this mean in practice? What sort of signs did physicians look for in the early modern period to determine whether a crime had occurred? Although Paolo Zacchia provided guidance for legal cases ranging from demonic possession to whether a disability was disqualifying for standing trial, two areas in particular—the investigation of violent murder and unusual deaths involving poison—demonstrate especially well how medical knowledge and practice had developed since the first testimonies in the fourteenth century.

Zacchia provided clear guidance in how to assess cases of violent crime in the second section in Book 5 of his *Quaestiones Medico-Legales,* which was simply titled "On Wounds." Zacchia walked his reader through a number of factors in determining the danger in which a wound placed the victim. This was all useful information for a forensic witness, who seems most routinely to have been called to assess whether a person had died from their wounds or from some other ailment. Zacchia started this section by noting that dealing with wounds was a matter that required especially both medical and legal expertise, for it was the physician who could comment on the nature of wounds and "the imminent danger from them," as well as whether they would lead to "scars, deformities, mutilations, or impediments" for the rest of the victim's life. However, it was up to the jurist to decide the meaning of this information: that is, whether the defendant should be condemned on the basis of the new evidence that a medical examination had brought to light, or whether there were other, extenuating circumstances?[38]

After this preamble about the respective roles of the physician and the jurist, Zacchia turned to explaining the various factors that a doctor must consider when determining the gravity of a wound. The first issue he raised was the location of the wound, which had been an accepted way to assess an injury even in far earlier cases. A wound to the head, for example, should almost always be seen as more serious than one to the foot or the arm.[39] He then stated that a doctor must assess whether a wound was "simple or combined," by which he meant that the medical examiner must consider whether the tissue or bones lying beneath a wound could have been injured. This mandate required the physician to probe beneath the superficial nature of a wound and thus assumed a detailed knowledge of anatomy.[40] Next, the doctor should consider the weapon used to make the wound and whether or not—if the person was not yet dead—it was likely to develop into or pose a "hindrance" to healing.[41] Here, Zacchia seemed to be indicating the need to determine if the injury would grow infected and become gangrenous. Although the nature of infection and the role of bacteria in it would not be discovered for more than 200 years, physicians at this point recognized different kinds of infection and the issues that gangrene could raise.[42] Zacchia's criteria for understanding the nature of a wound and its threat seems to simply put into an organized format the standards that had already been employed, quite literally, for centuries by medical experts.

Contemporary cases demonstrate that they adhered to the same standards put forward by Zacchia in the day-to-day work of a forensic expert. For example, a 1644 report before the Governor's Tribunal in Rome states that a medical practitioner was called when "a cadaver of the masculine gender was found lying dead by the door of a building." A surgeon, named as Antonio Giustino, was asked to look at the wounds to determine whether his death could have been accidental.[43] Giustino started with the location of the wounds to the man, noting that they were focused on the face and even the cheek of the deceased. He then probed the extent of the damage and concluded that although "the cuts were not very deep," the man had been murdered. Someone had beaten him with "a hoe or something similar" and wounded "his cheek, his jaw, his head, and throat" to the extent that his "right cheek had totally collapsed."[44] The surgeon's testimony followed quite clearly the criteria laid out by Zacchia by looking into the location of the wound, the danger to underlying tissue, and the weapon used to cause the injury. Although this testimony does seem to follow a formula that had been in place for centuries, it nevertheless highlights the distance between the expert and non-expert view of the human body. Giustino could immediately deduce that beyond the apparently superficial wounds, there had been deep trauma; he was able to identify that a weapon had been used, and thus he removed any suggestion that the death could have been accidental.

Of greater difficulty was an area that demonstrated more clearly the difference between seventeenth-century and earlier forensic investigations—a suspected poisoning. As historian Alessandro Pastore has observed, poisoning cases required specialized skills because they lacked visible signs and might only be proven by an expert who could probe the interior of the body.[45] It was, after all, a poisoning case that led to the first known forensic autopsy in 1302, bringing a new set of skills and anatomical knowledge to bear on legal questions.

Forensic autopsies for cases of poisoning expanded in number and importance during the early modern period. This increase owed to both the increased confidence of medicine and the politics of the moment. During the fractious wars of the sixteenth and seventeenth centuries, political rivals frequently accused each other of murdering via poison, and burgeoning news sources had no trouble spreading rumors of such deaths, even if they were not true.[46] Indeed, nearly every pope in the sixteenth and seventeenth centuries had an autopsy performed on them after death to dispel any suspicion of poisoning, and the results were frequently widely circulated.[47] These medical-legal investigations thus achieved a high level of public interest.

Paolo Zacchia echoed this political concern and awareness when he turned to write about poisoning, noting that the nefarious nature of murders caused by poisoning made it a worse crime than a normal murder.[48] Zacchia explained that the serious nature of this crime and the difficulty of its detection were why medical testimony was so important in cases of suspicious deaths.[49] A first difficulty, according to Zacchia, was that depending on the type of poison used, it could have many effects on the body. Such effects might include ulcerating the digestive tract, altering the composition of the humors, inflaming the body, causing a person to choke, and damaging the body in a range of other ways.[50] One could not judge, however, whether poisoning had occurred simply by finding signs in the body that fit these ailments. As Zacchia acknowledged, many of these symptoms could also occur due to natural causes.[51]

Given this difficulty of discerning between poisoning and other bodily ailments, for Zacchia the key in diagnosing poison lay in a reading of both the symptoms and the behavior of the deceased. Had the patient been ill for some time, or was death sudden? Were the symptoms not normally ones that coincided? According to Zacchia, certain forms of illness went together, such as fever and vomiting. But others—he listed, for example, "dysentery with difficulty breathing, vomiting with bruised nails, [or] swelling of the tongue with burning urine"—were not natural pairings and thus should always have raised the suspicion of a medical professional.[52] He argued that these unusual symptoms were not products of natural diseases but rather produced by artifice and hence were a significant key to recognizing when a poisoning had occurred. For Zacchia, case history and an experienced physician were the main methods by which poisoning could be detected.

The concerns voiced by Zacchia for diagnosing poisoning were present a generation earlier and can be seen in a number of Ambroise Paré's case studies. A key case in which Paré used patient history and a reading of symptoms to overturn a suspicion of poisoning occurred specifically on March 10, 1575. Paré was called in, with "M. Greaulme, Regent Physician in the Faculty of Medicine to the house of M. du Hamel, Advocate in the Court of Parlement at Paris," for a case in which two of Hamel's servants, a clerk and a groom, appeared to be dead, but there was no indication as to how they died.[53] Paré reported that he was called because the "dispute was in the manner of death, for du Hamel said they had been suffocated; others thought them to have murdered one another; others philosophized [sic] their having been taken with apoplexy."[54] Poison was also suspected as being the culprit since there were no overt wounds.

In evaluating the conundrum, Paré and his colleague started with a careful bodily examination. Though the injured men were insensible to prodding and touch, Paré nevertheless found a faint pulse in each of them. After realizing they were alive, the medical practitioners queried the witnesses to learn what had happened. On the basis of those witnesses' statements and the appearance of the unconscious men, Paré judged that this was a case of smoke inhalation.[55] A partially burned brazier was found nearby; Paré administered a series of treatments that brought the two men back to consciousness; he was immediately acclaimed for his correct diagnosis.[56] This account, though not actually a case of poisoning, demonstrates the difficulty that early modern physicians and laypeople would have in discerning between possible causes and signs of death. Poisoning, apoplexy, and suffocation were all proposed as possible explanations before Paré was able to effectively judge the case and, in fact, save the two men's lives. It also demonstrates the process whereby a medical practitioner would investigate supposed cases of poisoning and eliminate other causes by careful consideration of other possibilities.

Although case history and symptoms were clearly useful in assessing cases of unusual deaths, autopsy remained a central means with which to verify the possibility of poison. Zacchia's warning that there were many natural causes of death that resembled poisoning was a major concern for forensic anatomists, even during an autopsy. One sign, however, that early modern medical experts employed in these cases was to look for damage to the gastrointestinal tract. If there was damage, it did not absolutely mean poisoning had happened, though it strongly indicated the possibility. On the other hand, if the gastrointestinal tract seemed otherwise healthy, then this was considered a pretty sure way to rule out poisoning.[57]

The use of autopsies that focused on the gastrointestinal tract to rule out poisoning appears in numerous case studies from the early modern period. In one late sixteenth-century example, Paré reported that he was called in to examine the unusual death of a man following a dinner party. Although Paré was not explicit about which witnesses he interviewed, he clearly conducted the sort of questioning to obtain additional details about what happened. From the outset, Paré told the reader that he strongly suspected poisoning. First, there was the timing: before dinner, the deceased "had been well, not having any pain." However, "soon after supper he complained of a great pain in his stomach, crying that he was suffocating and his body became yellow and bloated."[58] Then the deceased developed a series of unusual symptoms, including shortness of breath, vertigo, spasms, and, eventually, heart failure.[59] Given these strong suspicions, Paré and a colleague opened the body in an attempt to use autopsy to confirm or deny the poisoning. As soon as they cut into the body, a foul odor filled the room, and "the intestines and the internal parts in general were inflated and filled with gas."[60] Accompanying this gaseous bloating was blood that had filled the intestine. Combined with the symptoms and the sudden onset, such symptoms could only be attributed to poisoning, and Paré was able to identify a specific type of poison that he thought was responsible.[61]

Such confirmation could be especially important in cases in which an autopsy was performed to clear a party of suspicion of poisoning. One such case occurred in 1624, when the eminent Roman physician Giovanni Faber (1574–1629) was called upon with another physician, Giulio Mancini, to perform an autopsy on Marco Antonio de Dominis.[62] De Dominis had been considered a heretic by the Catholic Church and had been imprisoned in the Castel San Angelo, where he died in 1624.[63] In fact, according to a later letter that Faber sent to Galileo, members of the Roman Inquisition watched Faber perform the autopsy without telling him why they were doing so.[64] De Dominis had been a churchman who was well-loved by a large number of parishioners; it seems likely that inquisition officials sought to clear themselves of any accusation of murder by ordering a postmortem exam.[65] Indeed, Faber wrote to Galileo that he suspected that this was why he had been summoned. In the end, Faber reported that the interior cavity of the body was "clean" (*netto*) and that only the lungs were inflamed. This was an autopsy in keeping with de Dominis' symptoms. It helped clear Church authorities of any accusation of poisoning.

As these case studies and examples have shown, by the early modern period, there were clear medical guidelines and accepted medical practices to follow when examining injuries in judicial proceedings. Guidebooks such as Zacchia's *Quaestiones Medico-Legales* established general criteria; a number of recorded case studies provided practical advice. Through these case studies, it is clear that although the early modern autopsies had procedural and intellectual precedents with medieval ones, by the seventeenth century, a certainty about the role of autopsy and anatomy in providing definitive information about the life and death of the victim became an important tool in forensic cases. This increased medical confidence in turn meant that medicine was deployed with greater frequency in criminal trials.

Notes

1 Paolo Zacchia, *Quaestionum Medico-Legalium Tomus Posterior* (Ioan. Ant Huguetan & Marci Amnt, 1671), 320.
2 Zacchia, *Quaestionum*, 320–23. The case is also discussed in a few modern secondary sources that I draw on here. See Silvia de Renzi, "Witnesses of the Body: Medico Legal Cases in 17th century Rome," *Studies in History and Philosophy of Science* 33 (2002): 219–42, with the case on 227–29; Cecilia Pedrazza Gorlero, "La ferita incriminante: due consilia de vulneribus di Paolo Zacchia (1584–1659)," in *Paolo Zacchia alle origini della medicina legale 1584–1659,* eds. Alessandro Pastore and Giovanni Rossi (Franco Angeli, 2008), 212–19.
3 For more information on Zacchia, see, De Renzi, "Witnesses of the Body," 221–22; Silvia de Renzi, "Per una biografia di Paolo Zacchia: nuovi documenti e ipotesi di ricerca," in *Paolo Zacchia alle origini della medicina legale 1584–1659,* 50–73.
4 Zacchia, *Quaestionum*, case 74, 320–23.
5 For information about the popularity and extensive afterlife of this text, see Maria Gigliola and Renzo Villata, "Paolo Zacchia, la medicina come sapere globale e la 'sfida' al diritto," in *Paolo Zacchia alle origini della medicina legale 1584–1659,* cit., 12–14. Gigliola and Villata are explicit that they are not exhaustive in their cataloging but found that editions of Zacchia's work were published across the Italian peninsula, in major French cities including Lyons and Avignon, in Amsterdam, and in German cities such as Frankfurt and Nuremberg.
6 De Renzi, "Witnesses for the Body," 223.
7 Katherine D. Watson, *Forensic Medicine in Western Society: A History* (Routledge, 2011), 11.
8 Watson, *Forensic Medicine*, 11.
9 Watson, *Forensic Medicine,* 13.
10 Ynez Violé O'Neill, "Innocent III and the Evolution of Anatomy," *Medical History* 20 (1976): 430. Although the clergy was generally not supposed to wield weapons or shed blood, there had long been exceptions allowed, which included the defense of a church and its property. See Lawrence G. Duggan, *Armsbearing and the Clergy in the History and Canon Law of Western Christianity* (Boydell Press, 2013), 119–23.
11 Duggan, *Armsbearing and the Clergy,* 430–31.
12 Luigi Papi, "The First Reported Medieval Judicial Autopsy on Azzolino degli Onesti: Poisoning or Budd-Chiari Syndrome," *Medicina Historica* 6 (2022): 2–3; Francesco Paolo de Ceglia, "Introduction: Corpses, Evidence and Medical Knowledge in the Late Middle Ages and the Early Modern Age," in *The Body of Evidence: Corpses and Proofs in Early Modern European Medicine,* ed. Francesco Paolo de Ceglia (Brill, 2020), 2; Watson, *Forensic Medicine,* 34.
13 Papi, "First Reported," 3.
14 Alessandro Pastore, *Il medico in tribunale: La perizia medica nella procedura penale d'antico regime (secoli XVI-XVIII)* (Edizioni Casagrande, 1998), 81.
15 De Ceglia, "Introduction," 2; Guido Ruggiero, "The Cooperation of Physicians and the State in the Control of Violence in Renaissance Venice," *Journal of the*

History of Medicine 33 (April 1978): 156–66. Joseph Shatzmiller, "The Jurisprudence of the Dead Body: Medical Practitioners at the Service of Civic and Legal Authorities," *Micrologus: Nature, Sciences and Medieval Societies* 7 (1999): 223–30.

16 Ruggiero, "Cooperation," 158.

17 Ruggiero, "Cooperation," 160.

18 Papi, "First Reported," 3; De Ceglia, 1–2.

19 Katharine Park, "The Criminal and the Saintly Body: Autopsy and Dissection in Renaissance Italy," *Renaissance Quarterly* 47 (1994): 3–4; Nancy Siraisi, "Signs and Evidence: Autopsy and Sanctity in Late Sixteenth-Century Italy," in Siraisi, *Medicine and the Italian Universities, 1250–1600* (Brill, 2001), 356–80. See also Katharine Park, *Secrets of Women: Gender, Generation, and the Origins of Human Dissection* (Zone Books, 2006), 50, where Park observes that it was the exception, rather than the rule, to have holy bodies examined by a medical practitioner in the medieval period.

20 Maria Pia Donato, "Il Normale, il patologico, e la sezione cadaverica in età moderna," *Quaderni Storici* 46 (2011): 75–98; De Renzi, "Witnesses of the Body," 223.

21 Nancy Siraisi, *Medieval and Early Renaissance Medicine: An Introduction to Knowledge and Practice* (University of Chicago Press, 1990), 3.

22 For a comprehensive discussion of the changing view of anatomy in dissection and its importance to Renaissance culture more broadly, see Jonathan Sawday, *The Body Emblazoned: Dissection and the Human Body in Renaissance Culture* (Routledge, 1995).

23 Siraisi, *Medieval and Early Renaissance Medicine,* 81–86; Andrea Carlino, *Books of the Body: Anatomical Ritual and Renaissance Learning,* trans. John Tedeschi and Anne C. Tedeschi (University of Chicago Press, 1999), 2; Mondino dei Liuzzi, *Anatomies de Mondino dei Luzzi et de Guido de Vigevano* (E. Droz, 1926).

24 Siraisi, *Medieval and Early Renaissance Medicine,* 88; Carlino, *Books of the Body,* 2.

25 Carlino, *Books of the Body,* 32.

26 Carlino, *Books of the Body,* 20.

27 Allen Shotwell, "Dissection Techniques, Forensics and Anatomy in the 16th Century," in *The Body of Evidence*, ed. Francesco Paolo de Ceglia (Brill, 2020), 107.

28 Carlino, *Books of the Body,* 2; Roger K. French, *Dissection and Vivisection in the European Renaissance* (Ashgate, 1999), 96.

29 Shotwell, "Dissection Techniques," 110.

30 Shotwell, "Dissection Techniques," 113.

31 Numerous authors have written about the importance of Vesalius and debated to what extent 1543 counts as a turning point. See Carlino, *Books of the Body,* 1, 44; French, *Dissection and Vivisection,* 163–79; Lindemann, *Medicine and Society, 92–95*; Charles O'Malley, *Andreas Vesalius of Brussels, 1514–1564* (University of California Press, 1964). The works I am referring to by Colombo and Estienne are Realdo Colombo, *De re anatomica libri XV* (Venice, 1559), and Charles Estienne, *De dissectione partium corporis humani libri III* (Paris, 1545).

32 Pamela O. Long, *Artisan/Practitioners and the Rise of the New Sciences, 1400–1600* (Oregon State University Press, 2011), 56–58.

33 Roy Porter, "Medical Science," in *The Cambridge History of Medicine,* ed. Roy Porter (Cambridge University Press, 2006), 136–75, here 138. On the increasingly important role of anatomy in medical education, see Cynthia Klestinec, "Practical Experience in Anatomy," in *The Body as Object and Instrument of Knowledge: Embodied Empiricism in Early Modern Science,* eds. C.T. Wolfe and O. Gal (Springer, 2010), 33–57.

34 I am referring here to the publications of Fabricius of Acquapendente, who described the valves present in human veins in 1603; Gasparo Aselli of Padua (d. 1626) and Franciscus Sylvius of Leiden (d. 1672), who uncovered the workings of digestion; Gabriele Falloppio (d. 1562), who made significant contributions to both the anatomy of the ear and of female genitalia; and ultimately William Harvey, who in 1628 demonstrated the circulation of blood in the human body.
35 Watson, *Forensic Medicine,* 22.
36 Gigliola and Villata, "Paolo Zacchia," 42–43.
37 Gigliola and Villata, "Paolo Zacchia," 42–43.
38 Zacchia, *Quaestiones Medico-Legales* (Avignon, 1660), Lib V, Tit. 2, Quaest. 1, 297.
39 Zacchia, *Quaestiones Medico-Legales* (Avignon, 1660), Lib V, Tit. 2, Quaest. 2, 299.
40 Zacchia, *Quaestiones Medico-Legales* (Avignon, 1660), Lib V, Tit. 2, Quaest. 2, 299.
41 Zacchia, *Quaestiones Medico-Legales* (Avignon, 1660), Lib V, Tit. 2, Quaest. 2, 299.
42 Heidi Hausse, "Bones of Contention: The Decision to Amputate in Early Modern Germany," *Sixteenth Century Journal* 47 (2016): 327–50.
43 Archivio di Stato di Roma, Tribunale Criminale del Governatore (hereafter ASR), Processi 387, 1644, f. 484r: "cadaver cuiusq[ue] hominis masculi generis in via prostrat. prope Janua d.nus."
44 ASR, Processi 387, 1644, ff. 484r, 485r.
45 Pastore, *Il medico in tribunale,* 93; see also Alessandro Pastore, *Veleno: credenze, crimini, saperi* (Il Mulino, 2010).
46 Alessandro Pastore, "Casi di venefici tra Cinque e Seicento: teoria medico-legale e pratica penale," in *Paolo Zacchia alle origini della medicina legale*, eds. Alessandro Pastore and Giovanni Rossi (FrancoAngeli, 2008), 249–50.
47 Bradford A. Bouley, "Papal Anatomy in the News: Bodies and Politics in the Early Modern Catholic World," *The Sixteenth Century Journal* 49 (2018): 643–62.
48 Zacchia, *Quaestiones* (Avignon, 1660) Lib 2., Tit. 2, Quaest. 1, 57. "Non inutiliter ergo pro ipsis Iurisconsultis ad hoc de venenis argumentum petractandum accedemus; praecipuè quia apud illos venendandi crimen gravissimum delictum existimatur, ut verè est, & gravius homicidio."
49 Zacchia, *Quaestiones Medico-Legales* (Avignon, 1660) Lib 2., Tit. 2, Quaest. 1, 57.
50 Zacchia, *Quaestiones Medico-Legales* (Avignon, 1660) Lib 2., Tit. 2, Quaest. 2, 59–60.
51 Zacchia, *Quaestiones Medico-Legales* (Avignon, 1660) Lib 2., Tit. 2, Quaest. 6, 69.
52 Zacchia, *Quaestiones Medico-Legales* (Avignon, 1660) Lib 2., Tit. 2, Quaest. 6, pg. 70.
53 Ambroise Paré, *The Case Reports and Autopsy Records of Ambroise Paré,* ed. and trans. Wallace Hamby (Charles C. Thomas, 1960), 151.
54 Paré, *The Case Reports,* 151.
55 Paré, *The Case Reports,* 151–52.
56 Paré, *The Case Reports,* 152–53.
57 Pastore, *Veleno,* 161–89.
58 Paré, *The Case Reports,* 154.
59 Paré, *The Case Reports,* 154.
60 Paré, *The Case Reports,* 155.
61 Paré, *The Case Reports,* 155.

62 Giovanni Faber, Rome to Galileo, Florence, 14 September 1624, in *Le Opere di Galileo Galilei*, ed. Giuseppe Saragat, vol. XIII (G Barbèra Editore, 1968), 207.
63 For an early modern biography of De Dominis, see British Library (BL), Additional Manuscripts (Add.) 8357, fols. 63v-68r.
64 Faber to Galileo, 207. "Morì nel nono d'una febre malgina, et alle 7 hore venne a casa mia Giulio Mancino, d'ordine *Sanctissimi* [sic], et mi menò seco al Castello, volendo che anche io assistessi quando fu aperto il cadavero di quest'Arcivescovo in presenza d'un notaro del S. Uffizio. Credo fosse fatto acciochè il mondo non potesse dire che fosse stato avelenato."
65 BL, Add. 8357, fol. 64v.

Select Bibliography

Carlino, Andrea. *Books of the Body: Anatomical Ritual and Renaissance Learning*. Translated by John Tedeschi and Anne C. Tedeschi. University of Chicago Press, 1999.
de Ceglia, Francesco Paolo, ed., *The Body of Evidence: Corpses and Proofs in Early Modern European Medicine*. Brill, 2020.
de Renzi, Silvia. "Witnesses of the Body: Medico-Legal Cases in Seventeenth-Century Rome." *Studies in the History and Philosophy of Science* 33 (2002): 219–42.
Donato, Maria Pia. "Il Normale, il patologico, e la sezione cadaverica in età moderna." *Quaderni Storici* 46 (2011): 75–98.
French, Roger K. *Dissection and Vivisection in the European Renaissance*. Ashgate, 1999.
Gentilcore, David. *Healers and Healing in Early Modern Italy*. Manchester University Press, 1998.
Klestinec, Cynthia. *Theaters of Anatomy: Students, Teachers, and Traditions of Dissection in Renaissance Venice*. The Johns Hopkins University Press, 2011.
O'Neill, Ynez Violé. "Innocent III and the Evolution of Anatomy." *Medical History* 20 (1976): 429–33.
Park, Katharine. "The Criminal and the Saintly Body: Autopsy and Dissection in Renaissance Italy." *Renaissance Quarterly* 47 (1994): 1–33.
Park, Katharine. *Secrets of Women: Gender, Generation and the Origins of Human Dissection*. Zone Books, 2006.
Pastore, Alessandro. *Il medico in tribunale: La perizia medica nella procedura penale d'antico regime (secoli XVI-XVIII)*. Edizioni Casagrande, 1998.
Pastore, Alessandro, and Giovanni Rossi, eds. *Paolo Zacchia Alle origini della medicina legale, 1584–1659*. Franco Angeli, 2008.
Pomata, Gianna. *Contracting a Cure: Patients, Healers, and the Law in Early Modern Bologna*. The Johns Hopkins University Press, 1998.
Ruggiero, Guido. "The Cooperation of the Physician and the State in the Control of Violence in Renaissance Venice." *Journal of the History of Medicine and Allied Sciences* 33 (1978): 156–66.
Shatzmiller, Joseph. "The Jurisprudence of the Dead Body: Medical Practitioners at the Service of Civic and Legal Authorities." *Micrologus: Nature, Sciences and Medieval Societies* 7 (1999): 223–30.
Siraisi, Nancy G. *Medieval & Early Renaissance Medicine: An Introduction to Knowledge and Practice*. University of Chicago Press, 1990.
Watson, Katherine D. *Forensic Medicine in Western Society: A History*. Routledge, 2011.

PART II

Urban Violence

4

ON HOMICIDE IN BOLOGNA

Colin Rose

For many years now, historians have mined the voluminous records of early modern Italian courts for fruitful evidence of the daily life and times of ordinary people living in the peninsula's densely packed cities and agricultural zones. Early methodological collections showed how this work could itself constitute a "crime" if careful reflection on the structures and constructions of those judicial records was not foremost in historians' analyses.[1] Historians working with these materials have noted the inherently unequal relationship between the highly educated and literate judges and notaries of courts such as Bologna's *Tribunale del Torrone*, and the illiterate victims of and witnesses to crime whom they interviewed behind closed doors. At the same time, Thomas Cohen and others have argued that the ordinary participants in judicial processes were themselves possessed of a variety of strategies for crafting strong narratives to press their case with the authorities.[2] We now understand that there existed in early modern Italy a wide degree of common legal literacy that gave both authorities and those under their authority a starting point for participation in the ongoing debates about causation, fault, and guilt that trial processes constituted.

Both judicial authorities and ordinary people understood legal processes, judicial right and wrong, and cultural ideals of "justice" in ways that allowed them to drive their own particular narratives. Bolognese urbanites and *contadini* had relatives, friends, and neighbors who engaged with the court's processes and could share insight and experiences, including how best to shape particular suits to particular ends. Italian courts, then, also relied upon forms of expertise to help ascertain and verify some of the basic "facts" around which narratives coalesced. Chief among those, and already noted in a growing body of literature, were the physicians and surgeons who provided courts

DOI: 10.4324/9781003486404-7

with expert opinions on the nature of wounds and causes of death in cases of violent crime.[3] These experts can shed light on both the nature of violence, through the surgeon's reports Peter Blastenbrei deployed to document violent crime in Rome, and the nature of early modern expertise, which Silvia de Renzi argues was hedged against both the legal knowledge of judicial authorities and the lay knowledge of ordinary supplicants and witnesses.[4] Physicians and surgeons worked at the beginnings of criminal *processi* to ascertain the condition of bodies and injuries and the probable ages of victims; assisted by lay witnesses to corporeal inspections, they also give insight into the material histories of bodies by noting the clothing people wore, the hair and facial hair styles prevalent at the time, and the forms of bodily ornamentation, such as jewelry, that people displayed. As experts in the body, medical men in early modern Bologna provided an invaluable service to a criminal court deeply concerned with its own legitimacy.

Legitimacy, or at least the presentation of such, was at the core of the work of early modern Italian tribunals. In Bologna, papal legates and their judicial officers devoted significant energies to public reform of institutions with an eye toward improving access to and the delivery of justice for *Bolognesi* of all stripes and stations. The history of Bologna weighed heavily on this process: the medieval city was fractious and factional, dominated by a few oligarchic families who deployed justice to their own political ends in both town and country.[5] Justice here was personal, not impartial, and ordinary *Bolognesi* lacked a solid institutional basis to pursue conflict resolution or redress for harms done outside of the sponsorship of feudal structures. After the papal conquest in 1506–09, rule of Bologna passed from the Bentivoglio oligarchs to the supposedly detached papal legates, and the delivery of justice from podestarial and feudal tribunals to the centralizing, institutional *Tribunale del Torrone*.[6]

An overarching goal of the *Torrone*'s officers was to supplant the partial justice of the medieval period with a central, singular judicial authority unbeholden to the factional politics of the city's oligarchs. This process could not be achieved through force and politics alone, as *Bolognesi* needed to be drawn away from old practices of clientage and sponsorship and toward use of the new papal institution. To effect that shift, the *Tribunale del Torrone* needed to be seen as a reliable, legitimate alternative to past forms of justice. Pacifying and "disciplining" the fractious nobility of the city was a starting point: much of the *Torrone*'s early decades were concerned with bringing the vendettas and violence of Bologna's elites to heel in order to demonstrate that papal authority could bring stability and therefore accessibility to the city's judicial landscape.[7] But nativist impulses reached deep into the Bolognese collective memory, and the *Torrone* also needed to demonstrate the legitimacy of its position and the legitimacy of the papal claim to govern Bologna. Drawing the city's professional classes, especially the graduates of its medical and legal university, into the tribunal's processes helped to communicate that legitimacy, as their expertise contributed to the institutional weight of its investigations and sentencing.

That legitimacy could be conceived in more than one way. On the one hand was the political legitimacy of the papal state and, by extension, its institutions. That legitimacy was established, tenuously, in 1509 with the final expulsion of the Bentivoglio monarchs and the recapitulation of the Bolognese senate to papal rule.[8] While pockets of resistance to papal rule persisted, and open defiance occurred periodically, by the end of the sixteenth century, Bolognese republicanism was a dead letter. There was no going back to the halcyon days of oligarchic factionalism, and while the descendants of the fractious Pepoli, Malvezzi, and Aldrovandini who so troubled Bologna's streets occasionally rode in force against their traditional nemeses, and despite a resurgence of factional violence in the mid-seventeenth century, no credible alternative to papal governance was ever seriously considered until Napoleon.[9]

On the other hand was the legitimacy of an institution seen to be doing its work assiduously and with access to the best resources at hand. In a series of reforms over the sixteenth and seventeenth centuries, the officers of the *Torrone* made distinct efforts to improve the visibility and image of the central court in the public eye. Reforms targeted the perceived corruption of its notaries, the affordability and therefore accessibility of its conflict resolution services, and the jurisdiction and competency of its judges.[10] Legitimacy here means not simply an undisputed claim to jurisdiction and territorial authority; it refers to the positioning of the institution within people's options and choices. Legitimacy meant providing better and more effective judicial solutions to the conflicts and troubles of ordinary people. Alongside the continual public reforms of the *Torrone*'s processes, court officials involved a number of experts and *buon'uomini* in its processes to present an image of professionalism and accuracy.

Non-medical experts also gave court processes an air of factuality by deploying their skills to create thick, deeply evocative descriptions of the times and places of violent crime. The notaries of the *Tribunale del Torrone* were university-trained, long-term employees of the city and court, skilled at recording all of the necessary elements of *Torrone* criminal processes. This included an intensive fidelity to the words of witnesses and supplicants during interrogations. Questions were asked in Latin and Italian and recorded in a Latin third person; answers were recorded in a vernacular first person. Publicly distributed rules for notaries periodically emphasized the need to ensure the fidelity and security of all copies of documents.[11] Though not beyond reproach and noted sometimes for corruption in the recording of supplementary materials, *Torrone* notaries were, by and large, assiduous in their creation of a dense documentary record of the acts of court officials. In their investigations of homicides, notaries developed a skill at rudimentary forensic examination of the scenes of crimes. Their twin expertises—faithful written reproduction of oral processes and thick description of the physical settings and characteristics of crimes—made notaries a critical element of early modern judicial processes.[12] They were present at investigations and described in their own words the settings and contexts of the manifold conflicts their court adjudicated. Like the work of physicians and surgeons, the expertise of notaries allowed the *Tribunale del Torrone* to achieve a widely accepted legitimacy as an inquisitorial court, one whose processes and conclusions could plausibly be said to be based on facts and evidence rather than on the weight of personal status, as in the network of accusatorial courts the *Torrone* displaced.

A third set of experts lent their skills to the *Torrone* as a means of legitimizing the activities of a hegemonic government body whose work could threaten the freedom and lives of the people of Bologna and its environs. The court exercised the power of life and death over its subjects through capital punishment. This fraught process needed to be handled with care, and two sets of experts buttressed the court's violence with a veneer of humanity. The comforters of the confraternity of *Santa Maria della Morte*, a mixture of elite patricians and artisan men, worked assiduously to bring condemned men and women to an acceptance of the justice of their fate and, thereby, to the gates of heaven through repentance and confession. This extraordinarily difficult work was the product of an education in both ecclesiastical and secular strategies for comforting the condemned, with a dedicated manual followed by the comforters.[13] The expertise they developed meant that the comforters were agents of the court's legitimacy, ensuring that executions could proceed peacefully and orderly to avoid inflaming the tension of a crowd that was always one thrown rock away from a riot. Their work was completed by executioners who were skilled in the delivery of death, both in the elaborate theaters of mutilation and symbolic punishment that preceded an execution and in the swift (or not) act of hanging itself.[14] Like medical men and notaries, the expert services of these men bolstered the perceived legitimacy of the *Torrone* in its treatment of the bodies of *Bolognesi* and *stranieri* in the *Legato*.

The records of early modern criminal process, then, cast a bright light, not without shadow, on the histories of ordinary people and their bodies—dead and injured bodies, bodies in physical and social contexts, and bodies as they prepared for and were sent to their deaths. These records do so because of the legitimate right of a court to investigate and exercise control over those bodies, a legitimacy that, in Bologna, was developed over a long struggle between various forms of judicial institutions.[15] Critical to its success was the *Torrone*'s ability to provide a more reliable, neutral, and fact-based form of justice than its predecessors; whether this claim to factual superiority is true or not is debatable. But it rested nonetheless on the contributions of various forms of expertise to buttress its claims of truth. In dealing with suspicious bodies—a body out of place being the most basic definition of homicide—the court adjudicated evidence and proceeded in its investigations with the assistance of experts both directly in its employ and acting in auxiliary roles to provide medical and spiritual expertise to developing homicide cases. Through their intensive engagement with suspicious bodies and the circumstances of their passing, medical men, notaries, comforters and executioners both rendered the history of bodies clearer to future historians and bolstered the legitimacy of a powerful agent of papal authority in the northern papal state. At the same time, they gave the officers of the court an outlet toward which they could redirect popular dissatisfaction with justice, by spreading the responsibility for judicial judgment across a body of non-judicial experts.

On June 27, 1632, in the neighborhood of Santa Maria Mascarella in Bologna, Italy, a woman named Margherita Parisina and her husband, Annibale Cesare, ate dinner at home, went to vespers at the church of San Giacomo, and then returned to their home where Margherita passed some minutes chatting with her neighbors in her doorway. Sometime during that night, Margherita dropped dead, "all of a sudden," as the neighborhood bailiff reported to the city's central criminal court the next day. Here, a mystery unfolded: how did Margherita die?[16]

The morning of June 28, the *Tribunale del Torrone* dispatched a notary and a judge to the location of the body in order to try to gather some answers. The judge, Prospero Prossi, had his notary investigate the body for any signs of foul play. The notary recorded that he saw a woman's body, approximately 40 years of age, facing toward the door of the kitchen, with no obvious injuries and no apparent cause of death. He added that a physician was needed to determine how Margherita met her end. Indeed, two physicians from the university medical school were called, Honorio Bensi and Lorenzo Arsinati. One of these physicians noted that Margherita had a black discoloration of her skin extending from her ears down the sides of her neck to her shoulders. He believed this to be a sign of possible poisoning. Both physicians agreed that in order to determine whether Margherita had indeed been poisoned, a full autopsy would be necessary. The judge duly ordered Honorio Bensi to perform such an autopsy and to submit his report to the court in a formal interrogation.

The physician Honorio and a colleague, Bartolomeo Bonacursio, assisted by two barber-surgeons affiliated with the university's anatomy theater, duly performed this autopsy and reported back to the court of the *Torrone* on July 4, 1632. In that report, Honorio described how they had "cut, opened and diligently observed" Margherita's cadaver; how she had "a large bruise, and very ugly, around the ears and down to her shoulders"; and, more importantly, how her insides smelled so bad that the surgeons performing and the students observing the dissection were made sick, and how her stomach and intestines were deeply inflamed and discolored. There was blood in her lungs, and in her stomach a large quantity of a yellow, bilious liquid. They judged that the inflammations of her organs and the internal bleeding that accompanied it had caused Margherita to stop breathing, which accounted for the discoloration of her skin around her face, and that the illness had probably begun seven or eight hours prior to her death. From these signs, they concluded Margherita Parisina had been poisoned, likely at dinnertime on June 27, the evening before she died. Both doctors, in their individual reports, hedged that "there are, however, many types of poison, some simple, some from animals, some artificial," and thus they could not render an exact verdict as to the particular poison. They agreed, however, that Margherita had indeed been poisoned, sometime on the evening of June 27.[17]

This graphic tale of inflamed organs illustrates one of the major problems facing the *Torrone*, and the courts of other Italian cities, in the seventeenth century: how to determine the cause of death, when a body itself did not display obvious signs of violence such as stab wounds or evidence of significant physical trauma? The inquisitorial judicial process employed by seventeenth-century courts relied significantly upon the evidence provided by bodies themselves: the first step in any potential homicide case was an official inspection of the corpse, performed by an official of the court and at least two witnesses. In obvious cases of homicide, these witnesses were generally local witnesses who knew the deceased and could identify him or her, give his or her approximate age, and perhaps point the court's agents toward possible witnesses to interrogate in the course of investigation. However, not all bodies displayed obvious signs of trauma or apparent cause of death. In these cases, such as the poisoning death of Margherita Parisina, the notaries and judges of the court relied upon the expertise of the city's medical school to assist in the judgment of homicide as the cause of death. This expertise provided the court with legitimate jurisdiction to pursue a homicide investigation.

The literature on medical expertise as an aspect of Italian judicial processes has often focused on the use of physician's testimony to bolster the authority of courts and states, as in the early work of Guido Ruggiero on Venice and the more recent work of Joanna Carraway Vitiello on medieval Modena.[18] Certainly the criminal courts of the late medieval and early modern periods existed as part of a nexus of institutions involved in the grand projects of state-making that many Italian governments undertook from the fourteenth through eighteenth centuries. The involvement of physicians and laypeople in the investigation of cadavers, however, has a more complex significance than simply the bolstering of court claims to authority. As they engaged in the investigation of bodies, the sites where they were found, and the social milieu that had brought them there, court authorities were not merely attempting to enhance the scientific expertise, and thereby the legal authority, of centralizing criminal courts. They were also engaged in a process of risk mitigation, that in many ways removed responsibility for judgment from the court itself, and diffused the possibility of dissatisfaction with court process into both the university medical school and the local communities who participated in these judicial inspections. The medical expertise of physicians and surgeons thereby legitimized the court at the same time as it drew the responsibility for court decisions away from individual court officers. This fact had significant ramifications, as judges, *sbirri* [cops], and notaries were repeatedly targeted by the disgruntled relatives of men they had accused of or condemned for violent crimes.

The inspection of a body was the first step in the process of investigating a murder; upon receipt of a denunciation or a report of a suspicious death, an officer of the court would be dispatched to the scene. Often, as in the Roman *relazioni dei Barbieri* studied by Peter Blastenbrei, these reports and denunciations themselves came from physicians at one of Bologna's two major hospitals, *Santa Maria della Vita* and *Santa Maria della Morte*, where many of the city's homicide victims were taken prior to their expiration.[19] In many, perhaps most, of the body inspections that followed the report of a suspicious death, local friends, family, and acquaintances of the victim aided the notary in inspecting the corpse and detailing its visible wounds. They were judged equally as reliable in identifying both the body and the significant injuries that it exhibited, and they thus accepted a share of the responsibility for that judgment. That is to say: in adjudicating cause of death, the court involved local participants of the deceased's kin and community network, not simply to bolster the authority of the state as with the use of physicians, but to lay the responsibility of declaring a homicide on more shoulders than just the notary's.

We see this in countless homicide trials within the city's urban core as well as the plains, villages, and mountain hamlets that make up the city's hinterland. A notary first describes the body as he sees it; following this, two acquaintances, usually though not exclusively men, were called upon to adjudicate what they saw: "I see and have seen well this body" [*vedo e ho veduto benissimo questo cadaver trovato qui*]. These witnesses went beyond the description provided by the notary to note the material surroundings, the clothes, the age of the victim, and, perhaps most importantly, the name. Like the notary, they described the wounds visible on the body. Unlike the notary, they often speculated on which wounds had caused the death—as did physicians—and even who might have caused the death or who the court might interrogate to learn more. Both physicians and lay witnesses in body inspections expanded upon the notary's cursory description of the body to make judgments about the cause of death and the person responsible for causing it. In doing so, they became participants in the judicial process in a way that also made them responsible for its effects on their local communities.

This did not necessarily improve their popularity. In the 1652 murder of a judge of the *Torrone* in one of the city's *piazzas*, the court relied upon the body inspection of only one physician, with the documentation implying that no one else would participate.[20] In a 1690 case in which two men were shot during the course of an argument over cows in the rural hamlet of Monzone, the judge of the *Torrone* was left to perform the inspection himself when nobody in town would participate.[21] A sense of resistance to participation in the court process is clear in some cases, but in the vast majority of homicides, witnesses collaborated with, or were compelled to participate in, the court's investigation in order to bring some clarity to the matter at hand. Frequently, the kin networks of the deceased filled this role; other times, business acquaintances, local religious figures, or simply town notables did. The important element is that the court drew in users as participants in criminal processes as a means to establish a broad legitimacy alongside the expertise provided by medical men.

If the judgment of locals and experts could be used to diffuse responsibility for a declaration of homicide, it was also necessary to absolve the court of that declaration; that is, even in cases of accidental death, expert testimony was used to allow the court to declare a death as such and cease their investigation. In 17 suspicious cases of drowning across the seventeenth century, expert testimony from physicians or surgeons declaring the drowning an accident was used to bring the investigation to a close. In 26 cases of "accidental death," mostly involving self-inflicted gunshot wounds or carriage accidents, locals testified to the absence of enmity, and barber-surgeons testified to the accidental nature of wounds in order to render the accidental verdict. In these cases, it was not a court official making the judgment but either prominent locals or medical authorities. These participants bolstered the authority of the court, yes, but they also shielded it from the criticism of kin dissatisfied with the judicial process. The expertise of medical authorities was brought in almost as an efficiency measure to ensure both that the *Torrone*'s judgment of cause of death was sound and legitimate and also to ensure that the court did not spend any more time and resources than strictly necessary.

In other cases, the opposite was true: testimony on the cause of death was brought in to ensure that a body received the full investigation its discovery warranted. In 1660, an incomplete skeleton was discovered in the garden of Girolamo Brigola on the banks of the Riva di Reno in Bologna.[22] The notary and two witnesses called to investigate the bones agreed that they were old, too old to have been of recent deposit, and likely predated Brigola's inhabitation of the property. Rather than let the discovery lapse, however, the court sought earlier residents of the area and reached out to neighbors for clues as to whom the bones might have belonged. Brigola's neighbors had long memories: one of them recalled that in 1647 a young girl, Teresa Fantazzi, had gone missing in the neighborhood and no trace of her had been found. In the

Torrone's records of the disappearance, the former resident of the property had fallen under suspicion but had never been formally accused of the girl's disappearance. That resident, Matteo Fantuzzi, was a water porter who had been disliked by his neighbors, and 13 years later, they recalled their distaste for him. The character judgment of the locals as well as the situational and forensic evidence of the discovered bones led the court to seek out Fantuzzi and level a charge of homicide 13 years later. The testimony of both experts and laypeople regarding the status of the bones, discovered in a backyard in 1660, led the court to reopen a cold case that had lain dormant since 1647. These witnesses gave the *Torrone* sufficient grounds—including judgment on the size of the skeleton—to make a determination of homicide as the cause of death and to turn the force of its authority onto a man who had remained unmolested by the court for nearly 15 years. Without this testimony, the court would not have had firm grounding upon which to do so.

Which was the same need served by our poor doctors in the case of Margherita Parisina, up to their elbows in viscera in the pursuit of a poison diagnosis? Following the determination that she died by poisoning and working on their judgment that the poison had been administered some seven or eight hours before she died, the *Torrone* leveled an accusation of murder against her husband, Annibale Cesare. But this was not their only information. While interrogating Catherina's neighbors, the court's agents learned that she and Annibale had a strange relationship and that he had recently argued, publicly and offensively, with his brother, intimating that Catherina was at the core of the argument. Over the course of July 1632, they interrogated Annibale repeatedly, but he stuck to his story: Catherina had first sickened while he was on a trip to Budrio two weeks prior to her death, and he did not know what the cause was, much less poisoned her himself. Unable to get a confession and unwilling to torture on what they deemed a flimsy pretext, the court eventually let him go.

Lurking in the background of these cases were the notaries of the *Torrone*, university-educated experts in their craft. The criminal archive of this ambitious criminal court runs to a total of approximately 12,000 bundled volumes from c. 1550 to 1796. Each bundle ranges from 300 to over 1,200 folios, creating a massive and unwieldy archival trove of documentation, a boon to historians in the twenty-first century and a fundamental element of the *Torrone*'s claims to legitimacy. In any given year, eight notaries handled the work of managing and recording the activities of themselves and other court officers and of keeping a reliable documentary record of the testimonies and depositions of suspects, witnesses, and affiliated experts. The notaries were ultimately responsible for the integrity of the *Torrone*'s work, and thereby, its legitimacy as the hegemonic criminal authority in the *Legato*.

Still, they were not above reproach, and throughout the latter half of the sixteenth century and into the seventeenth, their work was regulated in response to ongoing complaints about corruption and graft. Through a long process of reform, their professional status was confirmed and placed under scrutiny to ensure that the *Torrone*'s acts were as close to trustworthy as possible.[23] Legislation dating from the 1560s, 1580s, 1590s, and 1620s repeatedly laid out the responsibilities of notaries, the emoluments and fees they were allowed to collect for their work, and the limits on their actions. At the heart of this legislation was the *Torrone*'s continued push to gain ultimate authority over the bodies of the *Legato*.

The notaries, as the most visible public face of the *Torrone*, were critical to its image of legitimacy. In 1607, the Cardinal-Legate Giustiniano laid out his "Orders to be Observed by the Notaries of the Torrone, both concerning Causes and their Salaries."[24] In elaborate detail, the Legate established a process by which notaries were bound to follow a case from beginning to end without neglecting their duties. Notaries were commanded to render each process faithfully ad verbum, to interrogate witnesses singly and not in groups, to turn serious matters over to the judge for assistance, to promptly transfer all written materials to the archive once completed, and to properly inventory their materials for the entirety of their tenure as notaries. All of these rules were designed to promote a safe chain of custody for judicial materials that eliminated as many avenues as possible for tampering with documents or for deliberately clogging up the judicial system with slow work. In the same document, the Legate reiterated a fee schedule from 1580, which kept the emoluments that notaries received for various services, such as copying, deliberately low as a matter of access to justice for the poor. Finally, the Legate instituted a formal oath for notaries of the *Torrone* to swear upon entering the office, pledging to provide justice without bias and by their own hand. If they broke the oath, they were charged a stiff fine by the *Monte di Pietà* and were banned from employment in the city for at least two years.

The professionalization of the notarial staff of the court was a key plank in its claim to legitimacy and authority in the *legato*. By continually promoting the public image of the *Torrone* as a reliable, efficient, and trustworthy forum for conflict resolution, its judges knocked a key resource out from under anti-papal noble factions, who used rural justice to wield influence and patronage over their feudal tenants. By the beginning of the seventeenth century, there was no doubt that the *Torrone* was the most powerful court in Bologna, though it still faced competition. The Papal Legation was solidified, and while further threats to papal rule of Bologna in the seventeenth century could reach significant levels of violence, those threats did not meaningfully challenge the jurisdiction of either the popes or the *Torrone*'s notaries and judges.

At the heart of the consolidation of the *Torrone* in Bologna was the campaign to draw clients away from feudal courts and the patchwork of medieval urban tribunals into the orbit of the forbidding Great Tower. By continually heralding the professionalism of its notarial staff, the overseers of the *Torrone* promoted the notion that the *Torrone* was more accessible, more neutral, and more efficient than a justice beholden to networks of patronage and cronyism. In the early seventeenth century, the volume of documentation created by the notaries in the course of their duties began to grow rapidly as more clients brought more, and more petty, complaints and conflicts to be adjudicated by *Torrone* notaries. Where sixteenth-century *processi* were drafted directly into casebooks alongside denunciations, and continued on whichever blank page a notary might next have when he returned to the next interrogation, by 1630 *processi*—that is, those cases extracted for an extended trial and not dealt with summarily at denunciation–were prepared in separate *fascicoli*, integral to themselves and appended to a notary's casebook only when all investigation and sentencing was complete. Not only does this make the historian's job easier, but it also allows notaries to create significantly longer *processi* as they are no longer limited by casebooks: at this point homicide trials begin to regularly stretch past 60 folios. Moreover, even this new system grew to be inadequate as clients from the *contado* continued to flock to the *Torrone*'s benches, and sometime in the 1660s notaries began recording *processi* in separate casebooks from summary denunciations *entirely*, with the result that both the denunciation books grew to well over 300 folios and the *processi* continued to expand as the court solidified its position as the sole forum for conflict resolution in Bologna. The expertise of notaries in producing this massive volume of documentary material became a critical hinge for the *Torrone* around which its legitimacy turned.

Taken together, we can make some broad conclusions about the relationship between expert testimony from physicians, situational analysis provided by lay people with an interest in the body, and the power of the early modern court to investigate suspicious death as homicide. While we can see the growth of the centralized state and its coercive power as one element of this process, viewing the early modern state as a cynical, perhaps sinister, body with the power to effectively coerce participation often falls flat. In relying upon outside testimony to make the judgment of homicide, the officers of the *Torrone* were legitimizing their own office as much as they were imposing its authority on local communities. We can ask how these judgments shaped the reputation of the court as a site of truthful investigation, and we can ask whether it deployed these sorts of testimonies deliberately to do so.

The answers are not firm here, but in the body inspections of *Torrone* homicide trials, we see less a machinery of state power and more an institution attempting to establish legitimacy. The legitimacy of an institution, far more than its mere power, shapes its effectiveness in early modern societies, and the *Torrone*, by the end of the seventeenth century, had established a degree of legitimacy that allowed it to draw in a body of users from a wide swath of society to seek justice for wrongs done. The apparent rigor with which they determined homicide, buttressed by both expert and lay investigation of the sites of suspicious death, was perhaps a contributing factor to this legitimacy. The bodies of evidence these witnesses mustered in many ways shielded the court from the consequences of those decisions and eased the extension of court power into communities that were indeed deeply protective of their members against the exercise of arbitrary power.

Notes

1 Edward Muir and Guido Ruggiero, eds., *History from Crime: Selections of Quaderni Storici* (The Johns Hopkins University Press, 1994), Introduction.
2 Thomas V. Cohen, "The Case of the Mysterious Coil of Rope: Street Life and Jewish Persona in Rome in the Middle of the Sixteenth Century," *The Sixteenth Century Journal* 19 (1988): 209–21; Thomas V. Cohen, "Three Forms of Jeopardy: Honor, Pain, and Truth-Telling in a Sixteenth-Century Italian Courtroom," *The Sixteenth Century Journal* 29 (1998): 975–98; Thomas V. Cohen, "Reflections on Retelling a Renaissance Murder," *History and Theory* 41 (2002): 7–16; Thomas V. Cohen, "A Daughter Killing Digested," in Trevor Dean and K.J.P. Lowe, eds. *Murder in Renaissance Italy* (Cambridge University Press, 2017), 62–80; Daniel Lord Smail, *The Consumption of Justice: Emotions, Publicity, and Legal Culture in Marseille, 1264–1423* (Cornell University Press, 2003).
3 Silvia De Renzi, "Medical Expertise, Bodies, and the Law in Early Modern Courts," *Isis* 98 (2007): 315–22; Peter Blastenbrei, "Violence, Arms and Criminal Justice in Papal Rome, 1560–1600," *Renaissance Studies* 20 (2006): 68–87.
4 Silvia De Renzi, "Witnesses of the Body: Medico-Legal Cases in Seventeenth-Century Rome," *Studies in History and Philosophy of Science Part A* 33 (2002): 219–42.
5 Sarah Rubin Blanshei, "Crime and Law Enforcement in Medieval Bologna," *Journal of Social History* 16 (1982): 121–38; Sarah Rubin Blanshei, "Homicide in a Culture of Hatred: Bologna 1351–1420," in *Murder in Renaissance Italy*, eds. Trevor Dean and K.J.P. Lowe, 1st ed. (Cambridge University Press, 2017), 106–22; Sarah Rubin Blanshei, *Politics and Justice in Late Medieval Bologna* (Brill, 2010); Paolo Broggio, "Narrazioni Della Vendetta e Della Giustizia: Articolazioni Di Potere, Cultura Politica e Acculturazione Religiosa Nell'Europa Della Prima Età Moderna," *P. Broggio, S. Carroll, Introduction. Violence and Peacemaking in Early Modern Europe: A Comparative Perspective 4 A. Musin, Le Droit de Vengeance et Son Déclin Dans Les Pays-Bas (XIV e-XVI e Siècles)*; Trevor Dean, "Police Forces in Medieval Italy: Bologna, 1340–1480," *Social History* 44 (2019): 151–72; Daniel Lord Smail, "Factions and Vengeance in Renaissance Italy. A Review Article," eds. Edward Muirr and Osvaldo Raggio, *Comparative Studies in Society and History* 38 (1996): 781–89.
6 Giancarlo Angelozzi and Cesarina Casanova, *La giustizia criminale in una città di antico regime: il tribunale del Torrone di Bologna, secc. XVI-XVII* (CLUEB, 2008); Colin Rose, "Violence and the Centralization of Criminal Justice in Early Modern Bologna," in *Violence and Justice in Bologna, 1250–1700*, edited by Sarah Rubin Blanshei (Lexington, 2018), 101–22.
7 Giancarlo Angelozzi, *La Nobiltà Disciplinata: Violenza Nobiliare, Procedure Di Giustizia e Scienza Cavalleresca a Bologna Nel 17. Secolo* (CLUEB, 2003).

8 Angela De Benedictis, *Repubblica per Contratto: Bologna: Una Città Europea Nello Stato Della Chiesa* (Il Mulino, 1995).
9 On the Pepoli riding in force against the Marchese di Bevilacqua in 1640, see Archivio di Stato di Bologna (ASBo hereafter), *Tribunale del Torrone, Atti e Processi*, 6243, unnumbered fascicolo. On the murder of a *Torrone* judge amid rising factional violence, see ASBo, *Torrone*, 6612/1; the entire volume is occupied with the case. See also Colin Rose, *A Renaissance of Violence: Homicide in Early Modern Italy*, 1st Edition (Cambridge University Press, 2019), 181–83.
10 Rose, "Violence and the Centralization of Criminal Justice in Early Modern Bologna"; Giancarlo Angelozzi and Cesarina Casanova, *La giustizia criminale a Bologna nel XVIII secolo e le riforme di Benedetto XIV* (CLUEB, 2010).
11 See, for instance, ASBo, *Bandi e Notificazione*, Serie 1, No. 6, no folio, decree of 10/11/1595, which stipulated that all copies of *processi* stored with the court's archive must match in length and folio count the originals produced by the notary.
12 Irene Fosi, *Papal Justice: Subjects and Courts in the Papal State, 1500–1750* (Catholic University of America Press, 2011), 207–23.
13 Nicholas Terpstra, ed., *The Art of Executing Well: Rituals of Execution in Renaissance Italy* (Truman State University Press, 2008), chapters 6, 7.
14 While we don't know much about individual Italian executioners, a particularly rich "hangman's diary" from Nuremberg tells us that German executioners, at least, perceived themselves as skilled artisan experts at their work. See Joel F. Harrington, *The Faithful Executioner: Life and Death, Honor and Shame in the Turbulent Sixteenth Century* (Picador/Farrar, Straus and Giroux, 2014).
15 Blanshei, "Crime and Law Enforcement in Medieval Bologna"; Sarah Rubin Blanshei, "Cambiamenti e Continuità Nella Procedura Penale a Bologna, Secoli XIII-XVII. Parte I. Le Procedure Del Processo Penale in Età Comunale e Signorile," *Documenta* 1 (2018): 9–38; Colin Rose, "Cambiamenti e Continuita Nella Procedure Penale a Bologna, Secolo XIII-XVII, Parte II: Il Tribunale Del Torrone," *Documenta* 1 (2018): 39–60.
16 ASBo, *Torrone*, 5876, f. 432r–453r.
17 ASBo, *Torrone*, 5876, fols. 434v–436r. On poisoning in Italy, see Henri Bresc, "Knives and Poisons: Stereotypes of Male Vendetta and Female Perfidy in Late Medieval Sicily, 1293–1460," in *Murder in Renaissance Italy*, eds. Trevor Dean and K.J.P. Lowe, 1st ed. (Cambridge University Press, 2017), 41–61; Matthew Lubin, "Poisoning as a Means of State Assassination in Early Modern Venice," in *Medieval and Early Modern Murder: Legal, Literary and Historical Contexts*, ed. Larissa Tracy (Boydell & Brewer, 2018), 227–53; Alessandro Pastore, "Poison and Poisoning in Renaissance Italy," in *Murder in Renaissance Italy*, eds. Trevor Dean and K.J.P. Lowe (Cambridge University Press, 2017), 228–46; C. Lansing, "Poisoned Relations: Marital Conflicts in Medieval Bologna," in Gian Mario Anselmi, Angela De Benedictis, and Nicholas Terpstra, *Bologna: Cultural Crossroads from the Medieval to the Baroque: Recent Anglo-American Scholarship* (Bononia University Press, 2013), 129–42. The gist of most of the literature on poisoning is that many more husbands *believed* their wives were poisoning them than wives were actually poisoning their husbands.
18 Guido Ruggiero, *Violence in Early Renaissance Venice* (Rutgers University Press, 1980); Joanna Carraway Vitiello, *Public Justice and the Criminal Trial in Late Medieval Italy: Reggio Emilia in the Visconti Age* (Brill, 2016), 54–87.
19 Blastenbrei, "Violence, Arms and Criminal Justice in Papal Rome, 1560–1600."
20 ASBo, *Torrone*, 6612/1, f. 39r–v.
21 ASBo, *Torrone*, 7351, *in fine*.
22 ASBo, *Torrone*, 6794, *in fine*.

23 Rose, "Cambiamenti e Continuita Nella Procedure Penale a Bologna, Secolo XIII-XVII, Parte II: Il Tribunale Del Torrone."
24 ASBo, *Assunteria del Torrone*, 3c. *Constitutiones e bolle del Torrone,* 1607.

Select Bibliography

Angelozzi, Giancarlo. *La Nobiltà Disciplinata: Violenza Nobiliare, Procedure Di Giustizia e Scienza Cavalleresca a Bologna Nel 17. Secolo*. CLUEB, 2003.

Angelozzi, Giancarlo, and Cesarina Casanova. *La giustizia criminale in una città di antico regime: il tribunale del Torrone di Bologna, secc. XVI-XVII*. CLUEB, 2008.

Angelozzi, Giancarlo, and Cesarina Casanova. *La giustizia criminale a Bologna nel XVIII secolo e le riforme di Benedetto XIV*. CLUEB, 2010.

Anselmi, Gian Mario, Angela De Benedictis, and Nicholas Terpstra. *Bologna: Cultural Crossroads from the Medieval to the Baroque: Recent Anglo-American Scholarship*. Bononia University Press, 2013.

Blanshei, Sarah Rubin. "Cambiamenti e Continuità Nella Procedura Penale a Bologna, Secoli XIII-XVII. Parte I. Le Procedure Del Processo Penale in Età Comunale e Signorile." *Documenta* 1 (2018): 9–38.

Blanshei, Sarah Rubin. *Politics and Justice in Late Medieval Bologna*. Boston: Brill, 2010.

Blastenbrei, Peter. "Violence, Arms and Criminal Justice in Papal Rome, 1560–1600." *Renaissance Studies* 20 (2006): 68–87.

Bresc, Henri. "Knives and Poisons: Stereotypes of Male Vendetta and Female Perfidy in Late Medieval Sicily, 1293–1460." In *Murder in Renaissance Italy*, edited by Trevor Dean and K.J.P. Lowe. 1st ed., 41–61. Cambridge University Press, 2017.

Cohen, Thomas V. "The Case of the Mysterious Coil of Rope: Street Life and Jewish Persona in Rome in the Middle of the Sixteenth Century." *The Sixteenth Century Journal* 19 (1988): 209–21.

Cohen, Thomas V. "Three Forms of Jeopardy: Honor, Pain, and Truth-Telling in a Sixteenth-Century Italian Courtroom." *The Sixteenth Century Journal* 29 (1998): 975–98.

Cohen, Thomas V. "Reflections on Retelling a Renaissance Murder." *History and Theory* 41 (2002): 7–16.

De Benedictis, Angela. *Repubblica per Contratto: Bologna: Una Città Europea Nello Stato Della Chiesa*. Il Mulino, 1995.

De Renzi, Silvia. "Witnesses of the Body: Medico-Legal Cases in Seventeenth-Century Rome." *Studies in History and Philosophy of Science Part A* 33 (2002): 219–42.

De Renzi, Silvia. "Medical Expertise, Bodies, and the Law in Early Modern Courts." *Isis* 98 (2007): 315–22.

Dean, Trevor. "Police Forces in Medieval Italy: Bologna, 1340–1480." *Social History* 44 (2019): 151–72.

Dean, Trevor, and K.J.P. Lowe. *Murder in Renaissance Italy*. Cambridge University Press, 2017.

Harrington, Joel F. *The Faithful Executioner: Life and Death, Honor and Shame in the Turbulent Sixteenth Century*. First Picador edition. Picador/Farrar, Straus and Giroux, 2014.

Lubin, Matthew. "Poisoning as a Means of State Assassination in Early Modern Venice." In *Medieval and Early Modern Murder: Legal, Literary and Historical Contexts*, edited by Larissa Tracy, 227–53. Boydell & Brewer, 2018.

Muir, Edward, ed. *History from Crime*. Johns Hopkins University Press, 1994.

Pastore, Alessandro. "Poison and Poisoning in Renaissance Italy." In *Murder in Renaissance Italy*, edited by Trevor Dean and K.J.P. Lowe, 228–46. Cambridge University Press, 2017.

Polverini Fosi, Irene. *Papal Justice: Subjects and Courts in the Papal State, 1500–1750*. Catholic University of America Press, 2011.

Rose, Colin. "Cambiamenti e Continuita Nella Procedure Penale a Bologna, Secolo XIII-XVII, Parte II: Il Tribunale Del Torrone." *Documenta* 1, no. 1 (2018): 39–60.

Rose, Colin. "Violence and the Centralization of Criminal Justice in Early Modern Bologna." In *Violence and Justice in Bologna, 1250–1700*, edited by Sarah Rubin Blanshei 101–22. Lexington, 2018.

Rose, Colin. *A Renaissance of Violence: Homicide in Early Modern Italy*. Cambridge University Press, 2019.

Ruggiero, Guido. *Violence in Early Renaissance Venice*. Rutgers University Press, 1980.

Smail, Daniel Lord. "Factions and Vengeance in Renaissance Italy. A Review Article." *Comparative Studies in Society and History* 38 (1996): 781–89. Edited by Edward Muir and Osvaldo Raggio.

Smail, Daniel Lord. *The Consumption of Justice: Emotions, Publicity, and Legal Culture in Marseille, 1264–1423*. Cornell University Press, 2003.

Terpstra, Nicholas, ed. *The Art of Executing Well: Rituals of Execution in Renaissance Italy*. Truman State University Press, 2008.

Vitiello, Joanna Carraway. *Public Justice and the Criminal Trial in Late Medieval Italy: Reggio Emilia in the Visconti Age*. Medieval Law and Its Practice. Vol. 20. Brill, 2016.

5

ON HOMICIDE, FORENSIC PRACTICE, AND FORENSIC DISCOURSE IN MADRID

Blanca Llanes Parra

Introduction

The creation of the Chairs of Legal Medicine and Toxicology at the Universities of Madrid and Barcelona in the mid-nineteenth century was a very important milestone in the history and development of forensic science in Spain. Its founder was the medical doctor and politician Pedro Mata y Fontanet, who became the first professor of legal medicine at the Central University of Madrid in 1843. He had previously worked in Paris with the Spanish scientist Mateo José Buenaventura Orfila, considered the father of forensic toxicology. Mata y Fontanet was also responsible for the organization and institutionalization of forensic medicine in Spain, promoting the creation in 1862 of the Corps of Forensic Doctors [*Cuerpo de Médicos Forenses*]. This corps of career civil servants was established with the aim of "assisting the administration of justice in all cases and proceedings in which the intervention and services of their profession may be necessary or useful."[1] This is the same role that forensic medical doctors play in Spain today, where they continue to assist courts and tribunals in their areas of expertise, incorporating the latest scientific, technical, and legal advances into their work.[2]

Pedro Mata y Fontanet was also a prolific writer. In the fourth edition of his influential *Tratado de Medicina y Cirugía Legal* (*Treatise on Legal Medicine and Surgery*), published in 1866, Mata y Fontanet emphasized the "heterogeneous" and "encyclopedic" nature of legal medicine. According to this author, legal medicine borrowed "facts, knowledge and principles" from other sciences "to solve certain problems proposed by the administration of justice in order to improve the accuracy of its verdicts."[3] This group of sciences belonged to the natural, medical, social, and human sciences and

DOI: 10.4324/9781003486404-8

included "physics, chemistry, natural history, anatomy, physiology, hygiene, medicine, pathology, obstetrics, ethics, art history, psychology, philosophy and law." In the words of Mata y Fontanet, legal medicine was defined as "a body of scientific knowledge, mainly medical and physical, the purpose of which is to give due value and significance to certain legal facts and to contribute to the formation of certain laws."[4]

The development of forensic science in nineteenth-century Spain owed much to the scientific advances and judicial work of the previous two centuries. In this respect, the judicial and legal records of early modern Spain are a valuable source of information on forensic practices prior to the emergence of modern forensic science in the nineteenth century. Using, among other archival materials, the records of the Sala de Alcaldes de Casa y Corte, Madrid's highest tribunal during the early modern period, this study will look at violent crime cases in order to explore and shed light on the investigative process and the forensic activities carried out by justice officials, physicians and surgeons in the search for criminal evidence. It will also examine written testimonies in the form of *memoriales* and "forensic discourses" left by the judges and prosecutors of the Sala, with the aim of highlighting the importance of the forensic function in the resolution of criminal cases, not only as a means of "knowing the truth" but also as an essential component of the administration of justice. Particular attention is paid to cases of spousal homicide. Women were more likely to be the victims of such violence. However, they could also be the perpetrators. These violent crimes were very serious offenses, punishable by the most severe penalties. It is not surprising, therefore, that these cases are frequently mentioned by judges and prosecutors in their writings. These crimes were often difficult to solve. For example, the use of poison to commit these murders meant that the resolution of these cases often depended on the testimony of witnesses and indirect evidence, in the absence of modern forensic toxicology techniques.[5] By covering a period of two centuries, the primary sources used in this study also reveal the main trends in forensic practice applied to the investigation and resolution of these crimes over time (Figure 5.1).

The Sala de Alcaldes de Casa y Corte and the Regulation of Forensic Practice in the Early Modern Period

In July 1862, just two months after the passing of the royal decree creating the corps of *médicos forenses*, Pedro Mata y Fontanet wrote an article published in the journal *Revista española* in which he identified the shortcomings and criticized the lack of ambition of the measures contained in the law to institutionalize forensic medicine in Spain. For Mata y Fontanet, this was a missed opportunity that would have placed the country at the forefront of the field.[6] In this article, however, Mata y Fontanet offered interesting

FIGURE 5.1 Palace of Santa Cruz, the seat of the Sala de Alcaldes de Casa y Corte. © The Reading Room/Alamy Stock Photo 2ANC2BJ.

comments and reflections on the need to organize the discipline and activity of forensic doctors in an attempt to adapt the administration of justice to new social demands and to overcome past deficiencies in forensic practice. Following Mata y Fontanet, the creation of forensic doctors in Spain was intended to provide "courts, plaintiffs and defendants" with all the necessary "guarantees" expected from the administration of justice, whose main function was to protect the "great interests" of society. The experience of previous centuries had already shown the value of these professionals and their expert assistance in the proper resolution of legal matters, hence the importance of organizing their activity.[7] Mata y Fontanet also praised the efforts made by the Spanish government in this direction, by giving forensic doctors a certain official status and introducing rules to regulate aspects of their profession, such as their appointment or their salaries and fees, which could put an end to the "disorder" and "anarchy" that, in his opinion, had characterized the "forensic medical service" in Spain.[8]

Medical and forensic practice in early modern Spain was strongly influenced by the legal and scientific advances taking place in Europe, some of the earliest examples being the promulgation of the *Constitutio Criminalis Carolina* in 1532 and the publication of the first scientific treatise on legal medicine on the continent by the French royal surgeon Ambroise Paré in 1575. The importance of medicine in providing expert assistance to judges in Spain in the sixteenth century is also demonstrated by the work of the Spanish surgeon and physician Juan Fragoso. Decades before Paolo Zacchia published his influential book *Quaestiones medico-legales* (1621–51), the Spanish royal surgeon and physician Juan Fragoso had already written his book *Cirugía Universal* (*Universal Surgery*), first published in Madrid in 1581 and later republished in both Spanish and Italian in several editions throughout the sixteenth and seventeenth centuries. This book contains a detailed and precise guide for the instruction of surgeons and physicians in assisting judges and magistrates in cases of death, illness, and injury.[9] More than a century later, in 1783, the Spanish surgeon Domingo Vidal published his *Cirugía forense, o Arte de hacer relaciones quirúrgico-legales* (*Forensic Surgery or the Art of Making Surgical-Legal Reports*), which provided guidelines for surgeons, physicians, and other experts on how to write legal reports and carry out their forensic work.[10] Vidal's manual once again highlights the important role of forensic expertise in the investigation of legal cases in early modern Spain, while also revealing the existence of a foundation for the future professionalization of legal medicine.

In early modern Madrid, the activities of surgeons and physicians, including their assistance in the administration of justice, were regulated by the *Sala de Alcaldes de Casa y Corte* (the Hall of Judges of the Royal House and Court). The Sala was a political and judicial institution dependent on the Council of Castile with criminal and civil jurisdiction over the Spanish court and capital and its surrounding area of five leagues, known as the *rastro*. In addition to these judicial prerogatives, the Sala was also in charge of the government and administration of the city of Madrid, supervising economic and commercial affairs and regulating prices and other aspects of daily life, including public health and sanitation and leisure activities. The officers who served in the Sala included the *alcaldes*, or judges, the prosecutor of the royal prison, the bailiffs, the scribes, the gatekeepers, a lawyer and a solicitor of the poor, the warden of the court prison and the gatekeepers, a steward for the poor, an accountant and a treasurer, the court prison doctor and surgeon, and a prison chaplain.[11] The court prison surgeon and doctor were in charge of the prison infirmary. They assisted prisoners, prescribed and administered medications, and carried out other duties. For example, in the seventeenth century, when female prostitution was a legal activity in Madrid, the court prison doctor regularly visited registered prostitutes to examine them medically and effectively monitor the presence of venereal disease in the Spanish capital. The prison surgeon was also responsible for visiting injured victims of assault in Madrid's hospitals to assess their wounds and draw up a legal report or declaration.[12]

All other doctors and surgeons working in Madrid were also subject to the rules and regulations of the Sala. They had to report to the *alcaldes* or the city's judicial authorities immediately after treating a wounded person. However, doctors and surgeons in Madrid do not seem to have strictly adhered to this norm, given the numerous orders and decrees issued by the Sala during the seventeenth and eighteenth centuries, reminding them of this obligation and urging them to comply with it.[13] Similarly, the archives of the Sala reveal another of the concerns expressed by Pedro Mata y Fontanet in his writings in the nineteenth century, that of the salaries or fees received by these professionals for their expert work in the administration of justice. Difficulties and delays in the payment of fees were a constant problem for prison doctors and surgeons, as well as other medical professionals who offered their judicial services at the request of the Sala.[14] In fact, this is one of the reasons why doctors and surgeons refused to provide the Sala with the legal reports on the state of the injuries suffered by victims of physical violence when they were treated in Madrid's hospitals.[15] As a result, this task had to be carried out by the prison court surgeon, as mentioned earlier. This was not without difficulty, as he regularly encountered resistance and opposition from the medical professionals working in these hospitals. The Sala denounced this situation on May 1667 and ordered these hospitals to grant access to the prison court surgeon so that he could make the declarations and reports accompanied by surgeons or nurse practitioners from these institutions.[16]

Although relations were strained at times, the information provided by these sources, as well as the records of the Sala, shows the extent to which the administration of justice, as elsewhere in continental Europe, relied on the expertise of these professionals to solve crimes and legal problems.[17] The eighteenth-century Spanish surgeon Domingo Vidal was very clear about this when, in the prologue to his book on forensic surgery, he stated that this collaboration or "relationship" was "established by the law in order to thoroughly investigate the truth behind the facts."[18] According to Vidal, judges do not have a universal knowledge of all the scientific disciplines or arts (*artes*), which leads them to seek the opinion of experts (*peritos*) in order to decide on legal matters, and thus benefit society.[19] Vidal's words and writings in the eighteenth century undoubtedly express a conception of forensic activity and justice in line with Paolo Zacchia's assumptions about the importance of medicine and the new ideals of Enlightenment thought.[20] There is, however, one theme that seems to be common to the thinking of the previous century, and that is the desire to know "the truth behind the facts," the true goal to be pursued by justice and judges, as the *alcalde* of the Sala Juan de Quiñones expressed in a memorial he wrote to the king in the 1640s.

Facts, Evidence, and Truth

In 1643, Don Juan de Quiñones y Daza, *alcalde* and judge of the Sala de Alcaldes de Casa y Corte, wrote a memorial to King Philip IV in which he listed the most important accomplishments of his long career, as well as his literary work, with the aim of receiving from the monarch the reward he deserved for his services. The account of his professional achievements as a judge covers a period of almost 30 years in the service of the Spanish monarchy, 21 of which he had spent in Madrid. He had been *teniente de corregidor* [lieutenant of the *corregidor*, or chief magistrate of the city] between 1622 and 1625, and then *alcalde* of the Sala from 1625 on. (He would die in 1646.) Quiñones devoted around 30 pages of this work, almost half of the memorial, to recounting the most famous cases in which he acted as judge. His account of the most emblematic criminal trials of his entire career is of great interest. They represent a selection of the relevant cases in which his role as judge would have been particularly appreciated and valued by the monarch.

Throughout his memorial, Quiñones also gives us glimpses of his understanding of criminal procedure and forensic practice. In the opening pages of his memorial, for example, Quiñones shows that he was no stranger to debates about the appropriateness of an aristocratic background for public office when he emphasizes his noble status as both a quality and a prerequisite for being a judge.[21] Drawing on the work of the Spanish jurist Pere Belluga, Quiñones argues that loyalty is essential for judges and that "nobles are more likely to observe it."[22] However, when Quiñones discusses the criminal cases in which he has been involved as a judge, he points to other qualities that a judge should possess in order to do his job well. He also reflects on the role and importance of the use of forensic evidence in criminal investigations, particularly in homicide cases. And while Quiñones' account of his forensic work tends to focus on his personal achievements and actions, it also reveals the crucial contribution that forensic experts made to solving criminal cases.

An example of the latter was a murder committed in the city of Madrid, which Quiñones investigated and wrote about in his memorial.[23] Although

Quiñones does not specify the year in which the homicide was perpetrated, it seems to have occurred during his time as *alcalde* of the Sala de Alcaldes de Casa y Corte. Quiñones recounts that it was shortly after midnight when he received the news that the body of a man had been found near the convent of Nuestra Señora de Atocha in Madrid. He immediately rushed to the crime scene, where he saw that the victim's face had been mutilated so that he could not be identified. In order to establish the victim's identity, Quiñones ordered that the man's dead body, along with the disfigured remains of his face, be taken to Madrid's General Hospital, where surgeons were able to reconstruct his face with more than 60 stitches. The body was then taken to the Santa Cruz square, where the Sala and the court prison were located, for public viewing so that the victim could be identified. The deceased's wife, a shop-keeper who lived in front of the court prison, recognized him. On the basis of the information provided by the widow and subsequent investigations, the *alcalde* Quiñones concluded that the perpetrator of this brutal murder was a Portuguese resident of Vallecas, a small village on the outskirts of Madrid, who had collected the sum of 4,000 *reales* with a false bill of exchange, a fact known to the victim. This was the motive that led the Portuguese criminal to end the man's life and tear up his face for fear of being denounced. The murderer wanted to get away with his crime, which he did by fleeing Vallecas before the judicial authorities could arrest him.

In the eyes of the criminal law, the cases listed by Quiñones in his memorial were particularly serious crimes that required severe punishment. An analysis of these cases shows that the crimes he was most interested in were mainly those against property and homicide. In fact, of the 29 cases that Quiñones mentions in his memorial, 13 were property crimes and nine were violent deaths. It is also worth noting that the cases that opened and closed his list are homicides. Perhaps these were the crimes that concerned Quiñones most throughout his judicial career. The first case mentioned in the memorial relates to the prosecution and subsequent execution of a dangerous murderer whom Quiñones had arrested when he was mayor of the village of El Escorial, north of Madrid.[24] The last case cited was again a homicide, a double murder committed in 1635 in the town of Parla, located south of Madrid, which Quiñones was ordered to investigate by the Council of Castile when he was already *alcalde* of the Sala.[25] The victims of this last crime, a priest and his sister, were found dead in their home. The cause of death was severe blows to the head, made with stone slabs found next to the bodies. It also appears that the murderers inflicted these fatal wounds in order to rob the victims. This fact and the brutality of the attack alone justified the seriousness of the crime and its inclusion in the memorial. This last case, however, has a peculiarity that distinguishes it from the others mentioned by Quiñones. This may be the reason why he chose this case to conclude his account of his professional achievements. Quiñones presents himself first and foremost as a fair judge in search of the truth, and this is the main axis that articulates his narrative of the case.

Following this line of argument, Juan de Quiñones describes how, after investigating the priest's and sister's deaths and finding no conclusive evidence or clues, he arrested a homeless man to subject him to torture. The man, more afraid of torture than of the gallows, quickly confessed to the crime, leaving Quiñones with certain doubts about the veracity of his testimony. Quiñones' suspicions were confirmed when the prison guard told him that he had heard the prisoner say in his cell that he had not committed the crime and that he had confessed out of fear of torture. According to the beggar, he had spent the night of the crime in the hospital of Torrejón de Velasco, his hometown, one league from Parla. For these reasons, Quiñones went to Torrejón de Velasco to conduct a secret investigation into the case. At the town's hospice, he was able to corroborate that the poor man had been there on the night of the double murder, in a room with other beggars, thanks to the information provided by witnesses, including the hospital's steward (*mayordomo*), the hospitaller (*hospitalero*), and the doctor (*médico*). Twenty-four hours after his confession, the homeless man ratified his previous declaration and was taken from Parla to Madrid's court prison. It was then that Quiñones presented the Council of Castile with a report on the secret investigation carried out in Torrejón de Velasco, with the aim of freeing the prisoner, as was eventually done. Quiñones ends his account of this event by saying that the Council "thanked him for his diligence in seeking the truth with Christian zeal" and defending the legal principle of "when in doubt, rule for the accused" [*in dubio pro reo*].[26]

The nine cases of homicide and attempted homicide cited by Quiñones in his memorial reflected extremely serious criminal behavior because of the way in which the crimes were committed (with malice and treachery, either by poison or by assassination), the relationship between the perpetrator and his victim (spousal homicide), and their instrumental component, as in the case of robbery with homicide. These were also murders that were very difficult to investigate and trace, which would explain Quiñones' eagerness to highlight his achievements in solving these particular cases.

One homicide case stands out in Quiñones' account, as it contains many of the aggravating factors mentioned earlier. It was a premeditated homicide triggered by marital infidelity. The victim was a clothier (*ropero*) whose wife was having an extramarital affair with one of his craftsmen. After a first failed attempt to end the clothier's life by giving him a poisoned drink, and with the help of another craftsman, the lovers decided to hire two soldiers to carry out the murder. These hitmen, or assassins, achieved their goal of killing the clothier. The investigation carried out by Quiñones led to the arrest of all those involved in the crime, except for the "adulterous" craftsman, who managed to escape. The clothier's wife, the craftsman who supplied the poison, and the two soldiers were hanged for manslaughter. However, Quiñones does not elaborate on the poisoning attempt, depriving us of valuable information about the complexities and difficulties of investigating and solving these crimes in the early modern period.

The same complexity over poisoning is well illustrated by a criminal case, which was not in Quiñones' memorial but which was brought before the mayor's court of the town of Barajas, near Madrid, in 1666. Here, Bernabé Ruiz del Castillo, a falcon and prey retriever (*catarribera*) of the Royal Hunt of Falconry (*Real Caza de la Volatería*), was accused of having an affair with María Herla and of attempting to poison her husband, Francisco López Sanz.[27] The summary of the proceedings of this trial stated that Doña María Herla was a cousin of Bernabé Ruiz del Castillo's wife and that the poisoning of her husband was due to the affair María was having with Bernabé. Witnesses confirmed that the relationship between the accused couple was well known in the town of Barajas, and that María's husband himself had even had a conversation with Bernabé in which he warned him not to enter his house again. According to the same sources, on January 19 or January 20, 1666, Francisco López Sanz, María's husband, ingested the poison in a laxative prepared by the defendants. After taking the laxative, the man began to suffer from nausea and anxiety (*ansias* and *bascas*). The doctor who treated him, Doctor Juan de Cabañas, testified that these symptoms were not the result of the poison itself, but that "they could have been caused either by the malignity of some medicine or by the quality of his humors, which mixed with the purgative to produce these effects" on his health. Doctor Francisco de Ordeñano, a doctor in the town of Torrejón de Ardoz, stated on January 30 that, based on the information provided by Doctor Cabañas, he could not confirm that Francisco López Sanz's state of health was due to poisoning. The same doctor added that if this had been the case, and if the poison had been administered through the laxative, the lethal effects would have been immediate and would have been detected in less than 24 hours, and not in the ten or 12 days that had passed since the purgative had been taken.

Francisco López Sanz's health continued to deteriorate, and he died on February 1, 1666, almost two weeks after he was allegedly poisoned. At the request of the mayor of Barajas, Francisco's body was examined by two doctors, the aforementioned Juan de Cabañas and Diego Rodríguez de Castro, and a surgeon, Juan Sánchez, who concluded that there were signs of poison ("hot poison") in the victim's body, which could have been the cause of death. The dead man's wife, María Herla, sought an additional expert opinion from Doctor Francisco de Vivar, a professor at the University of Alcalá de Henares, who testified that he had found no evidence of poison in the victim's body and that he had died as a result of "a malignant and pestilential fever." However, when Barajas' judicial authorities confiscated María's belongings, they found some papers containing powder and water in a pair of boots.

According to the doctors and pharmacists who examined them, this white powder was made from hyacinth mixed with poisonous ingredients. María Herla told the authorities that these white powders were only facial waters (*aguas de rostro*) and other substances used to clean her teeth.

Witnesses for the dead victim testified that it had been publicly known that Francisco's health had worsened after he had taken the purgative and that he had died from the poison that Bernabé Ruiz del Castillo had given him. According to the same witnesses, Bernabé Ruiz del Castillo had gone to a local chemist's shop (*botica*) to buy the poison and stated that he had asked the chemist not to give him the exact amount prescribed by the doctor but to leave out half of a compound called *géminis*, made of basic lead carbonate and wax.[28] After hearing Bernabé's testimony, the mayor's court of Barajas sentenced him to pay the sum of 300 ducats and to be imprisoned in the North African garrison fort of Larache for six years, after which he was not allowed to return to the town of Barajas or within 20 leagues of its outskirts. María Herla, however, was acquitted. There is no information as to whether the sentence was actually carried out since the Marquis of Fresno, the Master of the Hunt (*Cazador Mayor*) of the *Real Caza de la Volatería*, who had the prerogative of hearing the civil and criminal cases against its members, ordered that the case be referred to him for investigation. Perhaps it was this confrontation between the two jurisdictions that led the judicial authorities in Barajas to accept the medical opinion of Juan de Cabañas and Diego Rodríguez de Castro and to impose an exemplary sentence on Bernabé Ruiz.[29] In this respect, this example shows the differences of opinion in solving poisoning crimes and how sentences in these may have been motivated by factors other than the search for the truth.

In other criminal cases of marital homicide, where poison was not used in the commission of the crime and where it was easier to gather conclusive evidence, there could be fewer discrepancies in the resolution of the case. This is exemplified by another case of marital homicide to which the *alcalde* Juan de Quiñones refers in his memorial.[30] The murder took place in the city of Madrid, although Quiñones does not specify the date or year. The victim was the wife of a liquor dealer, who died after being brutally beaten on the head with a club by her husband. Quiñones explains that after committing the crime, the murderer placed his wife's body in a trunk, which he later took to a friend's house, telling him that it contained only clothes. The judicial authorities soon discovered that the liquor dealer was selling his belongings with the intention of leaving Madrid and that his wife was missing. This led Quiñones to order his arrest in order to question him about his wife's whereabouts. The suspect's ambiguous answers did not convince Quiñones, who immediately sent him to the court prison. The killer's friend, knowing that the liquor dealer was in jail, informed the Sala that he had the trunk in his possession. Quiñones ordered the trunk to be opened, where he found the victim's body.

After burying the victim, Quiñones discovered a large club covered in blood in the couple's house. He therefore asked for the victim's body to be exhumed with the intention of examining the wound on her head, which appeared to have been caused by the club found in their home. This discovery prompted Quiñones to ask the suspect if he knew where the club had come from. The interrogation caused the suspect great anxiety and led him to confess that he had killed his wife by beating her with the club.

In his account of the murder, Juan de Quiñones once again sought to reinforce his image as a diligent judge and *alcalde*, always searching for the truth in the interests of the monarchy and society. As in the other cases mentioned in his memorial, Quiñones emphasizes his role as *alcalde* by highlighting his forensic skills in investigating and solving this murder. In this sense, his account focuses on finding and obtaining solid evidence in order to force the main suspect to confess to the crime and, finally, to solve the case and impose an exemplary punishment. Quiñones sentenced the parricide to be dragged in public and executed by garrote by the river. His body was then placed in a barrel and thrown into the river. This was the form of punishment that Castilian criminal law reserved for the most serious cases of parricide. It had its roots in the *culleus* punishment of ancient Rome.[31] As Quiñones stated in the first pages of his memorial, punishment should be used to "correct the wicked and put an end to them," pointing out the need to always apply justice to maintain social order.[32] With some variations, his vision of punishment would remain largely unchanged for the next century.

Crime, Criminals, and Victims

At the end of the eighteenth century, enlightened jurist, poet, and politician Juan Meléndez Valdés pursued his first criminal case as prosecutor of the Sala de Alcaldes de Casa y Corte and proposed a concept of punishment and forensics similar to those of Quiñones. The case was a very famous parricide that had occurred in Madrid in December 1797. The victim of the crime was Francisco del Castillo, a well-known canvas dealer with close ties to the artistic and cultural elite of the Spanish capital, including Meléndez Valdés himself, with whom he was friends. Francisco del Castillo was stabbed to death in his own home by his wife's lover, with her help and connivance; his death caused a great stir in Madrid and across the country. The formal accusation was published posthumously in 1821 in a work entitled *Discursos forenses* (*Forensic Discourses*), along with other accusations, opinions, and essays written by Meléndez Valdés.[33]

Meléndez Valdés claimed that in this type of murder, "justice should allow the sanctity of the law to triumph virtuously" and "set a healthy example to evil and immorality, which now seem to know no limits or restraints to their impudence."[34] Meléndez Valdés also demanded that once such a crime had been discovered, the facts established, and the accused admitted the deed, it should be punished with "the most severe penalties" in order to guarantee security and peace. He framed Castillo's murder as an attack on public virtue and morality as well as the institution of marriage and therefore called for "the avenging sword of justice to fall on the perpetrators."[35] For Meléndez Valdés, magistrates should always seek "to rebuke and persecute vice, to defend and celebrate virtue, to persuade and move to loathe the one and to love and practice the other."[36]

On these premises, Meléndez Valdés used his significant oratorical skills to build his case against the accused, confronting the figure of Francisco del Castillo, the murdered husband, with that of María Vicenta de Mendieta, the adulterous and parricidal wife. Instead of focusing solely on the crime itself, as Quiñones did in his memorial, Meléndez Valdés also placed the emphasis on both the criminals and the victims and on their moral behavior and character. In doing so, Meléndez Valdés offered an interesting insight into the roles of men and women in marriage according to the ideals of the Enlightenment.[37]

Before going into the details of the crime and the evidence in the case, Meléndez Valdés drew a very positive profile of Francisco del Castillo. On the basis of the testimony of "truthful and impeccable domestic witnesses," he presented Castillo as a "good man" and an exemplary husband, imbued with an enlightened spirit, in contrast to his "unfaithful and clumsy partner," who, according to the prosecutor, was characterized by a spiteful, daring character and "bloody rage."[38] In this way, Meléndez Valdés undermined the arguments that María Vicente had used in her testimony before the judge. In her defense, she had claimed that she had been "oppressed by a cruel husband, constantly insulted, run over and punished by his arrogant temper"; she therefore had "found no other way to protect herself than to resort to violence."[39]

Although Juan Meléndez Valdés focused his accusation on the moral aspect of the case, he also devoted several pages to defending the validity of the evidence that led to the discovery and arrest of the culprits and their subsequent confession to the crime.[40] This evidence was a letter written by María Vicenta to her lover, Santiago de San Juan, after the crime had been committed. On December 9, 1797, with the intention of putting an end to her husband's life, María Vicenta let her lover into the couple's home and hid him so that no one in the household would see him. When Santiago stabbed Francisco del Castillo in his bed, María Vicenta pretended to faint, causing a commotion and allowing the murderer to escape. After the crime, her lover remained hidden in the Madrid court. To keep him informed of the progress of the investigation, María Vicente wrote him a letter, addressed to a certain Don Tadeo Santisa, which she gave to one of her servants, Don Domingo García, to post. Domingo García, suspicious of the letter, brought it to the attention of Don Antonio Castillo, one of the victim's best friends, and they decided to take it to the judicial authorities. According to Meléndez Valdés, when María Vicenta was confronted with this "fatal letter, this merciless paper," she immediately "shuddered" and confessed to the crime, leading to her imprisonment along with her lover.[41] After Santiago's arrest, the bloody clothes he wore on the day of the crime were found in one of his belongings, a chest, which Meléndez Valdés considered to be "irrefutable evidence against its unfortunate owner."[42]

In his accusation, Meléndez Valdés refuted, one by one, the arguments put forward by the defense to invalidate the evidence contained in the letter. First, he pointed out that the letter was clearly incriminating because it suggested to the addressee that he should be very careful not to be discovered. The defense countered that it was illegal to open and read the letter; therefore, such evidence should be considered null and void. In response, Meléndez Valdés defended the validity of the evidence on the grounds that the letter was written by a "person accused of such a heinous crime" and was in the custody of the court. Furthermore, he questioned the fact that María Vicente would have written a letter to a person unknown to her entourage and that she would have intended to send it by post since the recipient lived in Madrid. He also praised the diligence of the servant in turning the letter over to the court, considering it a just and honorable action. Meléndez Valdés concluded by pointing out that María Vicenta did not deliver the letter to the "public trust of the post office, always inviolable, sacred to all," but entrusted it instead to one of her servants, who thankfully disobeyed the order of an "imprudent mistress." For Meléndez Valdés, the servant's disloyalty to María Vicenta was no obstacle to using this evidence against her and her lover Santiago since it had already been unsealed by the time it was presented in court.

Given the seriousness of the crime, Juan Meléndez Valdés requested the death penalty as punishment. He based his request on the case's many aggravating circumstances, including the existence of an adulterous relationship and the fact that the crime had been committed in Madrid, involved the perpetrator hiding in the Spanish Court, and occurred not only "in the conjugal bed" but was carried out by two of the closest and most intimate people to the victim. Meléndez Valdés therefore considered it as an attack on the "conjugal knot," friendship, morality, and the nation—in short, a crime that "outrage[d] and degrade[d] humanity."[43] In April 1798, María Vicenta de Mendieta and her lover Santiago de San Juan were finally executed in Madrid's Plaza Mayor for the murder of Francisco del Castillo.

A month after the sentencing of Maria and her lover, Meléndez Valdés had to issue another accusation for another case of spousal homicide, this time a wife-murder.[44] The murderer, Marcelo J., had killed his wife, María G., in September 1797: she had left the couple's home but had been forced to reunite with her husband after an ecclesiastical court order. As noted by the prosecutor, the murder was not premeditated but committed in a state of rage and intoxication. In his examination of the case, Meléndez Valdés once again focused on the characters of the perpetrator and the victim, contrasting here the "tolerance, peace, constant kindness, and good behavior" of Marcelo with the "hard and stubborn temperament" of María, which, according to the prosecutor, finally led her husband to become enraged and kill her during a drunken argument.[45]

It is possible that the prosecutor and Meléndez Valdés' negative opinion of María was originally grounded on the fact that she had left Marcelo and their domicile. On the basis of the circumstances and Marcelo's repentance and immediate surrender to justice after committing the crime, Meléndez Valdés took a much more lenient approach to the case than he did in his first as prosecutor of the Sala. While he started out by calling for the application of the "terrible punishment" prescribed by law for crimes of parricide, he concluded his accusation with an endorsement of leniency and compassion toward the murderous husband.[46]

These reports on the two cases of spousal homicide can be interpreted in the light of Enlightenment ideas about criminal justice and punishment, in particular Cesare Beccaria's principle of proportionality, which also takes into account the background and circumstances of the offender. In his *Forensic Discourses*, Meléndez Valdés not only revealed his legal knowledge but also sought to voice his enlightenment ideology, as the editor's note in the prologue to this work.[47] Perhaps for this reason, Meléndez Valdés was less concerned with the analysis of criminal evidence than Juan de Quiñones was in his memorial.

In this regard, it is worth noting that, in contrast to these two formal accusations by Meléndez Valdés, the deliberations of the Sala in the 1780s and 1790s on death sentences in cases of marital homicide demonstrated the importance of examining physical evidence in solving crimes as well as how crucial the expert opinion of medical professionals was in deciding on the correct punishment under the law. These reports reproduced the testimony of doctors and surgeons who, following the guidelines of Domingo Vidal's *Forensic Surgery*, gave a precise and detailed account of the fatal injuries sustained by the victims.[48]

Conclusion

Historians of crime and the law, as well as scholars of the history of medicine in the early modern period, have outlined the important role played by medical professionals and other experts in the resolution of legal problems and criminal cases, particularly violent and sexual crimes. In early modern Spain, the books and treatises on forensic surgery, by both foreign and Spanish authors, offered surgeons useful guidelines for assisting the administration of justice in the examination of wounds, deaths by hanging and suicide, poisoning, sexually related matters such as virginity, impotence, and sterility, and sexual crimes such as sodomy. Medical expertise also played an important role in the writing of legal reports or declarations for the courts. The increasing sophistication of these manuals reflected the relevance and value of their skills and work to the legal system and paved the way for the professionalization of forensic medicine in the nineteenth century. Judicial documentation from the Sala de Alcaldes de Casa y Corte reveals the interdependence between judges and physicians and provides information on how their forensic work was regulated in the city of Madrid.

Although their relationship with the Sala was not always harmonious, the fact remains that the expertise of surgeons and physicians was essential in resolving difficult cases. Though conceived and written for different purposes, both Quiñones' memorial and Meléndez Valdés' *Forensic Discourses* reflect their own views of the judicial function and of punishment, implicitly recognizing the need for cooperation between judges and medical professionals in the search for the truth. This is most evident in the case of Quiñones, whose account of some of his greatest achievements as *alcalde* served to highlight his forensic skills in collecting and analyzing evidence and in investigating and solving crimes. These tasks were aimed at assessing the seriousness of the crime in order to determine and impose an exemplary and appropriate punishment, as Quiñones and Meléndez Valdés noted when referring to cases of spousal homicide. Here, too, the role of surgeons and experts was important, as shown by the records of the Sala and the treatises on forensic surgery of the seventeenth and eighteenth centuries.

Acknowledgments

The research for this chapter was conducted as part of the project CIRGEN. *Circulating Gender in the Global Enlightenment: Ideas, Networks, Agencies*, funded by the European Research Council under Horizon 2020 (ERC2017-Advanced Grant 787015).

Notes

1 Royal Decree Law, 13 May 1862, published in the *Gazeta de Madrid*, no. 137 (17 May 1862), 1, available at https://www.boe.es/gazeta/dias/1862/05/17/pdfs/GMD-1862–137.pdf.
2 See Ángel Carracedo and Luis Concheiro, "Forensic science practice in Spain," in *The Global Practice of Forensic Science*, ed. Douglas H. Ubelaker (Wiley-Blackwell, 2015), 262–64.
3 Pedro Mata y Fontanet, *Tratado de Medicina y Cirugía Legal teórica y práctica seguido de un compendio de Toxicología*, 4th ed., vol. I (Carlos Bailly-Baillière, 1866), 15.

4 Mata y Fontanet, *Tratado de Medicina*, 25.
5 See Silvia De Renzi, "Medical Expertise, Bodies, and the Law in Early Modern Courts," *Isis* 98 (2007): 320–21 and Katherine D. Watson, *Forensic Medicine in Western Society: A History* (Routledge, 2011), 63–69.
6 Pedro Mata y Fontanet. "Del servicio médico-forense en España," *Revista española política, científica, y de artes, viajes, comercio, etc.* 2, no. 8 (1862): 81–90.
7 Mata y Fontanet, "Del servicio médico-forense," 82–83.
8 Mata y Fontanet, "Del servicio médico-forense," 84.
9 *Tratado de las declaraciones que han de hacer los cirujanos acerca de muchas enfermedades y muchas maneras de muertes que suceden* (*Treatise on the declarations to be made by surgeons about many diseases and many ways of deaths that occur*). Juan Fragoso, *Cirugía Universal, ahora nuevamente enmendada, y añadida en esta quinta impresión. Por el Licenciado Juan Fragoso Médico y Cirujano del Rey nuestro Señor y de sus Altezas* (Juan Gracián, 1592), 286v–305v.
10 Domingo Vidal, *Cirugía forense, o Arte de hacer las relaciones chirúrgico-legales. Obra útil a los médicos, cirujanos y jurisperitos, así seculares como eclesiásticos. Por el Licenciado Don Domingo Vidal, Profesor y Bibliotecario del Real Colegio de Cirugía de Barcelona* (Carlos Gibert y Tutó, 1783). This manual was the Spanish translation and adaptation of the 1745 edition of Jean Devaux's *L'Art de faire les rapports en chirurgie* (*The art of making surgical reports*), first published in 1703. It soon became the reference work for surgeons who had to report to the courts in both Spain and Spanish America. See Irina Podgorny, "Los médicos de muertos y la paleontología en el Plata. Medicina Legal, Cirugía Militar y Observación de Campo en la Obra de Francisco X. Muñiz, 1830–1850," *Anuario IEHS: Instituto de Estudios históricos sociales* 25 (2010): 313.
11 José Luis de Pablo Gafas, *La Sala de Alcaldes de Casa y Corte (1583–1834). Justicia, gobierno y policía en la Corte de Madrid* (Libros del Taller de Historia, 2017), 305–25.
12 Archivo Histórico Nacional [AHN], Consejos, Book 1252, ff. 77r–77v, 79r–79v.
13 See, for example, [AHN], Consejos, Book 1200, f. 497r; Book 1223, f. 164r; Book 1257, ff. 280r–281v; Book 1267, f. 49r; Book 1286, f. 158r; Book 1292, f. 308r; and Book 1354, ff. 328r–329v.
14 AHN, Consejos, Book 1214, ff. 62r–62v, 132r–132v, 276r–276v; Book 1294, ff. 70r–71v; Book 1304, ff. 118r–118v; Book 1307, ff. 86r–86v, 243r–245v; Book 1313, f. 374r–374v; Book 1317, ff. 260r–268v; and Book 1322, ff. 236r–238v, 256r–257v.
15 AHN, Consejos, Book 1252, f. 77r.
16 AHN, Consejos, Book 1252, ff. 77r–77v, 79r–79v.
17 For the case of seventeenth-century France and Italy, see Silvia De Renzi, "Witnesses of the Body: Medico-Legal Cases In Seventeenth-Century Rome," *Studies in History and Philosophy of Science* 33 (2002): 219–42 and Katherine Dauge-Roth, "Bodies of Evidence: Judges and Surgeons at the Crime Scene in Early Modern France," *Journal of Medieval and Early Modern Studies* 54 (2024): 137–63.
18 Vidal, *Cirugía forense*, prologue.
19 Vidal, *Cirugía forense*, prologue.
20 De Renzi, "Witnesses of the body," 223.
21 Juan de Quiñones, *Memorial de los servicios que hizo al Rey Don Felipe III nuestro Señor, que santa gloria aya, y que ha hecho a V. Magestad, que Dios guarde, el Doctor Don Juan de Quiñones Alcalde de Casa y Corte, más antiguo, en diferentes jornadas, causas graves que ha averiguado contra delinquentes, y castigos que se les dieron. Y de otras ocupaciones que ha tenido, tocando al servicio de V. Magestad, y en beneficio del bien público* (n.p., 1643), 11–15.
22 Quiñones, *Memorial de los servicios*, 12.
23 Quiñones, *Memorial de los servicios*, 70–71.

24 Quiñones, *Memorial de los servicios*, 43–45.
25 Quiñones, *Memorial de los servicios*, 71–75.
26 Quiñones, *Memorial de los servicios*, 74–75. The phrase *in dubio pro reo* can also mean "benefit of the doubt."
27 AHN, Consejos, Legajo 7124, no. 4.
28 For a definition of the term *géminis*, see *Diccionario de Autoridades*, vol. IV (1734), 38.
29 See Rosa Isabel Sánchez Gómez, *Delincuencia y Seguridad en el Madrid de Carlos II* (Secretaría General Técnica del Ministerio del Interior, 1994), 117.
30 Quiñones, *Memorial de los servicios*, 49–51.
31 The *poena cullei* involved sewing a convict into a sack with wild animals; the sack was then thrown into water with the expectation that the animals would claw the convicted killer to death in their attempt to escape drowning. It may have reflected more of a belief by ancient Romans about customary punishments that their ancestors had used, rather than serving as a real punishment that was ever used.
32 Quiñones, *Memorial de los servicios*, 41.
33 The Archivo Histórico Nacional in Madrid holds a manuscript copy of this report ([AHN], Diversos-Colecciones, 1, no. 50).
34 Juan Meléndez Valdés, *Discursos forenses de D. Juan Meléndez Valdés, fiscal que fue de la Sala de Alcaldes de Casa y Corte é individuo de las Academia Española y de San Fernando, y de la de San Carlos de Valencia* (Imprenta Nacional, 1821), 1. In October 1797, after serving in various positions in the judiciary, Juan Meléndez Valdés had been appointed prosecutor of the Sala de Alcaldes de Casa y Corte. He held this post for a short time before being dismissed in August 1798 following the fall of Melchor Gaspar de Jovellanos as Minister of Grace and Justice.
35 Meléndez Valdés, *Discursos forenses*, 2.
36 Meléndez Valdés, *Discursos forenses*, 3.
37 Fernando Durán López, "Humanidad y justicia: el ensayismo en los *Discursos Forenses*," in *Juan Meléndez Valdés y su tiempo (1754–1817)*, eds. Jesús Cañas Murillo, Miguel Ángel Lama, and José Roso Díaz (Editora Regional de Extremadura, 2005), 317–28; and Mónica Bolufer Peruga, "De violentar las pasiones a educar el sentimiento: el matrimonio y la civilidad dieciochesca," in *Conflictividad y violencia en la Edad Moderna*, eds. Antonio Jiménez Estrella and Julián J. Lozano Navarro, vol. 2 (Universidad de Granada, 2012), 349–60.
38 Meléndez Valdés, *Discursos forenses*, 4–7.
39 Meléndez Valdés, *Discursos forenses*, 29–30.
40 Meléndez Valdés, *Discursos forenses*, 17–28.
41 Meléndez Valdés, *Discursos forenses*, 17–18.
42 Meléndez Valdés, *Discursos forenses*, 20.
43 Meléndez Valdés, *Discursos forenses*, 29.
44 Meléndez Valdés, *Discursos forenses*, 45–70.
45 Meléndez Valdés, *Discursos forenses*, 48.
46 Meléndez Valdés, *Discursos forenses*, 69–70.
47 Meléndez Valdés, *Discursos forenses*, iv.
48 See, for example, the deliberation on the death sentence imposed by the Sala on Tomás Pérez in March 1794 for the murder of his wife, Anastasia Bernabé, in September 1793: "As for the body of the crime, it appears in the unanimous testimony of two surgeons and in the anatomical dissection they subsequently made of the body according to the rules of the art. They found that the wound had been made with a cutting instrument, that it was two fingers long and more than eight in depth, that it crossed the lower cartilage of the first true rib and was directed

toward the mediastinum, and that part of the main vessels of the heart and the nerves of the intercostal branch had penetrated and injured the pericardium. For these and other reasons that they discovered, they declared that it was necessarily fatal. After comparing the knife used, whose identity was recognized by three witnesses and by the perpetrator himself in his confession, with the cavity of the wounds, the surgeons had no doubt as to the instrument used." [AHN], Consejos, Book 1384, ff. 546r–546v.

Select Bibliography

Bolufer Peruga, Mónica. "De violentar las pasiones a educar el sentimiento: el matrimonio y la civilidad dieciochesca." In *Conflictividad y violencia en la Edad Moderna*, edited by Antonio Jiménez Estrella and Julián J. Lozano Navarro. Vol. 2. Universidad de Granada, 2012.

Carracedo, Ángel, and Luis Concheiro. "Forensic science practice in Spain." In *The Global Practice of Forensic Science*, edited by Douglas H. Ubelaker. Wiley-Blackwell, 2015.

Dauge-Roth, Katherine. "Bodies of Evidence: Judges and Surgeons at the Crime Scene in Early Modern France." *Journal of Medieval and Early Modern Studies* 54 (2024): 137–63.

De Renzi, Silvia. "Witnesses of the Body: Medico-Legal Cases in Seventeenth-Century Rome." *Studies in History and Philosophy of Science* 33 (2002): 219–42.

De Renzi, Silvia. "Medical Expertise, Bodies, and the Law in Early Modern Courts." *Isis* 98 (2007): 315–22.

Durán López, Fernando. "Humanidad y justicia: el ensayismo en los *Discursos Forenses*." In *Juan Meléndez Valdés y su tiempo (1754–1817)*, edited by Jesús Cañas Murillo, Miguel Ángel Lama, and José Roso Díaz, 27. Editora Regional de Extremadura, Colección Estudio, 2005.

Fragoso, Juan. *Cirugía Universal, ahora nuevamente enmendada, y añadida en esta quinta impresión. Por el Licenciado Juan Fragoso Médico y Cirujano del Rey nuestro Señor y de sus Altezas*. Juan Gracián, 1592.

Mata y Fontanet, Pedro. "Del servicio médico-forense en España." *Revista española política, científica, y de artes, viajes, comercio, etc.* 2, no. 8 (1862): 81–90.

Mata y Fontanet, Pedro. *Tratado de Medicina y Cirugía Legal teórica y práctica seguido de un compendio de Toxicología*. 4th ed., Vol. I. Carlos Bailly-Baillière, 1866.

Meléndez Valdés, Juan. *Discursos forenses de D. Juan Meléndez Valdés, fiscal que fue de la Sala de Alcaldes de Casa y Corte é individuo de las Academia Española y de San Fernando, y de la de San Carlos de Valencia*. Imprenta Nacional, 1821.

Pablo Gafas, José Luis de. *La Sala de Alcaldes de Casa y Corte (1583–1834). Justicia, gobierno y policía en la Corte de Madrid*. Libros del Taller de Historia, 2017.

Podgorny, Irina. "Los médicos de muertos y la paleontología en el Plata. Medicina Legal, Cirugía Militar y Observación de Campo en la Obra de Francisco X. Muñiz, 1830–1850." *Anuario IEHS: Instituto de Estudios históricos sociales* 25 (2010): 305–32.

Quiñones, Juan de. *Memorial de los servicios que hizo al Rey Don Felipe III nuestro Señor, que santa gloria aya, y que ha hecho a V. Magestad, que Dios guarde, el Doctor Don Juan de Quiñones Alcalde de Casa y Corte, más antiguo, en diferentes jornadas, causas graves que ha averiguado contra delinquentes, y castigos que se les dieron. Y de otras ocupaciones que ha tenido, tocando al servicio de V. Magestad, y en beneficio del bien público*. N.p., 1643.

Sánchez Gómez, Rosa Isabel. *Delincuencia y Seguridad en el Madrid de Carlos II*. Secretaría General Técnica del Ministerio del Interior, 1994.

Vidal, Domingo. *Cirugía forense, o Arte de hacer las relaciones chirúrgico-legales. Obra útil a los médicos, cirujanos y jurisperitos, así seculares como eclesiásticos. Por el Licenciado Don Domingo Vidal, Profesor y Bibliotecario del Real Colegio de Cirugía de Barcelona.* Carlos Gibert y Tutó, 1783.

Watson, Katherine D. *Forensic Medicine in Western Society: A History.* Routledge, 2011.

6

ON FEUDING IN VENICE

Andrew Vidali

In late April 1515, the Quarantia Criminale rendered an *in absentia* verdict against the young Venetian nobleman Alessandro Marcello, son of Lorenzo, who lived in the Santa Marina district. This tribunal comprised 40 patricians typically selected from the middle and lower echelons of the lagoon nobility, and it stood as one of the most important judicial bodies in Venice for addressing criminality and violence, in addition to being a court of appeal. Its judgments were based on evidence collected by other judiciaries, particularly the Avogaria di Comùne, and debates between prosecutors and defense attorneys, which the public could also attend.[1] The charge against Alessandro was having killed Nicolò Sosina, a *fante*, or officer of the Council of Merchants. This magistracy, though ancient, now focused primarily on commercial disputes.[2] The sentence detailed how Nicolò had gone to the house of Lorenzo Marcello in the context of such a lawsuit. Upon opening the door and seeing the officer, Alessandro's response was immediate: he struck Nicolò on the head and nape, bringing about his death. For this heinous act, the young patrician was summoned by the tribunal; however, he did not appear for trial and was banished from Venice and all territories of the Republic up to Corfu. If apprehended within these boundaries, his right hand was to be severed and his head cut off.[3] This case, along with its judicial management and resolution, serves as a basis for examining how violent disputes between individuals and families from significantly different social strata were addressed by premodern judicial institutions.

This chapter will not offer insights that can be extrapolated to all of Europe but rather seeks instead to situate its analysis within a peculiar polity, the aristocratic Republic of Venice, whose scholarship has not

DOI: 10.4324/9781003486404-9

sufficiently problematized inter-class violence and its management.[4] In such conflicts, status disparity was crucial, as ambiguities and expectations surrounding one's standing in society were a powerful trigger for violence, and the resolution of such conflicts shaped new sociopolitical balances that initially had been disrupted.[5] At the same time, even making peace was potentially troublesome whenever the social gap was considerable.[6] At the heart of this investigation lies the ambiguity between reconciliation, status, and interpersonal violence. But in the capital of the Republic, such uncertainty was—supposedly—absent: membership in the Venetian ruling elite, the patriciate, was in fact rigorously codified and closely supervised and further regulated at the early sixteenth century.[7] Alessandro Sosina's case proves paradigmatic in revealing how ambiguities persisted, particularly in questions of resolution. By examining cases of violent conflict involving, on one side, patrician families and officers of the Republic's institutions as well as members of other privileged Venetian groups on the other, particularly *cittadini originarii*, this chapter provides a fresh perspective on the relationship between social status and violence through the lens of reconciliation among unequal parties.

Before exploring such cases of inter-class violence, it is necessary to clarify what peace agreements were, their role within the criminal justice system (particularly in relation to pardon requests), and their implications concerning social hierarchies. A fundamental notion to bear in mind is the intertwining of religious and political dimensions: these were equally present in late medieval and early modern notarial deeds, where ritualistic elements, such as the kiss of peace, were derived from the religious sphere but had explicit political and judicial implications.[8] The church and its hierarchies played a pivotal role in the Late Middle Ages in fostering peace within the community of the faithful; meanwhile, Italian civic institutions increasingly prioritized the promotion of social reconciliation policies, particularly in response to the turbulent factional struggles that characterized the city-states.[9] More broadly, European rulers positioned themselves as defenders and guarantors of peace within their territories, prohibiting private warfare. While this did not curb violence, it empowered sovereigns and judicial institutions to intervene more effectively in reconciling disputing parties. The fourteenth century thus emerged as a crucial period when the concept of public crime arose and replaced the earlier notion of private wrongdoing.[10] The religious notions of peace and forgiveness became embedded in the sphere of public justice, permeating both statutes and local customs, and associated with petitions for leniency submitted by offenders to court or the ruler.[11] The legal translation of renewed harmony materialized in the form of the aforementioned peace agreements; these could also involve monetary compensations as reparation for the damages suffered by the victim as well as symbolic gestures and rituals that intertwined and lent substance to such notarial deeds.[12]

Violence Against an Officer of the Republic or an Ordinary Enemy?

The events involving the nobleman Alessandro Marcello and the officer Nicolò Sosina resonated significantly within the lagoon's community. Yet the episode was far from unique: in early September 1510, the Quarantia Criminal delivered a verdict on a remarkably similar case, which involved the wounding of the officer Grazioso, once again employed by the Council of Merchants. He had arrested and incarcerated the patrician, Andrea Arimondo, following orders from the judiciary. In retaliation, Andrea's son, Giacomo, ambushed and attacked Grazioso. What made this episode noteworthy was the explicit acknowledgment that the violence perpetrated by Giacomo Arimondo was indeed driven by a desire for *vindicta*, or revenge, against the officer who was following official legal orders.[13] There is a twofold set of issues attached to the use of this term in the judicial record, which brings to the fore the status of the two conflicting parties, a matter that will reappear in the resolution of the dispute between the Marcello patrician family and the late Nicolò Sosina's kinship group. First, scholarship on violence in premodern Europe has emphasized that revenge and enmity indicate a conflict resolution system that pitted individuals belonging to the same social rank against each other, or at least with a comparable social standing and reputation.[14] It is difficult to think that a young patrician could be equated with a fante, that is, a modestly salaried official. The social distance was evident and recognized by contemporaries, including the judges who sat in the Quarantia.

This raises the second issue, namely, the judicial interpretation of the incident by authorities: was it an act of *lèse-majesté* because it was committed against an individual performing a public function who embodied the authority of the Republic and its institutions? Or was it a matter of private violence motivated by personal disputes?[15] It is precisely in the extrajudicial management of Alessandro Marcello's case that we can find a more nuanced answer than expected. In particular, two pardon requests offered two different framings in addition to the official one embedded in the judicial record and echoed in contemporary ego-documents.[16] The official account attributed the violent actions of the patrician Alessandro Marcello to the defense of status and honor, specifically to prevent his father's imprisonment, yet the two petitions submitted by his father, Lorenzo, to the Council of Ten cited other reasons.[17] Slightly more than a year after the conviction, the tribunal assessed the content of the first petition, as it started doing with many other pardon requests sent by Venetian patricians to negotiate their sentences in the early sixteenth century.[18] However, the request for his son's absolution was denied. This decision was likely influenced by Lorenzo Marcello's description of the events. In his lengthy account, the patrician claimed that Nicolò's death resulted from a brawl: when his son opened the door to the officer, a verbal altercation ensued, quickly escalating into insults. The heated exchange led to physical confrontation, with Nicolò drawing a blade and pursuing the patrician inside the house and up the stairs, where the unarmed patrician was attempting to escape. The officer then stumbled and lost his weapon, which was seized by the patrician, who then struck the officer twice, though not fatally. According to Lorenzo, Nicolò's death was in fact due to other unspecified causes.[19]

At first glance, this version does not appear to diverge significantly from the official account, which is lacking in detail. It is likely that the reference to the two blows delivered by Alessandro with the weapon taken from the officer (which his father declared non-lethal) did not align with the judicial reconstruction and medical report, which have not been preserved.[20] Still, a closer examination of the text allows us to notice some legal nuances that contradicted the initial account of the events. In particular, the insistence on classifying the incident as a "simple brawl" was inherently problematic, for the legal argument presented to support this interpretation conflicted with the judicial verdict. The narrative provided by the father underlined the themes of provocation and self-defense, which, according to contemporary jurisprudence, rested on the absence of premeditation.[21] The members of the Council of Ten were presented then with a narrative grounded in legal aspects that did not match the evidence compiled during the trial: the verdict had declared that the assault on the officer occurred not after a prolonged exchange of words and not within the house, but at the door. The discrepancies were too pronounced: the judicial case pointed to a high degree of responsibility on the part of the young patrician; it was something more severe than a brawl, as evidenced by the involvement of the Avogaria di Comùne, an institution responsible for serious and premeditated cases. Ultimately, Alessandro's failure to appear at the trial ultimately prevented him from contesting the narrative framed by the judicial authorities, which emphasized the heinousness of the death of an officer acting within official capacity. This was acknowledged by Alessandro in his second petition, submitted in 1522 by his father, where he presented a drastically different account.[22]

The patrician persisted in characterizing the altercation between his son and Nicolò Sosina as a "very simple brawl." At the same time, he provided an alternative justification for his son's assault. Alessandro purportedly did not act in defense of his father's noble status nor following a verbal altercation: this third version emphasized the honor of his mother, which the young patrician allegedly defended by shedding the officer's blood. According to this account, Nicolò had insulted and demeaned Alessandro's mother, inciting great "wrath" in Alessandro, who, at 21 years of age, was unable to tolerate such a grievous affront. The implications of this new interpretation stand in stark contrast to the narrative presented in the first petition. This revised account shifts the focus from male to female honor, which the young patrician felt compelled to defend, reflecting notions about gender identities that are well documented by scholars, at least as they are articulated in premodern literary works.[23] The family probably thought this was a line of defense harder to counter. Another significant element was the appeal to the emotional sphere: anger provoked by an offense was regularly cited during trial or pardon requests to demonstrate the absence of premeditation. Premodern jurisprudence and courts recognized that such intense passion could induce a temporary mental infirmity, potentially absolving the individual of partial or total responsibility for actions committed in such a fit of rage, although this was not automatic.[24] This new version acknowledged the homicide and Alessandro Marcello's culpability but justified his actions in a manner more consistent with premodern notions about emotion, mind, and justice. Nonetheless, the Council of Ten hesitated: while most members were inclined to fulfill the request made by the head of the family, a qualified majority of members in agreement was lacking.[25]

What was still missing to persuade the tribunal? To grasp the Council of Ten's indecisiveness, one must reflect on the sociopolitical implications, not just strictly legal ones, of the third and final version: emphasizing the defense of maternal honor and the emotions associated with it meant framing the conflict within the paradigms of feud and enmity. In other words, through the second petition, the Marcello family asserted that the altercation between Alessandro and Nicolò Sosina transcended the latter's public role. A similar event unfolded in early sixteenth-century papal-ruled Reggio Emilia. Here, the Bebbi family, who were members of the pro-Este faction, successfully argued the private nature of their enmity with the former papal governor Gozzadini, which culminated in his heinous murder in the city cathedral in 1517.[26] While the Bebbi had killed someone who formally came from a higher socio-political hierarchy—for Giovanni Gozzadini embodied papal sovereign power—the opposite occurred in Venice. As patricians and members of the Venetian ruling elite, the Marcello family occupied a position far above that of Nicolò Sosina, a common member of the diverse Venetian population. However, if Officer Sosina's death stemmed directly from his challenge to the honor of Alessandro's mother and the provocation of such fury in the young man, that meant the social distance with Sosina had been theoretically bridged and outweighed. It's difficult to believe that the members of the Council of Ten, or other members of the Venetian patriciate, missed these subtleties embedded in the second petition. In fact, in order to secure the freedom of Alessandro Marcello, the tribunal carried forward the argument laid out by the nobleman to its natural consequence: two weeks after the initial rejection, on February 22, the tribunal reconsidered the second petition and added a further clause; a safe conduct of 100 years would be granted "having a peace agreement, and not otherwise."[27]

The requested document was indeed attached: *donna* Marietta, wife of the sailor Marco Soranzo and sister of the deceased, "granted pure, true, and sincere peace" to Giovanni Marcello, brother of Alessandro. The notarial deed had in fact been signed in the house of Marietta and her husband.[28] What complicates this already intricate scenario is the date on which the peace agreement was signed: June 4, 1516, just a few days before the submission of Lorenzo's first supplication to the Council of Ten. It is reasonable to hypothesize that the patrician family intended to formalize the end of hostilities in anticipation of Alessandro's imminent formal request.[29] The crucial issue is then the absence of any reference to reconciliation not only in the first supplication but also in the second. Why did the Venetian patrician neither mention that the conflict had been resolved nor provide clear evidence of that outcome? In voting on the first pardon request, the members of the Ten seemed to be aware of the notarial act, making the additional clause appear as redundant.[30] Even if the initial version of the conflict presented by Lorenzo Marcello—where his son Alessandro was absolved of any responsibility—did not match the notarial deed implying the exact opposite, it still remains unclear why, in the second petition, the patrician family showed reluctance to explicitly state the reconciliation. Peace represented the natural consequence of the new version of events as the most coherent means to ensure the non-perpetuation of violence. However, the tribunal had to urge the Marcello family members to offer evidence about the end of hostilities. Did the patrician house not wish to acknowledge an unbecoming peace, forged with people evidently much lower in the Venetian social hierarchy? And was this attitude shared by the rest of the Venetian patriciate?

Reconciling With Inferiors: Venetian Patricians and Native-Born Citizens

The interplay among class conflict, pacification, and social status can be better grasped by considering other cases comparable to those of the patrician Alessandro Marcello and the officer Nicolò Sosina, which highlight the flexibility of social status in connection to peace-making, particularly those involving members of the privileged *cittadini originarii*.[31] For example, in 1538, Giacomo Rizzo and his brother Vincenzo, a secretary at the Ducal Chancellery, granted forgiveness to the nobleman Giovanni Alvise Bragadin for a wound inflicted on Giacomo during a brawl.[32] The two native-born citizens directed the notarized peace agreement towards Alvise but also *omnibus eius fratribus de cha Bragadeno*, meaning his brothers and, by extension, his entire lineage.[33] The record does not fully convey the details of the physical altercation, but it aims to mitigate the patrician's culpability by depicting a broader tumult involving many armed participants. The summons for trial, issued by the Council of Ten at the end of January 1537, referred to insolent acts committed in a residence where a wedding celebration was taking place. Failing to appear, Giovanni Alvise was sentenced in absentia to 12 years of exile in Cyprus, where he went in May of the same year.[34] While Giovanni Alvise was on the island in the eastern Mediterranean, his brothers—Giovanni, Michele, Marino, Girolamo, and Lorenzo—did not remain inactive. A year later, in early May 1538, they managed to secure their sibling's release. In the petition submitted to the Council of Ten, the patricians offered a donation of 300 ducats and declared they possessed the aforementioned peace agreement. Although it is not included in the relevant archival collection, the Council's ruling specified that the nobles from the Bragadin house had indeed presented said notarial act.[35]

At first glance, this case appears much more straightforward than that of Lorenzo Marcello and Nicolò Sosina: Giovanni Alvise Bragadin had injured the native-born citizen and was exiled, thereby creating the conditions for the families to negotiate peace and communicate it to the authorities.[36] Once notified of the formal end of the conflict, the court acquitted the nobleman who had sought and obtained forgiveness from the injured party despite the social gap, which placed the former above the latter. However, this divide was considerably smaller than the one separating Lorenzo Marcello from the officer of the Council of Merchants. Figuratively, this episode of violence resulted in either the social demotion of the Bragadin family or the elevation of the Rizzo family, or a combination of both. Importantly, the decree summoning Bragadin referred to the transgression of both the law and good custom.[37] This was likely an explicit allusion to a law passed a few years earlier. On March 1532, the court lamented that some groups of young Venetians were causing many disturbances by attempting to enter houses where parties and dances were taking place against the will of the owners and residents, pounding on doors vehemently, and uttering insults and other scandalous words. To ensure the safety and freedom that the citizens of the lagoon were entitled to enjoy, the Council of Ten decreed that anyone attending banquets, weddings, dances, and similar festivities would incur specific penalties if they refused to leave at the host's request or engaged in even more offensive behavior. Refusal to leave would result in six months of imprisonment and a two-year banishment from Venice; abusive language would entail a five-year ban. Finally, if someone initiated a brawl, as Giovanni Alvise Bragadin did, or employed violence to enter the place where the party was being held, they would incur a ten-year exile.[38]

This measure was almost certainly inspired by a recent incident. In late January 1532, the Council of Ten ordered the arrest of the nobles Giovanni

Vendramin, Francesco da Mosto, and Pietro Grioni for entering the house of the native-born citizen Alvise Caolini and his brothers while celebrating a wedding and dining. The patricians caused considerable disturbance and murmuring among the guests.[39] The new law was enforced again on November 1535 when two other patricians were accused of using violence to enter the house of some other lagoon inhabitants, this time some apothecaries, once again during wedding celebrations.[40] After the case involving Bragadin, a similar case was also recorded in 1543, when Matteo Mocenigo, aided by Alvise Lion, violated the 1532 law by committing insolent acts inside a non-noble house during wedding festivities.[41] What motivations might have driven a number of patricians to disrupt the festive occasions of the lower classes? In the absence of trial records, we can only speculate on the sociopolitical significance of noble conflict.

Indeed, although legally equal, the Venetian patriciate was internally stratified according to political significance and the family's economic resources.[42] One can speculate that the patricians responsible for these transgressions were from the lower echelons of the Venetian ruling class and were therefore driven by envy toward those citizens who, despite being socially inferior, were perhaps more affluent or enjoyed connections with prominent patricians and influential families.[43] Indeed, Bragadin's family lacked significant political influence.[44] The picture, however, is even more complicated than that: though four nobles implicated in cases of infringement of the 1532 law were from families with little political power, the others came from more prominent ones, but they do not seem to have enjoyed a great political career themselves.[45] Regardless, what matters is that, among all these patrician families, the Bragadin family alone recognized the benefit of negotiating peace with the aggrieved party, or at least made such efforts explicit, thereby making the approach taken by this patrician house stand out even more.[46] The court had indeed stipulated that any eventual pardon request would require an exceptionally high majority vote but did not include any clause pertaining to reconciliation between the offended and the offenders. This would suggest that families from more precarious social strata had greater benefits from making peace agreements with anyone, higher or lower.

Equally compelling is a final case study taking place in early sixteenth-century Venice that pitted a branch of the Tiepolo patrician family against some members of the Benedetti citizen family.[47] Just like Alessandro Marcello and Nicolò Sosina's case, the Venetian community deemed this episode of violence so appalling that it drew the attention of not only the famous diarist Marin Sanudo but also some other important chroniclers.[48] However, there was a notable distinction: the victim of this violence was a woman. In late January 1516, Samaritana Zon, the wife of Giovanni Battista Benedetti, was assaulted after leaving the church of Santa Maria dei Miracoli. As she was preparing to board a boat to return home with her sister-in-law, a masked assailant who had been waiting nearby attacked her, "cutting her face from the eye to the mouth."[49] From a social perspective, contemporary writers presented the event as an illegitimate act of violence, which could not be understood within the framework of the tolerable punishment of an unfaithful woman. Sanudo noted that Samaritana was very beautiful but, more importantly, married to Giovanni Battista Benedetti, thereby implying her moral rectitude. Even more explicitly, Marcantonio Michiel wrote that the woman had been attacked "as if she were a vile whore," further stressing the unlawfulness of the violence committed by the anonymous masked person.[50] It is precisely in light of this community condemnation that we understand how the subsequent legal reaction further emphasized the heinous nature of the events. Despite the matter not falling within its usual jurisdiction, the Council of Ten decided to handle the case personally, offering a substantial reward and other incentives for information leading to the identification of the perpetrator.[51]

Suspicions quickly fell upon a patrician from a high-profile family: Andrea Tiepolo of Paolo, who enjoyed family connections with some members of the same Council of Ten, who had to recuse themselves from the case.[52] Andrea was indeed a member of a patrician group with excellent connections to the most influential circles of the ruling class. Nevertheless, this did not prevent his conviction, which was exacerbated by his failure to appear at his trial in late February 1516. He was banished for life from Venice and all of mainland Italy up to the Kvarner Gulf.[53]

His exile was short-lived: about a year later, in mid-January 1517, his brothers submitted a pardon request to the Council of Ten. Stefano and Pietro Tiepolo contended that the violence committed by Andrea was merely the result of "youthful fury," implying that the attack on the woman was an impulsive act, not part of a broader, structured enmity between the two families.[54] In a sense, this argument resembles the final version of events offered by the patrician Lorenzo Marcello regarding his son's murder of the officer Nicolò. The petitioners also asserted that their brother could safely return to his homeland, as the patrician family had already "made peace" and "reconciled with the Benedetti, who [were] the aggrieved party." To bolster their plea, they offered compensation of 600 ducats, of which 400 would serve as compensation for the damage inflicted on the native-born citizens. These funds were intended "for the marriage or convent entry of one or more daughters of said Benedetti."[55] Beyond the financial reparation, the claim that peace had already been achieved warranted further attention and likely ensured the swift resolution of the case. In a text attached to the petition, Giovanni Battista Benedetti himself, along with his brother Antonio, corroborated Tiepolo's version; in fact, he used the same words, "youthful fury," and then clarified that Andrea had "no legitimate cause against my said wife, as known to all." Giovanni Battista also confirmed that he had indeed "made good peace and reconciled with the said Tiepolos." The husband of the injured woman finally stated that granting Andrea Tiepolo's absolution "would be greatly appreciated by us."[56] Although a formal peace agreement was not attached, we must consider that this document signed by the offended parties was considered a sufficient alternative as evidence that the conflict had been resolved. Thus, in a similar fashion to what the Bragadin family members did in relation to the Rizzo affair, the Tiepolos did not hide the fact that they had questioned their own status and accepted the fact that they would ask forgiveness from someone socially inferior.

Conclusion: Providing or Withholding Evidence of Reconciliation?

Making peace was a delicate matter: some Venetian patricians did not consider it advantageous to explicitly acknowledge the reconciliation they had achieved with non-noble families before the Republic's legal institutions, while others did the exact opposite. The Marcello family had formalized peace with the victim's sister but did not leverage it in their negotiations with the Council of Ten, opting instead to focus on legal arguments. Nevertheless, the court insisted on the peace agreement to substantiate the arguments made by the noble family. On the other hand, the noblemen from the Bragadin and Tiepolo families incorporated evidence of newfound harmony into their petitions by presenting a copy of the signed notarial act or having the offended party submit a sort of memorandum. This essay has demonstrated how such a radically different strategy is to be traced back to the different degrees of social distance between victims and the aggressors: settling a conflict with members of a lower but contiguous class, which was still at the top of Venetian non-patrician society, did not pose the same challenge as dealing with a simple commoner. But Nicolò Sosina was more than just an individual when he was killed by Alessandro Marcello: as an officer of one of the Republic's institutions, the violence he suffered also constituted an affront to the honor of the Serenissima. The murderer's father, Lorenzo, aimed to deconstruct this interpretation of the conflict, reframing it as a purely personal matter, divorced from any public function. This tactic was successful but at the cost of the humiliation of giving proof about the reconciliation with Nicolò's sister, an element that implies the absence of closer male heirs or relatives, making this case even more peculiar.

The issue posed by the social gap is then further complicated by the element of gender, which connects the Marcello-Sosina affair to the Tiepolo-Benedetti one. At the same time, the two cases addressed gender in distinct ways: although Samaritana Zon, wife of Giovanni Battista Benedetti, was the victim of Andrea Tiepolo's assault, she had no role in the appeasement. Her own voice was not represented but rather implicitly absorbed within her husband's family, the Benedetti, who instead were depicted as the victims.[57] Even though similar cases of male-on-female violence occurred in early-sixteenth-century Venice, what makes these stand out is how the gender dimension was entwined with their resolution.[58] Women granting peace to men by signing notarial acts and engaging in the ritualistic aspects of reconciliation, such as the kiss of peace, were uncommon, though not unknown; and the Venetian notarial collections offer a number of examples from the mid-to-late sixteenth century.[59] Donna Marietta's case was therefore not unique: women, particularly widows or the sole surviving sibling, could have the right to grant peace to the offender, either independently or alongside other male relatives of the deceased, playing a significant role in both the ritual gestures and legal proceedings.

But between Marietta and the Marcello family, there was also a significant social distance. And it is perhaps this final piece of the puzzle that may shed light on the hesitation by the latter to submit evidence of reconciliation: a stark difference in status combined with assumptions about gender roles. Conversely, Tiepolo and Bragadin emphasized having achieved peace with male members of non-patrician yet reputable Venetian families, with far less embarrassment for the former. Presenting or withholding evidence of peace was thus one element of the strategy employed by groups, families, and factions when dealing with courts. In instances of violent conflict between members of distinct but well-defined social groups, multiple factors influenced their decision-making processes. The disparity in social status proved to be crucial and likely outweighed gender considerations, as proven by the Tiepolo-Benedetti case. Notably, Samaritana, the victim of the nobleman's armed assault, did not play any role in the peace agreement or the negotiations with the Council of Ten. That court, for its part, did not appear to handle pardon requests from patricians who perpetrated violence against inferior subjects in a markedly different manner when compared to disputes and quarrels between noble households from the lagoon. Providing evidence of peace remained a fundamental condition for a sentence reduction in the pre-modern era, even in cases involving inter-class violence.

Notes

1 Marco Bellabarba, "Giustizia, disciplina e ordine pubblico," in *Storia di Venezia. Dalle origini alla caduta della Serenissima, vol. 6, Dal Rinascimento al Barocco*, eds. Gaetano Cozzi and Prodi Prodi (Istituto della Enciclopedia Italiana, 1994), 833.

2 Piero D'Angiolini, ed., *Guida Generale degli Archivi di Stato Italiani*, vol. IV (Ministero per i beni culturali e ambientali, 1994), 979.

3 Archivio di Stato di Venezia (henceforth ASVE), Avogaria di Comùne (henceforth AC), reg. 3662, fol. 179.

4 A recent book that discussed the political stability and social legitimacy of the Venetian state in light of various instances of grassroots protest and revolt, without focusing on inter-class violence, is the one by Maartje van Gelder and Claire

Judde de Larivière, eds., *Popular Politics in an Aristocratic Republic: Political Conflict and Social Contestation in Late Medieval and Early Modern Venice* (Routledge, 2020).

5 Roger V. Gould, *Collision of Wills: How Ambiguity about Social Rank Breeds Conflict* (University of Chicago Press, 2003).

6 See the case involving Francesco Guicciardini, the famous humanist and Renaissance historian, acting as Papal governor in Reggio Emilia, and Domenico Amorotto, an outlaw and faction leader discussed in Carlo Baja Guarienti, *Il bandito e il governatore. Domenico d'Amorotto e Francesco Guicciardini nell'età delle guerre d'Italia* (Viella, 2014), 116–20. The former refused to make peace with the latter, granting him only forgiveness.

7 Stanley Chojnacki, *Women and Men in Renaissance Venice: Twelve Essays on Patrician Society* (The John Hopkins University Press, 2000), 7–8.

8 John Bossy, *Peace in the Post-Reformation* (Cambridge University Press, 2004); Kiril Petkov, *The Kiss of Peace. Ritual, Self, and Society in the High and Late Medieval West* (Brill, 2003).

9 Massimo Vallerani, *Medieval Public Justice* (Catholic University of America Press, 2012), 21–23.

10 Justine M. Firnhaber-Baker, "From God's Peace to the King's Order: Late Medieval Limitations on Non-Royal Warfare," *Essays in Medieval Studies* 23 (2006): 19–30; John Watts, *The Making of Polities. Europe, 1300–1500* (Cambridge University Press, 2009), 215.

11 Shona K. Wray, "Instruments of Concord: Making Peace and Settling Disputes through a Notary in the City and Contado of Late Medieval Bologna," *Journal of Social History* 42 (2009): 733–60; more comprehensive assessments of late medieval Italy in Joanna C. Vitiello, *Public Justice and the Criminal Trial in Late Medieval Italy: Reggio Emilia in the Visconti Age* (Brill, 2016), 177–201.

12 Ottavia Niccoli, *Perdonare. Idee, pratiche, rituali in Italia tra Cinque e Seicento* (Editori Laterza, 2007); Stephen Cummins, "Forgiving Crimes in Early Modern Naples," in *Cultures of Conflict Resolution in Early Modern Europe*, eds. Stephen Cummins and Laura Kounine (Routledge, 2016), 271–74.

13 AC, reg. 3661, fol. 149–50. Note that Giacomo Arimondo's exile was annulled a few years later upon payment of 200 ducats to the Republic, with no mention made of any reconciliation between the patrician house and the family of the deceased: ASVE, Consiglio dei Dieci, Deliberazioni (henceforth CD), Miste, Filze, reg. 32, fol. 257, with one attachment.

14 Claudio Povolo, "Feud and vendetta: customs and trial rites in Medieval and Modern Europe. A legal-anthropological approach," *Acta Histriae* 23 (2015): 199–207; Stuart Carroll, *Enmity and Violence in Early Modern Europe* (Cambridge University Press, 2023), 99–101.

15 On this crime in late medieval Italy, see Robert Fredona, "Baldus de Ubaldis on Conspiracy and Laesa Maiestas in Late Trecento Florence," in *The Politics of Law in Late Medieval and Renaissance Italy*, eds. Lawrin Armstrong and Julius Kirshner (University of Toronto Press, 2011), 141–60.

16 See, for instance, Marin Sanudo, *I Diarii di Marino Sanuto* (henceforth *Diarii*), eds. M. Allegri et al., vol. 20 (Stabilimento Visentini cav. Federico-Editore, 1879–1902), col. 154.

17 On petitions as a means of communication between subjects and rulers, there is a vast bibliography. See at least Cristina Nubola and Andreas Würgler, eds., *Suppliche e "gravamina." Politica, amministrazione, giustizia in Europa (secoli XIV-XVIII)* (Il Mulino, 2002). On pardon requests, see Natalie Z. Davis, *Fiction in the Archives: Pardon Tales and Their Tellers in Sixteenth-Century France* (Stanford University Press, 1990); Peter Arnade and Walter Prevenier, *Honor,*

Vengeance, and Social Trouble: Pardon Letters in the Burgundian Low Countries (Cornell University Press, 2015).

18 Andrew Vidali, *Giustizia e violenza delle élites in una repubblica aristocratica. Politica del diritto, tribunali e patriziato nel Cinquecento veneziano* (Unicopli, 2024), 89–95.

19 CD, Miste, Filze, reg. 37, fol. 216.

20 On forensic science and its relationship with criminal justice in late medieval Italy, see Joanna C. Vitiello, "Forensic Evidence, Lay Witnesses and Medical Expertise in the Criminal Courts of Late Medieval Italy," in *Medicine and the Law in the Middle Ages*, eds. Wendy Turner and Sara Butler (Brill, 2014), 133–56.

21 Consider, for instance, the opinion of a late sixteenth-century jurist, Lorenzo Priori, who was well-versed in Venetian criminal justice: Lorenzo Priori, *Pratica criminale secondo le leggi della Serenissima Repubblica di Venezia* (Venice: 1738), 83, 90, 133, 180, 195.

22 CD, Criminali, Registri, reg. 3, fol. 140.

23 Elizabeth S. Cohen, "Honor and Gender in the Streets of Early Modern Rome," *Journal of Interdisciplinary History* 22 (1992): 597–625; Scott K. Taylor, "Women, Honor, and Violence in a Castilian Town, 1600–1650," *The Sixteenth Century Journal* 35 (2004): 1079–97.

24 Claudio Povolo, *Furore. Elaborazione di un'emozione nella seconda metà del Cinquecento* (Caselle di Sommacampagna: Cierre Edizioni, 2015); Mònica Calabritto, *Murder and Madness on Trial: A Tale of True Crime from Early Modern Bologna* (Penn State University Press, 2023).

25 CD, Criminali, Registri, reg. 3, fol. 140; assembled with its *Zonta*, 16 members voted in favor and 12 against.

26 See Carlo Baja Guarienti, "Le 'guerre civili' di Reggio. Una faida tra guelfi e ghibellini all'inizio del XVI secolo," in Giambattista Bebbi, *Reggio nel Cinquecento. Le guerre civili fra guelfi e ghibellini del secolo XVI*, ed. Carlo Baja Guarienti (Antiche Porte, 2007), 37–45.

27 CD, Criminali, Registri, reg. 3, fol. 141.

28 CD, Criminali, Filze, b. 4, fasc. "1521", unfoliated, *1521 Die xxii Februarii In Consilio X cum Additione*, attached.

29 An insightful reflection on the relationship between the time when proof of pacification is submitted to a court and judicial outcome, albeit in a different context, is different; see Vallerani, *Medieval Public Justice*, 207–12.

30 CD, Miste, Registri, reg. 40, fol. 84.

31 This social group had access to the most prestigious offices within the Ducal Chancellery and established marital ties with Venetian noble families. See Andrea Zannini, *Burocrazia e burocrati a Venezia in età moderna: i cittadini originari (sec. XVI–XVIII)* (Istituto veneto di scienze, lettere ed arti, 1993); Dennis Romano, *Patricians and Popolani. The Social Foundations of the Venetian Renaissance State* (The John Hopkins University Press, 1987), 141–58; Alexander Cowan, *Marriage, Manners, and Mobility in Early Modern Venice* (Ashgate, 2007), 15, 48–55.

32 The Rizzo family tree is in ASVE, Miscellanea codici, Storia veneta, b. 15, fol. 160–61.

33 ASVE, Notarile. Atti (henceforth Notarile), b. 3347, cc. 65 r.-v.

34 CD, Criminali, Registri, reg. 5, fol. 96, 97–98.

35 The court's ruling is in CD, Comuni, Registri, reg. 13, fol. 19; the Bragadin brothers' petition is in CD, Criminali, Registri, Filze, reg. 25, fol. 93.

36 On the role of banishment as a means to promote conflict resolution, see Claudio Povolo, "The Public Rock of Cut Heads. Violence and Banditry in the Mediterranean: The Republic of Venice in the Sixteenth Century," in *Management*

and Resolution of Conflict and Rivalries in Renaissance Europe, eds. Jill Kray, Marc Laurey, and David A. Lines (V&R unipress-Bonn University Press, 2023), 115–17.
37 CD, Criminali, Registri, reg. 5, fol. 96: "contra legem et bonos mores."
38 CD, Comuni, Registri, reg. 8, fol 4. On violence during celebrations in the Republic of Venice, see Umberto Cecchinato, "Danza, contaminazione, conflitto. Risse e aggressioni durante i balli nelle ville rurali del Trevigiano (secoli XVI-XVII)," *Acta Histriae* 23 (2015): 29–42.
39 CD, Criminali, Registri, reg. 4, fol. 101.
40 CD, Criminali, Registri, reg. 5, fol. 69–70.
41 CD, Criminali, Registri, reg. 6, fol. 59–60.
42 The newly elected Doge Andrea Gritti himself spoke of "rich, middle-class, and poor" patricians in one of the first speeches he delivered in the Great Council in May 1523. See *Diarii*, vol. 34, col. 228–29.
43 As was generally the case with those employed in the Ducal Chancellery; see Giuseppe Trebbi, "Il segretario veneziano," *Archivio Storico Italiano* 144 (1986): 44, 68–69.
44 ASVE, Miscellanea codici, Storia veneta, reg. 18, fol. 141.
45 ASVE, Miscellanea codici, Storia veneta, reg. 20, fol. 163, 253; reg. 21, fol. 200, 397; reg. 23, fol. 178, 207, 208, 357.
46 Absolutions and pardon requests made by the noblemen convicted in 1535 can be found in CD, Comuni, Registri, reg. 13, fol. 19, 51; Filze, reg. 25, fol. 91, 92, 225. The petitions submitted by those sentenced in 1543 and the related court's rulings are in CD, Criminali, Registri, reg. 6, fol. 81, 86, 88.
47 The Benedetti family tree is in ASVE, Miscellanea codici, Storia veneta, reg. 9, fol. 261; Paolo, brother of the two male protagonists, became Cancelliere Ducale.
48 Venice, Biblioteca del Museo Correr, Codici Cicogna (henceforth Correr), reg. 2848, *Diarii di Marcantonio Michiel. 1511–1521*, fol. 219, 221.
49 *Diarii*, reg. 21, col. 477.
50 Correr, reg. 2848, fol. 219.
51 CD, Criminali, Registri, reg. 2, fol. 159–60. On the growing interference of the Council of Ten in Venetian criminal matters, see Vidali, *Giustizia e violenza*, 123–36.
52 CD, Criminali, reg. 2, fol. 161. On this aspect of Venetian republicanism, see Gasparo Contarini, *Della Republica e magistrati di Venetia libri V. di M. Gasparo Contarini, che fu poi cardinale* (Venice: 1591), 158, 182–83.
53 CD, Criminali, reg. 2, fol. 164.
54 CD, Miste, Registri, reg. 40, fol. 213.
55 CD, Miste, Registri, reg. 40, fol. 213.
56 CD, Miste, Filze, reg. 38, fol. 237, attached.
57 See Julian A. Pitt-Rivers, *The Fate of Shechem or the Politics of Sex: Essays in the Anthropology of the Mediterranean* (Cambridge University Press, 1977).
58 Some examples of Venetian noblemen assaulting and injuring low-born women in the early sixteenth century are *Diarii*, vol. 20, col. 126; vol. 22, col. 446; vol. 27, col. 317, 328, 671; vol. 33, col. 608, 620, 630; and vol. 34, col. 8.
59 Notarile, reg. 5834, fasc. 5, fol. 222; reg. 8353, fol. 67–68; reg. 4911, fasc. 1, fol. 17–18; reg. 5755, fol. 53–54; reg. 4909, fasc. 1, fol. 101–2.

Select Bibliography

Arnade, Peter, and Walter Prevenier. *Honor, Vengeance, and Social Trouble: Pardon Letters in the Burgundian Low Countries*. Cornell University Press, 2015.
Baja Guarienti, Carlo. "Le 'guerre civili' di Reggio. Una faida tra guelfi e ghibellini all'inizio del XVI secolo." Giambattista, Bebbi. *Reggio nel Cinquecento. Le guerre*

civili tra guelfi e ghibellini del secolo XVI, edited Carlo Baja Guarienti. Antiche Porte, 2007.
Baja Guarienti, Carlo. *Il bandito e il governatore. Domenico d'Amorotto e Francesco Guicciardini nell'età delle guerre d'Italia.* Viella, 2014.
Bellabarba, Marco. "Giustizia, disciplina e ordine pubblico." In *Storia di Venezia. Dalle origini alla caduta della Serenissima, Vol. 6: Dal Rinascimento al Barocco*, edited by Gaetano Cozzi and Prodi Prodi. Istituto della Enciclopedia Italiana, 1994.
Bossy, John. *Peace in the Post-Reformation.* Cambridge University Press, 2004.
Calabritto, Mònica. *Murder and Madness on Trial. A Tale of True Crime from Early Modern Bologna.* Penn State University Press, 2023.
Carroll, Stuart. *Enmity and Violence in Early Modern Europe.* Cambridge University Press, 2023.
Cecchinato, Umberto. "Danza, contaminazione, conflitto. Risse e aggressioni durante i balli nelle ville rurali del Trevigiano (secoli XVI-XVII)." *Acta Histriae* 23 (2015): 29–42.
Chojnacki, Stabley. *Women and Men in Renaissance Venice. Twelve Essays on Patrician Society.* The John Hopkins University Press, 2000.
Cohen, Elizabeth S. "Honor and Gender in the Streets of Early Modern Rome." *Journal of Interdisciplinary History* 22 (1992): 597–625.
Contarini, Gasparo. *Della Republica e magistrati di Venetia libri V. di M. Gasparo Contarini, che fu poi cardinale.* Venice, 1591.
Cowan, Alexander. *Marriage, Manners and Mobility in Early Modern Venice.* Ashgate, 2007.
Cummins, Stephen. "Forgiving Crimes in Early Modern Naples." In *Cultures of Conflict Resolution in Early Modern Europe*, edited by Stephen Cummins and Laura Kounine. Routledge, 2016.
D'Angiolini, Piero, ed. *Guida Generale degli Archivi di Stato Italiani.* Vol. IV. Ministero per i Beni Culturali e Ambientali, 1994.
Davis, Natalie Z. *Fiction in the Archives: Pardon Tales and Their Tellers in Sixteenth-Century France.* Stanford University Press, 1990.
Firnhaber-Baker, Justine M. "From God's Peace to the King's Order: Late Medieval Limitations on Non-Royal Warfare." *Essays in Medieval Studies* 23 (2006): 19–30.
Fredona, Robert. "Baldus de Ubaldis on Conspiracy and Laesa Maiestas in Late Trecento Florence." In *The Politics of Law in Late Medieval and Renaissance Italy*, edited by Lawrin Armstrong and Julius Kirshner. University of Toronto Press, 2011.
Gould, Roger V. *Collision of Wills: How Ambiguity about Social Rank Breeds Conflict.* University of Chicago Press, 2003.
Niccoli, Ottavia. *Perdonare. Idee, pratiche, rituali in Italia tra Cinque e Seicento.* Editori Laterza, 2007.
Nubola, Cristina, and Andreas Würgler, eds. *Suppliche e 'gravamina.' Politica, amministrazione, giustizia in Europa (secoli XIV-XVIII).* Il Mulino, 2002.
Petkov, Kiril. *The Kiss of Peace: Ritual, Self, and Society in the High and Late Medieval West.* Brill, 2003.
Pitt-Rivers, Julian A. *The Fate of Shechem or The Politics of Sex: Essays in the Anthropology of the Mediterranean.* Cambridge University Press, 1977.
Polecritti, Cynthia. *Preaching Peace in Renaissance Italy. Bernardino of Siena and His Audience.* Catholic University of America, 2000.
Povolo, Claudio. "Feud and vendetta: customs and trial rites in Medieval and Modern Europe. A legal-anthropological approach." *Acta Histriae* 23 (2015): 195–244.
Povolo, Claudio. *Furore. Elaborazione di un'emozione nella seconda metà del Cinquecento.* Cierre Edizioni, 2015.
Povolo, Claudio. "The Public Rock of Cut Heads. Violence and Banditry in the Mediterranean: The Republic of Venice in the Sixteenth Century." In *Management and*

Resolution of Conflict and Rivalries in Renaissance Europe, edited by Jill Kray, Marc Laurey, and David A. Lines. V&R unipress-Bonn University Press, 2023.
Priori, Lorenzo. *Pratica criminale secondo le leggi della Serenissima Repubblica di Venezia*. Venice, 1738.
Romano, Dennis. *Patricians and Popolani: The Social Foundations of the Venetian Renaissance State*. The John Hopkins University Press, 1987.
Sanudo, Marin. *I Diarii di Marino Sanuto*, edited by Rinaldo Fulin, Federico Stefani, Nicolò Barozzi, Guglielmo Berchet, and Marco Allegri. Stabilimento Visentini cav. Federico—Editore, 1879–1902.
Taylor, Scott K. "Women, Honor, and Violence in a Castilian Town, 1600–1650." *The Sixteenth Century Journal* 35 (2004): 1079–97.
Trebbi, Giuseppe. "Il segretario veneziano." *Archivio Storico Italiano* 144 (1986): 35–73.
Vallerani, Massimo. *Medieval Public Justice*. Catholic University of America Press, 2012.
van Gelder, Maartje, and Claire Judde de Larivière, eds. *Popular Politics in an Aristocratic Republic: Political Conflict and Social Contestation in Late Medieval and Early Modern Venice*. Routledge, 2020.
Vidali, Andrew. *Giustizia e violenza delle élites in una repubblica aristocratica. Politica del diritto, tribunali e patriziato nel Cinquecento veneziano*. Unicopli, 2024.
Vitiello, Joanna C. "Forensic Evidence, Lay Witnesses and Medical Expertise in the Criminal Courts of Late Medieval Italy." In *Medicine and the Law in the Middle Ages*, edited by Wendy Turner and Sara Butler. Brill, 2014.
Vitiello, Joanna C. *Public Justice and the Criminal Trial in Late Medieval Italy: Reggio Emilia in the Visconti Age*. Brill, 2016.
Watts, John. *The Making of Polities. Europe, 1300–1500*. Cambridge University Press, 2009.
Wray, Shona K. "Instruments of Concord: Making Peace and Settling Disputes through a Notary in the City and Contado of Late Medieval Bologna." *Journal of Social History* 42 (2009): 733–60.
Zannini, Andrea. *Burocrazia e burocrati a Venezia in età moderna: i cittadini originari (sec. XVI-XVIII)*. Istituto veneto di scienze, lettere ed arti, 1993.

PART III
Gendered Violence

7

ON SPOUSAL MURDERS AND HONOR KILLINGS IN SPAIN

Edward Behrend-Martínez

One function of any judicial system is to bring resolution—however unsatisfactory—to society's ugly, inexplicable, and chaotic events. In the case of gruesome early modern spousal murders, Spanish courts began constructing possible explanations for the violence through an initial investigation, an arrest, and a trial of the murderer. To find such meaning, however, it was just as necessary to judge the murdered spouse—their behavior as a wife or husband leading up to the killing—as it was the killer. This study seeks to better understand spousal murder cases by scrutinizing the way contemporaries described and made meaning of them. Many people collaborated in writing these wife-murder tragedies, including notaries, witnesses, and lawyers. Notaries, bailiffs, and especially prosecutors, lawyers, and witnesses all struggled to make a murder into a tale with a clear message; murders became stories with a beginning, a conflict, a resolution, maybe a conclusion, but most importantly, a moral. In the process of constructing a morality play from real situations of abuse and violence, communities had to assign moral guilt as well as simply determine who killed whom. Often husbands were both guilty of the murder and morally guilty. But just as often, trials suggested that the victim was guilty, and the murdering spouse became the judge and executioner.

When one spouse killed another, the murder usually initially confounded and frightened witnesses. Take the experience of 12-year-old servant Ana de Labar, living in Cartagena in 1649, as an example.[1] She worked for Leandro Báez and Clara Musante, husband and wife, though she mainly attended to Clara. Adults abruptly removed Ana from her home on the night that Leandro murdered Clara because the house had turned into a gruesome crime scene. The next morning, Ana returned to the setting of the murder.

DOI: 10.4324/9781003486404-11

She, like everyone involved, needed to see and find a meaning for the brutal violence that traumatized her world. Providing testimony in this case gave Ana an opportunity to create, in a formal way, meaning from the violence. Not only did investigations and prosecutions of murders satisfy community demands that justice be done, but they also provided reasons, explanations, and meanings for the survivors of violence. Bit by bit, when witnesses like Ana recounted the events leading up to the murder and when lawyers devised explanations for the murder, they made the murders fit into their understanding of how their world functioned. In an unpredictable world, people needed to know what would and would not cause violence, or what did and did not justify it. Criminal investigations and trials, then, did much more than determine whether a husband was guilty or not and what was to be done with him, his property, and his children. Court cases were a forum for resolving many other questions: was the killer right or wrong to kill? Had the wife merited her fate, or was she the victim of an evil man? Were other people to blame, in whole or in part? Were either of their souls going to Heaven or Hell?

In most cases, officials used these killings to illustrate to townspeople a general conclusion that to avoid the worst social disorder, women had to contain their sexuality and obey their husbands, while men had to contain their rage. Although everyday gossip likely spread the trials' proceedings and events, the court publicized its views through the final pronouncement and the meting out of the punishment, usually in the town square. The rhetoric of wife-murder trials—all the language, questions, and testimonies taken to construct a murder—did not necessarily expose the true motivations of killers for us or contemporaries. Rather, they gave these horrible killings a purpose. Either the rhetoric held up these murders as evidence to prove what ugly, violent chaos ensued when women were unfaithful, or the murders illuminated the ugly, violent chaos caused by bad men, men who were undisciplined, who could not control their passions, temper, or perhaps their drinking.

Though honor may have been a rhetorical justification for murder, it is clear that other factors motivated these killings. Wife-murders horrified Spaniards, however the crimes occurred. In fact, it was that very horror that brought drama to the well-known wife-murder plays that were so popular at the turn of the seventeenth century.[2] By blaming the wife for her own murder, the rhetoric of honor could transform the ugly crime of murder into a justified execution, something early modern Spaniards understood well. Honor was a facile excuse, even though that might be what murderers claimed and how playwrights portrayed such killings. In cases that defense attorneys today might explain as the result of "temporary insanity" rather than a "defense of honor," honor neatly explained such killings.[3] The rhetoric of honor also invalidated women's defenses in killing an adulterous husband: a woman could not lose honor due to a philandering spouse. At most, honor might have provided an excuse to kill; honor was a cultural justification to act out violently feelings of anger and rage.

In fact, many historians as well as contemporaries recognized that killing in the name of "honor" might just as easily have been a pretext to kill for other reasons: money, hatred, or other hidden motives.[4] And in any case, honor killings were rare. According to Victor Uribe-Uran's study of 65 spousal murders in Spain from the very end of our period and just after (1750–1824), the stereotypical "honor killing" that had a man murdering a wife for her infidelity only occurred in a minority of cases (6.6%).[5] Much more common in his study were spouses who killed in order to free themselves to be with another lover (33.3%). Even more unlike honor killings, in Uribe-Uran's study, a surprising percentage of the total spousal murders were wives murdering husbands (30.8%). Often these women were motivated by the ardor of an extramarital love to rid themselves of their husband.[6] It may be that these statistics from the late eighteenth century reflect a change in attitudes regarding honor since the sixteenth century. At least one scholar of the medieval period argues that honor killings were quite common.[7] However, the variety of motives that we find in spousal murder trials from earlier centuries support Uribe-Uran's conclusion that honor killing was hardly as widespread or condoned as a transparent reading of Golden Age wife-murder plays would suggest.

Wife-murder cases often involved accusations of infidelity. Contemporary legal understanding of adultery began with the assumption that a husband held legal jurisdiction to judge and punish a wife, or, for that matter, any household member.[8] Consequently, women had no direct legal recourse against an adulterous husband, though many wives complained about adulterous husbands in separation trials for abuse. But the growing power of Spain's early modern judicial system could not allow husbands to have arbitrary power over wives. This, in part, motivated Isabella and Ferdinand to prod courts to adjudicate cases of an unfaithful wife when they could, rather than permit a husband to act as his own judge and executioner. The Catholic Monarchs also made it against the law for a husband to inherit the dowry or property of the wife he had murdered.[9] Even before Isabella and Ferdinand's efforts to intervene in cases of adultery and honor killings, medieval peninsular law codes had only allowed a husband to kill his wife if she were caught in bed with a lover, in which case he might legally kill them both.[10] Castile had harsher punishments for adulterous wives than other parts of Iberia, and different legal jurisdictions (secular or ecclesiastical) varied in how they treated such women.[11] While secular courts might go so far as to excuse a husband for killing his adulterous wife, church courts could not prosecute adultery itself but could offer a spouse a marital separation. Ecclesiastical institutions such as convents or monasteries might shelter adulterous wives when they fled their husbands. In fact, church buildings and institutions often offered asylum (*asilo*) to an array of individuals seeking sanctuary from other jurisdictions.[12] According to Mendoza Garrido, ecclesiastical institutions also often became involved in spousal disputes because adulterous lovers were frequently clerics.[13] If an adulterous woman, having fled, was apprehended by the local *hermandad*, the militia would return her to her husband for punishment while they would execute the adulterous lover. Punishments like public shaming, whippings, cutting off a nose, exile, and prison were all more common than allowing a husband to execute his wife.[14]

Wife killings reveal early modern views of spousal abuse. Then, as now, a dead wife was often the saddest and worst consequence of a period of long-term abuse. How Spaniards prosecuted, tried, and punished wife-murders illuminates how seriously people really took the abuse of wives in early modern Spain. Witness statements especially show that physical and verbal abuse preceded most wife-murders.

A careful reading of the rhetoric of these trials demonstrates that authorities took two main approaches in adjudicating wife-murders: the first pursued such murders using the logic of a crime of passion and defense of honor. It was not the most common approach, but most recognizable. A husband killed a wife due to adultery or suspicion of adultery. Authorities mainly proceeded to investigate what led up to these kinds of murders by uncovering the alleged acts of infidelity that precipitated the final uxoricide. In these cases, authorities jailed the murdering husbands and prosecuted them, but they very clearly modified the husband's guilt in killing his wife through uncovering the wife's own crime of adultery. Rather than focusing on and asking questions about whether the husband was cruel, investigators queried whether or not the wife had been seen with, kissed, or had sex with a lover. While the word "honor" was rarely if ever mentioned in these cases, they still fit the stereotype of honor killings.

The second type of murder prosecution case was the more common one. The trials of these wife-murders depicted the crime as the final incident in a pattern of cruelty and abuse. The investigators focused on how the husband had treated his wife in the months and years prior to the murder. They explained how the husband's cruel nature resulted in the final killing. This approach squarely placed all the guilt for the murder on the husband. Unlike the cases for the murder of an adulterous wife, in cases of cruelty, communities in no way appeared to condone or excuse wife-murderers. Authorities asked questions about threats the husband had previously made to kill his wife and about incidents of physical and verbal abuse, broken bones, and bruises. They established whether or not the couple had fought, why they fought, and especially if there was any justification for the husband's mistreatment. They even asked whether or not the husband might have had a mistress who could have caused hatred and division between the couple. All such behavior was understood by local communities as shameful, wrong, and unchristian.

Murder by the Cruel Husband

As an example of a community's negative reaction to a cruel wife-murderer, we have the case of Antonio de Galarreta, whom the residents of the Basque town of Valle de Gordejuela suspected of killing his wife in 1705.[15] Dying from a massive blow to the head, her death caused local authorities to apprehend Antonio. They did not have enough evidence, however, and Antonio was soon freed. The suspicions of his neighbors, though, remained. Soon after winning his case, Antonio proposed marriage to his maid, María de Urriaga. Nevertheless, the parish clergy refused to allow the couple to marry, regarding the relationship as an illicit affair (*amancebamiento*). Antonio petitioned the bishop's court to compel the local parish to marry them. In order to make a decision about whether or not to allow the second marriage, the episcopal jurisdiction opened its own investigation. Antonio and María both claimed that his wife had gotten drunk, fallen down the stairs, and hit her head on the corner of a piece of furniture. But the church court uncovered the affair Antonio had had with his maid before his wife's death, including the detail that the wife had caught the couple in bed together. The church court did the only thing it could, charging the couple with publicly carrying on an affair and forcing them to pay the smallish fine of 1,000 maravedis each.

This case provides a glimpse into how a community could punish men for committing adultery, abuse, and murder outside of the law and the courts. Even though the secular court did not have enough evidence to try Antonio for murder, and church courts ultimately could not prevent him from marrying his mistress, this did not prevent neighbors and local clergy from carrying out their own forms of justice. If the local clergy refused to marry the couple, then it can be expected that other community members also shunned Antonio and María, perhaps denying them credit, business, and other forms of support. This was a time when one's reputation and standing often served as the only guarantee for the financial and physical aid that people needed to prosper and, when faced with the inevitable calamities of early modern life, even survive.

Long-simmering hatred could eventually lead one spouse to murder. Some marriages that never even began with the benefit of love or lust between husband and wife often only grew worse as time dragged on. Disputes over control of the house, food, money, children, servants, and sex all became issues in abuse cases. Occasionally such hatred and abuse resulted in murder. Control over sex and money were two factors that appeared, for instance, in the murder of Doña Manuela Josepha de la Pena by her husband in 1656.

The couple lived in the prosperous Andalusian town of Úbeda, in the province of Jaén.[16] On the afternoon that Manuela died, she was on the second floor of her house dressing while her young cousin Leonor, two other women, and a male servant named Luis waited patiently on the ground floor. They were preparing to take Manuela with them to a local convent in an effort to protect her from her husband. While they waited, Leonor and Luis began to hear screams. Shortly after, they saw Manuela's husband, Juan de la Torre, come running down the stairs and then out of the house. Luis immediately ran up the stairs, opened the bedroom door, and found Manuela collapsed in a pool of her own blood. Soon after the discovery of her body, neighbors Ana Ruiz and Bartolome de Baena said they heard young Leonora out in the street scream, "[M]y cousin has been killed by her husband!"[17] According to the local surgeon, Juan had stabbed Manuela five times. Most of the wounds were to her shoulders and back, but one had pierced her heart.

The constable immediately sent notices to surrounding towns and their jurisdictions to arrest Juan de la Torre. He set a bounty of 200 ducats for Juan's apprehension and organized a search. Úbeda's constable began his investigation by talking to neighbors and witnesses and taking their sworn testimonies. What emerged from the testimonies was the fact that Juan had been abusing Manuela for a long time before her unfortunate end. Several people had already intervened to try to bring peace to the troubled couple. In fact, 26-year-old neighbor Catalina de Quesada had heard Juan tell Manuela that he was going to kill her long before the actual murder. This threat, however, is unsurprising and rather common. In court cases in which couples sought separations, many wives described their angry husbands making similar threats to kill them. However, few men actually carried out such threats.

Before the murder, there had been growing tension between Juan and Manuela. They had recently taken a trip to Madrid to meet Leonor, Manuela's young cousin, and bring her back to Úbeda with them. The couple constantly bickered while traveling. In her testimony, Leonor painted an ugly picture of her cousin's husband: she said that on one occasion the three of them were walking down the street when they came upon a beggar. Manuela dug into her pockets for some money and started to hand it to the beggar. Juan quickly hit Manuela's hand and then proceeded to beat the poor man. Leonor's telling of this incident portrays Juan not only as an abusive husband but also as unchristian. After arriving in Úbeda, the day before the murder, Leonor said Juan yelled at Manuela for not lighting the stables to feed the horse. He threw her to the floor and broke one of her teeth. Leonor begged Manuela not to stay that night with her husband. But being obedient, and perhaps trying to placate her enraged husband, Manuela stayed in the house upstairs for the night.

That night Juan and Manuela went to bed together. Leonor recalled,

> [T]he said Juan de la Torre and his said wife went to bed and around midnight, I heard Juan de la Torres say to Doña Manuela, his wife "I won't let you enter the convent . . . now give me a hug," and they seemed to be making their embraces. Then this witness then heard Doña Manuela say "don't touch my head because it's hurt."[18]

After this last fight, the scandal caused by Juan's abuse appeared bad enough to Leonor and the neighbors that they sought help from a cleric, a local Franciscan monk, Francisco Franco. Francisco asked Juan, "Why do you abuse your wife so much?" and told him that "this [abuse] was not part of God's law."[19] Francisco scolded Juan, saying that if he did not love Manuela, she should be taken to a convent, and he said that he would make arrangements. Francisco even made Juan promise not to beat Manuela. After the meeting, Francisco went directly to the local authorities because he feared for Manuela's life.

Modern studies of intimate violence conclude that such violence is, in part, a symptom of an emotional need to control love objects.[20] The most dangerous time for abused women is the brief period when they attempt to separate and flee their abusers. When confronted with the reality that Manuela was leaving him, Juan perhaps became more enraged and killed her instead of allowing her to go. Over many months after her murder, Juan was never apprehended or even found. He was tried in absentia.

Authorities and witnesses, then, understood and wrote Juan de la Torre's killing of Manuela as a story of an unchristian, cruel, and murderous husband. They described the crime in contrasting hues of black and white, evil and good. Juan was unchristian and uncharitable; Manuela had been faultless, meek, honorable, and worthy of much better treatment. The trial did not include any defense of physical disciplining or violence. Investigators did not search for any misdeeds or misbehavior by Manuela that would have justified violence or her death.

One wife-murderer who did not succeed in escaping authorities was Juan Ortíz of Belmonte, a town near Córdoba.[21] In 1676, neighbors found Juan Ortíz's wife, María de Cantarero, lying dead in a brick kiln, stabbed many times. Juan possibly intended to hide his crime by having the body consumed by flames in the kiln when it was fired or by firing it himself. As it turned out, Juan Ortíz fled the mortally wounded María, the kiln, and the town right after the crime. Juan and María had been married only three years, but they already had a baby boy.

After the shocking discovery of the body, many residents in Belmonte said that they had seen María's death coming. Sixty-year-old Joseph Melendro, for instance, claimed that he had seen María on many occasions with bruises on her face and neck. And at one point, Joseph said his wife had even warned the local bailiff that Juan was going to end up killing María. The bailiff reputedly replied to Joseph's wife, "[G]et out of here, [Juan] couldn't kill a cat."[22] It was also Joseph Melendro who found María in the brick kiln still alive, with gashes to her face and throat, and a small knife "the size of an asparagus" in her breast.[23] Verbal abuse was also mentioned as evidence that the husband was a violent killer: Juana Martínez recalled that Juan said that María "was a bitch" and boasted "that if he were [really] a man he would stab her full of holes."[24] Once the authorities realized that Juan was gone, they sent word to all the surrounding jurisdictions. In this instance, the warrant worked. Around midnight in the town of Bujalance, the local bailiff apprehended Juan.

Both of these cases serve as examples of how neighbors and witnesses created stories to explain why murders happened. As in many other murder cases, the main theme was that these men were simply tyrannical; they were cruel, barbarous men who were miserable husbands. They used knives and fists to inflict wounds and kill. Their evil character and conduct made life for their wives a living hell—women whom Spaniards pitied with the name *malmariada* (the "badly married woman"). Townspeople deeply mourned such women, but they did not see these deaths as completely unexpected. These crimes were the bad endings of already bad circumstances.

Murders *en flagrante delicto*

The playwrights' trope of honor killing may have provided justices of the peace, lawyers, judges, and witnesses with a script with which they could interpret bloody and complicated murders. One wife-murder that took on the traditional trappings of the honor killing was the one that Ana de Labar witnessed in the opening of this chapter: that of Doña Clara Musante by her husband Leandro Báez in the Mediterranean coastal town of Cartagena in 1649.[25] According to witnesses working in the couple's household, Doña Clara had been having an affair with Francisco Lomelin. Twenty-four-year-old maid Josepha Ruiz served as the lovers' paid *alcahueta* (go-between); she facilitated the couple's illicit rendezvous.

No one saw the murder take place. The closest witness was 12-year-old servant Ana de Labar, who cared for Clara and Leandro's five-year-old boy. Ana testified that Don Leandro had been upset for nearly three weeks since he had begun to suspect his wife's adultery. Ana had retired to her room for the evening. She woke up at two in the morning when local authorities entered her room and told her to take her young charge out of the house. Ana was not able to sleep any more that night and returned to the house that morning, where she saw the murder scene: Doña Clara lying dead in her bed.

Investigating surgeon Jusepe Porreda described the corpse as having been stabbed in the kidneys with a dagger. The murderer had stabbed Clara 11 times. Leandro had fled the scene and was nowhere to be found.

Rather than uncover any earlier cruel treatment or angry temperament, the investigator's attention focused on the illicit affair between Francisco Lomelin and Doña Clara and the *alcahueta* Josepha Ruiz. In Josepha's testimony, she recalled the evening 20 days prior to the murder, when she was fired by her employer, Leandro Báez. Leandro had been sleeping upstairs in his bedroom while Francisco Lomelin was secretly downstairs spending time with Leandro's wife, Doña Clara. Hearing another man in the house, Don Leandro woke up and ran downstairs naked, something several witnesses commented on. He found a sword sitting downstairs and asked Josepha whose sword it was. Josepha claimed not to know. Leandro yelled at the uncooperative maid, but she would not tell him anything. Instead, Josepha decided to leave, at which point Don Leandro fired her. Despite no longer serving in the house, Josepha said that she knew Francisco Lomelin continued to visit Doña Clara regularly.

After the murder, the authorities searched for Don Leandro in local churches, convents, and monasteries. Seeking refuge or asylum in the jurisdiction of the church was a common strategy for early modern fugitives.[26] They could seek sanctuary under ecclesiastical jurisdiction, hope to persuade clerics that they were wrongly charged, or at least delay their arrest by the secular arm of the law. But Don Leandro could not be found. Only a year later was he arrested in front of a convent, heavily armed with a dagger, a sword, and two pistols. After first being uncooperative, Don Leandro finally admitted to the murder in a confession. His final punishment, however, was unfortunately not part of the case record.

The trial for the murder of Doña Clara Musante by her husband contains many tropes of the popular imagination. A paid go-between for the couple. Francisco Lomelin was the stereotype of the macho *majo*, dressed in a black cape and hat, smoking a cigarillo, and so on. It seems that witnesses were more traumatized by Don Leandro ranting naked in his slippers than anything else. Though it is important to point out that honor was never mentioned in the trial, Don Leandro predictably killed his wife in what might be called an "honor killing." Yet in witnesses' depositions as well as the prosecution, there was no hint of sympathy or justification for Leandro's actions. If anything, he was ridiculed. Like Antonio de la Torre and Juan Ortíz earlier, he instinctively fled justice and armed himself in a desperate—one might even say cowardly—attempt to escape. These were not husbands who stood their ground before the community and claimed that they had a right to kill their wives.

A great deal of evidence, in fact, shows that husbands often looked for alternatives to murder as a way to control women who had or were cheating on them. Church-sanctioned separations were one such way. A separation due to adultery would have allowed a husband to strip his wife of her property and right to his support, perhaps leaving her destitute. Such a separation would also allow him to live apart from his wife.

Another common way for a man to skirt the demands of the rhetoric of honor was for a cuckolded husband to reconcile with his wife formally using a *carta de perdón de cuernos* (literally "a cuckold's pardon"): this letter was a notarized document in which a wife would confess to adultery and her husband would officially forgive her and agree to take her back to live a married life.[27] Through such a letter, a husband relinquished his honor in order to avoid bloodshed and to secure a chance of some peace and, one assumes, stability. Such documents would have remained in the possession of the notary and so could be used in later litigation if a husband decided that he wanted to seek a legal separation from his wife, in which case proof of her adultery might allow him to keep her dowry and all the marital goods.

Murder threats could often have been more a warning used by a husband desperate to control a wife threatening to leave than they were a real option. A further factor that clouds our historical point of view is the fact that murders became documented while other solutions people found for infidelity were usually not; most cases in which an adulterous wife and husband came to some other resolution simply would not have been written down. We have no idea how many men chose to forgive or ignore the affair of adulterous wives.

None of the male murderers I have described earlier actually caught their allegedly adulterous wives in bed with their lovers, the kind of murder for which the law in Europe had traditionally been most sympathetic: the murder of lovers *en flagrante delicto*, caught in the act. Such cases were naturally rare, considering that lovers tried their best, we may assume, not to get caught.[28] One example of the stereotypical crime of passion occurred in Pontevedra, Galicia, in 1561.[29] According to the trial, Pedro Cunquiero had misgivings that his wife was having an affair with a cleric.[30] To test his suspicions, Pedro left his home using the pretext that he had to travel on business. He then returned home at an unexpected hour of the morning the next day. Pedro's distrust proved to be well-founded. When he entered his bedroom, he found his wife and Juan Pérez, a clergyman, asleep in his bed, lying naked under the sheets. In his confession, Pedro admitted, "and not being able to suffer such deep anguish I killed them both . . . and then I called the neighbors and authorities."[31] The local authorities immediately led him off to jail. The preliminary investigation found the murdered lovers in bed, naked, only covered by the now bloodied sheets. The investigator's testimony displayed a thorough forensic eye for detail: one of the corpse's heads was turned toward the window; the legs were twisted, and the bare chests were above the sheets. This corroborated the view that the couple was caught "in the act." The fact that the wife and the lover were adulterers obviously modified Pedro's murder charge and influenced the course of the trial and the prosecution's tack. There were no questions about Pedro's earlier treatment of his wife, whether they had ever quarreled, whether he abused her, or whether Pedro had had sexual liaisons of his own. Pedro's wife's adultery lessened his guilt.

The prosecution's questionnaire for witnesses implied that Pedro was not as culpable as he would have been for a different kind of murder: its second question asked "if the adulterers did not kiss and know one another carnally." Number three asked if the husband did not kill them. The implication was that the answer to question 3 was justified by the answer to question 2. The murder had been understandable and justified.

The real judgment had been against Pedro's wife and her lover. There was no final verdict against Pedro. We know this because the murdered clergyman's mother, Catalina Juárez, had to initiate a suit herself against Pedro and other officials involved in the case. She was not satisfied with the outcome of the investigation. Not only did her litigation prove that, in her eyes, justice for the murder of her son had not been done, but it also showed that authorities, even though they had apprehended the husband and undertook a long investigation, in the end condoned the murder of adulterous lovers caught in the act.

Aside from living as a cuckold and accepting his situation, with or without a notarized pardon, Spain's courts offered alternatives to husbands before they took justice into their own hands and killed adulterous women. One option was for a husband to go to the secular justices and ask that his wife and her lover be charged with adultery. Several cases in Spain's National Historical Archive attest to the possibility that a husband might forego uxoricide and seek the courts' help. In 1656, for instance, Gabriel Herrero sued his wife, María de Velasco, and her lover for adultery.[32] The adulterous affair had resulted from an already rocky marriage. Several witnesses testified that the married couple had already had a violent relationship. Town councilman Fernando Mortal Ruiz related an incident involving the three principals in the case:

> [O]ne day, hearing voices from their house, I came out to see what was going on, and I saw that Gabriel Herrero was quarreling with María de Velasco, his wife. And among other things he said to his wife, he called her a bitch and said that she should go with the said Francisco de Carrera to Madrid. And she told him he was a cuckold, and when she said these words, Francisco de La Carrera was there, and he also called Gabriel Herrero a picaro cuckold.[33]

Her lawyer responded to her husband's accusation that María was adulterous with the claim that Gabriel had treated her severely. She claimed that he had beaten and kicked her until she bled profusely. María went to the bailiff, accusing her husband of severe cruelty.

This overview of the rhetoric of wife-murder cases reveals a number of important facts. First, it demonstrates that the language used in court cases and especially witness testimonies created narratives that gave domestic violence and murder a useful social message, one that could have been repeated outside the court, given that no one in the secular jurisdiction was sworn to secrecy. Rather than proving to be anecdotal, a close reading of trials and testimonies turns up revealing patterns of thought and reactions in the language people used to understand these murders. Witnesses and courts deployed tropes with which they were already familiar: the cuckold, the adulteress, the *malmariada*, the abusive or drunk husband, and so on. They paid great attention to forensic evidence, eyewitness testimony, and history.

Second, how officials and witnesses chose to write their prosecutions, defenses, and testimonies varied in important ways. Court procedure was generally the same in all cases: officials made an arrest, they took initial testimonies, leveled a charge, created questionnaires for witnesses, and took more testimonies using the questionnaire; the defendant's representative then put forward a defense, and the court gave a verdict. But the rhetorical tack of the prosecution, questions, and testimonies differed enormously. There were two main patterns of court rhetoric surrounding wife-murder. One such rhetoric was indeed the typical crime of passion, a product of jealousy and anger. Were these honor killings if neither the culprits, nor witnesses, nor prosecutors used the word "honor" in their confessions, testimonies, or pleas? In any case, they were crimes of passion.

A second kind of rhetoric actually did focus on the cruel nature of an "unchristian" man, in which we see the outlines of the abusive husband. Informants used several other words to describe such vicious men: "harsh," a "man-child," "cruel," "base," "lowly," and so forth. Here the story was one of the badly married woman who suffered a bad husband. All the blame was placed on the husband for his lack of civility, moderation, sobriety, and self-discipline. Rather than try to excuse the murder as a freak mistake or a unique and odd circumstance, these cases explained the murder as part of a long-term condition or situation. Violence characterized the bad husband's nature and relationships with others. His actions were abusive because they went beyond all reasonable correction and led to the final murder. Court documents find this stereotype of the bad husband as the most likely culprit in wife-murders as well.

Judging the Victim

In early modern Spanish wife-murder cases, and abuse cases for that matter, the status and actions of the woman were integral in deciding whether the violence was abusive or not. Today, we often define and measure physical abuse according to its severity and method—whether, for instance, the actor struck with an open or closed fist, a wooden spoon, a belt, a switch, a rod, or a pan—and the frequency and extent of the violence. In the case of murder, modern prosecutors focus on the intent, motivation, and conscience of the murderer. Rarely do they consider the motivations of the murder victim. But what was just as important for Spaniards in the early modern period in a case of violence or murder was how much the victim allegedly deserved to be beaten or killed. In order to pass judgment and make a case meaningful, the actions, attitude, and conditions of the victim were as integral to the crime as those of the perpetrator. The idea of abuse, in other words, was severely modified, ironically, by the condition of the person who was the object of violence. This is not surprising if we take into account the basic principles of a Christian mindset: original sin established that, without God's grace, *every* person deserved eternal physical suffering in Hell. Therefore, every individual deserved some kind of penance, and that penance depended on the spiritual state of the individual. Whether or not punishment meted out to a child or wife by a husband constituted abuse, then, depended on the extent of their guilt. Thus, trials generally needed to evaluate the victims as much as they judged the abuser in order to establish if the punishments were truly cruel, if they were actually abuse.

From the perspective of early modern Spaniards, spousal abuse and even murder, then, could either be the fault of the wife or the husband, and prosecutors made this assumption very early on in these cases. By doing so, these murder trials helped define what was and what was not physical abuse. The actions themselves were defined as much by the status of the victim as the perpetrator. In other words, murder became legitimate if the wife somehow "deserved" it, but it was illegitimate if she had been a chaste Christian woman.

Notes

1 Archivo Histórico Nacional [AHN], Consejo de Castilla 5575–6, Indultos de Viernes Santo. Scott Taylor discusses this case in *Honor and Violence in Golden Age Spain,* and I thank him for directing me to the Good Friday pardons at the [AHN] in which it is found. Scott K. Taylor, *Honor and Violence in Golden Age Spain* (Yale University Press, 2008), 194–96.
2 For instance, see Matthew D. Stroud, *Fatal Union: a Pluralistic Approach to the Spanish Wife-Murder Comedias* (Bucknell University Press, 1990); Margaret Rich Greer, *María de Zayas Tells Baroque Tales of Love and the Cruelty of Men* (Penn State University Press, 2000).
3 Scott Taylor explores this use of the rhetoric of honor in *Honor and Violence.*
4 There is an extensive discussion of late medieval instances of adultery and honor killings in Iñaki Bazán Díaz, "Mujeres, delincuencia y justicia penal en la Europa medieval: una aproximación interpretativa," in *Mujer, marginación y violencia entre la Edad Media y los Tiempos Modernos*, ed. Ricardo Córdoba de la Llave (Servicio de Publicaciones Universidad de Córdoba, 2006), 58; Juan Miguel

Mendoza Garrido, "Sobre la delincuencia femenina en Castilla a fines de la Edad Media," in *Mujer, marginación y violencia entre la Edad Media y los Tiempos Modernos*, ed. Ricardo Córdoba de la Llave (Servicio de Publicaciones Universidad de Córdoba, 2006), 112–20.

5 Victor Uribe-Uran, *Fatal Love: Spousal Killers, Law, and Punishment in the Late Colonial Spanish Atlantic* (Stanford University Press, 2015), 132–72.

6 Uribe-Uran, *Fatal Love*, 139–40.

7 Bazán Días finds that 25% of murders in medieval Catalonia were uxoricides: "Mujeres, delincuencia y justicia penal," 56.

8 Lisa Vollendorf, "Reading the Body Imperiled: Violence against Women in María de Zayas," *Hispania* 78 (1995): 273, 275; Antonio Gil Ambrona, *Historia de la violencia contra las mujeres: misoginía y conflicto matrimonial en España* (Cátedra, 2008), 241. Uribe-Uran, *Fatal Love*, 80.

9 Bazán Díaz, "Mujeres, delincuencia y justicia penal," 59.

10 Law codes in early modern Spain vary regarding this right, whether the husband can kill only the lover, or his wife, or both. Gil Ambrona, *Historia de la violencia contra las mujeres*, 241.

11 Mendoza Garrido, "Sobre la delincuencia femenina en Castilla," 117.

12 Uribe-Uran, *Fatal Love*, 162–65.

13 Mendoza Garrido, "Sobre la delincuencia femenina en Castilla," 114.

14 Mendoza Garrido, "Sobre la delincuencia femenina en Castilla," 117.

15 Archivo Catedrálico y Diocesano de Calahorra [ACDC], Legajo 375/58, 1705.

16 AHN, Consejo de Castilla, Legajo 25630, Expediente 3.

17 AHN, Consejo de Castilla, Legajo 25630, Exp. 3, f. 22r–v.

18 AHN, Consejo de Castilla, Legajo 25630, Exp. 3, f. 43r–v.

19 AHN, Consejo de Castilla, Legajo 25630, Exp. 3, f. 44r–v.

20 Dorothy A. Counts, Judith K. Brown, and Jacquelyn C. Campbell, eds., *To Have and to Hit: Cultural Perspectives on Wife Beating*, 2nd ed. (University of Illinois Press, 1999).

21 AHN, Consejo de Castilla, Legajo 26062, Exp. 12.

22 AHN, Consejo de Castilla, Legajo 26062, Exp. 12, f. 8r–v.

23 AHN, Consejo de Castilla, Legajo 26062, Exp. 12, f. 8r–v.

24 AHN, Consejo de Castilla, Legajo 26062, Exp. 12, ff. 17r–18v, "que era su muger una puta que si era hombre la cosiera a punalados."

25 AHN, Consejo de Castilla, Legajos 5575–5576, one of the Good Friday Pardons (Indultos de Viernes Santo). Scott Taylor discusses this case in *Honor and Violence*, 194–96.

26 Antonio de Erauso describes using this strategy several times when he was running from the law. Catalina de Erauso, *Lieutenant Nun: Memoir of a Basque Transvestite in the New World*, trans. M. Stepto and G. Stepto (Beacon Press, 1997). See also Uribe-Uran, *Fatal Love*, 162–65.

27 Bazán Díaz, "Mujeres, delincuencia y justicia penal," 60–61.

28 For a discussion of murders of women *en flagrante delicto,* see Mendoza Garrido, "Sobre la delincuencia femenina en Castilla a fines de la Edad Media," 115.

29 Archivo Real de Galicia [ARG], Legajo 25137/55.

30 Allyson Poska has noted that in Galicia it was not uncommon for clergymen to be involved in sexual affairs. See Allyson M. Poska, *Women and Authority in Early Modern Spain: The Peasants of Galicia* (Oxford University Press, 2005), 76–81.

31 "y no pudiendo sufrir tan prieto dolor los mate astr ambos y dos y luego llame los vecinos y a la justicia par que biesen los susos dhos y debiendo de que areme . . . me prendieron y tienen presos." ARG, Legajo 25137/55, f. 4r–v.

32 AHN, Consejo de Castilla, Legajo 25609, exp. 12.

33 AHN, Consejo de Castilla, Legajo 25609, exp. 12, f. 19r-v, testimony of Don Fernando Ruiz.

Select Bibliography

Bazán Díaz, Iñaki. "Mujeres, Delincuencia Y Justicia Penal En La Europa Medieval: Una Aproximación Interpretativa." In *Mujer, Marginación Y Violencia Entre La Edad Media Y Los Tiempos Modernos*, edited by Ricardo Córdoba de la Llave. Servicio de Publicaciones Universidad de Córdoba, 2006.

Counts, Dorothy A., Judith K. Brown, and Jacquelyn C. Campbell, eds. *To Have and to Hit: Cultural Perspectives on Wife Beating*. 2nd ed. University of Illinois Press, 1999.

de Erauso, Catalina. *Lieutenant Nun: Memoir of a Basque Transvestite in the New World*. Translated by M. Stepto and G. Stepto. Beacon Press, 1997.

Gil Ambrona, Antonio. *Historia de la violencia contra las mujeres: misoginía y conflicto matrimonial en España*. Cátedra, 2008.

Greer, Margaret Rich. *María De Zayas Tells Baroque Tales of Love and the Cruelty of Men*. Penn State University Press, 2000.

Mendoza Garrido, Juan Miguel. "Sobre La Delincuencia Femenina En Castilla a Fines De La Edad Media." In *Mujer, Marginación Y Violencia Entre La Edad Media Y Los Tiempos Modernos*, edited by Ricardo Córdoba de la Llave. Servicio de Publicaciones Universidad de Córdoba, 2006.

Movellán, Tomás Antonio Mantecón. *Conflictividad Y Disciplinamiento Social En La Cantabria Rural Del Antiguo Régimen*. Universidad de Cantabria, 1997.

Poska, Allyson M. *Women and Authority in Early Modern Spain: The Peasants of Galicia*. Oxford University Press, 2005.

Stroud, Matthew D. *Fatal Union: A Pluralistic Approach to the Spanish Wife-Murder Comedias*. Bucknell University Press, 1990.

Taylor, Scott K. *Honor and Violence in Golden Age Spain*. Yale University Press, 2008.

Uribe-Uran, Victor. *Fatal Love: Spousal Killers, Law, and Punishment in the Late Colonial Spanish Atlantic*. Stanford University Press, 2015.

Vollendorf, Lisa. "Reading the Body Imperiled: Violence against Women in María De Zayas." *Hispania* 78 (1995): 272–82.

8

ON INFANTICIDE IN SPAIN

Jodi Campbell

In the fall of 1626, a horrific event shook Loeches, a small town about a day's journey east of Madrid. Ambrosia de Alvarado, the 40-year-old wife of the surgeon Lorencio Calvo, was found with the bloodied body of her three-year-old son Jusepe, whom she had just killed. This event set off an investigation during which Ambrosia confessed to the murder, and Lorencio demanded that she be held accountable and punished to the full extent of the law. Infanticide was one of the most abhorred crimes in early modern Europe, and Ambrosia was clearly guilty. Nevertheless, her neighbors argued that she was suffering from a temporary madness following the recent birth of her third child and that she therefore should not be held responsible. Following a year-long investigation, local authorities agreed with their defense, found her not culpable of any crime, and sent her home.[1]

This chapter uses Ambrosia's case to cast light on issues surrounding infanticide and madness, and the ways in which justice was understood, sought, and rendered in early modern Spain. Her story lands at the nexus of several issues that were ill-defined but at the same time of great interest to a society that had a well-developed legal system and a rich cultural interest in the workings of the mind. Neither infanticide nor madness had clear judicial definitions; both were open to interpretation and a great deal of flexibility on the part of local authorities. Infanticide was addressed very differently in theory than in practice, and what scholars are able to see in judicial records may be far from reflecting actual procedure. As for madness, understandings varied according to whether it was viewed through judicial, medical, religious, or literary lenses. Ambrosia's case is shocking and unusual, both to us and to her contemporaries. But it demonstrates the importance to scholars of considering lived experience and situational interpretations of justice

DOI: 10.4324/9781003486404-12

alongside formal institutional frameworks. Ambrosia is a data point in the larger picture of our evaluation of early modern crime and gender, but she was also a real individual, known to her friends and neighbors in the small community of Loeches, and they evaluated her crime in terms of the human being they knew. Far from being clear-cut, her case reveals a high degree of ambiguity and accommodation, and underscores the importance of a community in defining justice and seeking redress.

The murder of a child, especially by its own mother, was a disturbing violation of the social and moral order. In early modern Europe, it was not always distinguished legally from other forms of murder, but it was troubling enough to be an ongoing matter of concern in political, religious, and moral treatises.[2] The reaction to a child's unnatural death was colored by several assumptions: that the child was the result of an unplanned pregnancy and that the offender was its mother, who in turn was most likely to be an unmarried woman in a marginalized position, obliged to hide such a pregnancy. It was therefore a gender-specific crime, of which men were only very rarely accused. Mikel Berraondo Piudo notes an unusual case in 1610 of a man accused of impregnating his maid and killing her child: in his defense, the man's lawyer argued that "such weakness would never be seen in men, but only in women, to hide their dishonesty."[3] Young children may have died for other reasons, but the vast majority of the cases that attracted legal attention were associated with single women. Many of these women's pregnancies may have been the result of sexual coercion, as single women accused of infanticide were often poor servants. But the cultural and judicial perspective of infanticide was that the women were responsible, and legal punishments were harsh, penalizing the murder itself as well as the presumed moral laxity of the unwed mother.[4] Infanticide was one of the few crimes to merit a sentence of death, usually in a form that maximized the public message of shame and retribution, such as burning, drowning, or decapitation.[5] Sophie Bartels, a 20-year-old servant girl from a small German town, was found guilty of infanticide in 1764 and sentenced to "death by the sword and the impalement of her removed head" to serve as a warning to others.[6] In Navarre, those convicted of infanticide were sentenced to punishment by public whippings, and some legal writers argued for the application of the medieval *encubamiento,* in which the guilty party would be caged with a monkey, a rooster, a snake, and a cat, and thrown into the sea.[7] In its demand for theatrical public justice, punishment for the crime of infanticide was similar to that for witchcraft and poisoning, other crimes that were associated with women and the reversal of traditional expectations that they be submissive and nurturing.[8]

Harsh sentences were often based on the assumptions surrounding the crime rather than any real investigation or analysis of evidence. Infanticide could be hard to determine with certainty. Babies might be stillborn or die of natural causes or be accidentally smothered, and even if an infant were to have suffered an unnatural death, that alone would not be a guarantee that the mother was responsible.[9] Nevertheless, the presence of a dead child could easily lead to an assumption of criminal activity on the part of the mother. The *Constitutio Criminalis Carolina,* established in Germany by Charles V, for example, explicitly understood the murder of an infant to result from the evil intentions of its mother.[10] Seventeenth-century statutes in England and Scotland directed courts to convict women who gave birth to illegitimate children who subsequently died, on the presumption that murder had been committed, even without direct evidence of such.[11] The fueros of Navarre, assuming harmful intent on the part of mothers, defined the abandonment of a child as homicide.[12] These reactions were based on the presumption that an unmarried woman would abandon or smother her newborn to try to hide the evidence of an unwanted pregnancy.

In spite of this legal and social concern about infanticide, and the documentation of cases across early modern Europe, it is hard to know how often infanticide actually happened and how it was actually punished. From the juridical records, it did not seem to be a frequent crime: accusations of infanticide appear in both criminal and ecclesiastical courts, but they were always a tiny fraction of total criminal behavior. In Spain, it was not recognized as a specific crime (distinct from other forms of murder) until 1822, and the *Novísima Recopilación* of 1804 only mentions it indirectly in reference to the abandonment of children.[13] It may have been much more frequent, however, than the records suggest. Several historians suggest that crimes committed by women may have been substantially underrepresented in the historical record, since families (especially of the elite) had an interest in avoiding public scandal by not putting women on trial. A male head of the family generally had the power to discipline the women under his authority, thereby keeping both the crime and the punishment within the walls of his domestic space.[14] Accusations of infanticide were particularly unusual for married women, in whose case the death of an infant would not immediately arouse suspicion.[15] Therefore, the death of a child, rather than being clear evidence of wrongdoing, could be interpreted in various ways according to the status and social context of the mother. Still another possibility is that infanticide was more generally accepted than its reputation would imply. Demographic historians have argued that infanticide may have been a common way to control sex ratios and population and that it occurred more frequently than judicial records would indicate, particularly when people aware of the crime conspired to pretend that a child had been stillborn or accidentally smothered.[16] If this is the case, infanticide would not be the province only of unwed or otherwise socially marginalized mothers, nor would it be a crime committed exclusively by women. Given these possibilities, traditional judicial records probably fall short of giving us a true picture of the nature, frequency, and acceptability of infanticide.[17]

Even considering these broader possibilities for the realities of infanticide, the case of Ambrosia de Alvarado is not easy to explain or understand; it fits none of the patterns. She was a mature, married woman, by all evidence in a stable economic position, well known and supported in her community. Had she lost a child, especially a newborn, in any way that could have been interpreted as natural, such a death would have aroused sympathy more than suspicion. However, this was a clear case of murder: Ambrosia had taken one of the knives from her husband's surgical supplies and slit the throat of her son, making no effort to conceal the deed, and admitting to it when questioned. Although she had recently delivered a newborn, the victim was her middle son, the three-year-old Jusepe. There was no possibility that this death was accidental, or desirable, or attributable to someone else, or that it could have been covered up by the family to preserve their honor. In theory, Lorencio could have been juridically responsible for the actions of his dependents. Nevertheless, his demands for his wife to be prosecuted were ultimately dismissed, suggesting that the courts and the community could override the authority of the head of the household.[18] In the end, given the shocking nature of the crime, one would have every reason to anticipate the kind of severe, public punishment that the law promised to women such as Sophie Bartels. Such a punishment was sought by her own husband—and yet Ambrosia was determined to be not guilty.

Just as judicial records may not accurately record the actual number of infanticides, the same margin of error exists in relation to the possible punishments for the murder of children. Across early modern Europe, infanticide always carried the possibility of being penalized by death. But legal systems often maintained a degree of flexibility when it came to reducing sentences for this as well as other kinds of crimes. The intent of authorities was not only to maximize the display of their power, and therefore to inculcate obedience and good behavior, but also to leave room for humane treatment and magnanimity.[19] Even in cases of infanticide that did receive firm sentences of death, it is not always clear whether those were carried out. Häßler and Häßler express this doubt about the German dukedoms in their study, and scholarship on early modern England suggests that more than half of the accused served more lenient sentences than those initially handed down, and fewer than a third of death sentences for infanticide there were carried out.[20] In Scotland, even though women were given death sentences for child murder more than for any other crime, the courts did not always follow through on this punishment.[21] There was also a significant degree of regional variation. Spain seems to have been more lenient in regard to prosecuting infanticide as a result of extramarital pregnancies than France or England. In Navarre, out of 27 sentences for infanticide, 23 were sent into exile, and the other four were not punished. Courts in Prague and Paris imposed death penalties on fewer than a third of those accused of infanticide.[22] Laws of the Italian states prescribed exile or capital punishment for infanticide, but judges were reluctant to actually apply the death penalty.[23] These directions in recent scholarship remind us that while there was always the potential for dramatic forms of capital punishment, authorities did not jump at the opportunity to use it, and actual practice may have been far more forbearing. In the case of Ambrosia's murder of her child, though, there was not an adjustment to a harsh penalty but a refusal to penalize her at all.

This brings us to another key element of her case, the discussion of her mental state at the time of the murder. In the initial investigation, while Ambrosia was being held in chains in the public prison, she was asked whether she had killed her child, why she had done so, and whether she was solely responsible.[24] She confessed that not only had she killed Jusepe, but that she had attempted to cut her older son Lorenzo as well, and that she had acted alone, but that she could not explain why she had done so. She offered no further defense, and a confession, in early modern judicial systems, was essential to a conviction. However, rather than immediately declaring her guilty, as her husband requested, the judge proceeded to gather and question more witnesses. The trial then became centered, not on Ambrosia's guilt, but on the question of whether or not she was in her right mind—and how that could be determined.

There was no consistent and reliable definition of madness in the early modern period. As in most societies, it could be generally understood as any behavior that visibly and defiantly challenged social conventions, especially through unusual speech or behavior. Medieval understandings of madness saw it most often as a manifestation of sin or evil, but early modern thinkers embraced a wider range of possible ideas. Concerns about madness appeared frequently in early modern medical, religious, legal, and literary texts, where it might be perceived as an internal impediment to understanding, a disordered behavior, or a mystic vision or other connection to something others could not perceive. Renaissance Spaniards had a particular fascination with melancholy, which in a medical sense was understood as the depression and despair caused by an excess of black bile in the system of humors. The humoral interpretation also led people to see it as a state more transient than inherent, often described in terms of "deeds and demeanor" more than a chronic disease or condition.[25] Other humoral forms of mental instability included mania, expressed by excited and incomprehensible language, and frenzy, marked by shaking and fits of rage.[26] While humoral imbalances provided a way of explaining madness, there was no real plan for treatment of the mad beyond the dietary approaches that could help correct the excess of black or yellow bile that was associated with most mental disorders.[27] Generally those who suffered from these ailments were cared for by their own families. The earliest alternatives to this were *manicomios*, or madhouses, first established in the early 1400s; their goal was not treatment as much as it was to keep the ill housed and fed and to protect the rest of the community from the disorder they might provoke.[28]

It is telling that these institutions were known as *casas de los inocentes*, houses of the innocents, implying that their patients were not responsible for themselves or their actions. Theological and humanist thinking perceived madness as part of the human condition, a kind of opposite face of wisdom or a renunciation of the world.[29] The law did not have a clear definition of insanity, but it was generally agreed by lawyers and philosophers alike that the truly mad should not be held responsible for their actions.[30] How, then, did one determine whether someone was insane? The area where early modern Spaniards were most likely to seek a definition of madness, especially with the implications of whether one might be responsible for one's actions, was religion. In a society that had a particular concern about policing proper religious belief and practice, questions of mental competence and attempts to evade punishment were more likely to be addressed by priests and canon lawyers than other authorities.[31] The Inquisition, established as a branch of the Spanish state in the late fifteenth century, reached the height of its activity in the sixteenth century with the combined challenge of incorporating converted Jews and Muslims, dealing with the Protestant Reformation, and establishing its authority over new Christians in the Americas. When confronted with people who challenged religious convention or authority, officials needed to determine whether they were heretical, possessed, misguided, ill, or insane.[32] They were well aware that heretics might feign insanity to avoid a conviction, so they evaluated such potential cases with particular caution. An inquisitorial manual from 1654 included a section on distinguishing between genuine and contrived loss of reason, though it lacked official criteria with which to make this determination, suggesting instead that officials make their own determination. Authorities were therefore given wide discretion in how to interpret mental illness, often relying on the consensus of those who had the closest contact with the accused (witnesses, doctors, jail companions).[33]

What implications could this have, then, for Ambrosia's case? How could people judge the legal responsibility of the mad? Hers, of course, was not an investigation of heresy, but the law, like the Inquisition, lacked clear criteria for determining sound judgment, and in both systems the responsibility of determining motive and intent in uncertain cases fell on local authorities. As we have seen, Ambrosia's case lacked the factors that might have drawn sympathy or at least the benefit of the doubt from local authorities. She was in a legitimate marriage, economically stable, and not single and facing an unwanted pregnancy. The child who died was a three-year-old, not a newborn who might have died of other causes, and he clearly died of the injuries she inflicted. Ironically, though, these conditions may have helped her, because in such circumstances killing an older male child was the least rational thing she could have done; there was simply no way to explain it but by madness.

So Ambrosia's community sought to make sense of her deed, seeking evidence in the broader framework of her situation. Ambrosia's neighbors knew her as a real person, not a hypothetical criminal or a character from a broadside, and the case explored their perception and judgment of her actions and responsibility. In the investigation, each party presented questions to be asked of their witnesses. Beyond the required formulaic questions about what each witness knew of the case and what their relationship was to the people involved, Lorencio's witnesses were asked if Ambrosia "always was, has been, and is a woman of good judgment and natural understanding, without any evidence of madness or furor on any previous occasion."[34] The witnesses for Ambrosia's defense were asked if "she has always been a woman of good conduct and known virtue, quiet, of calm judgment, and very loving and generous with her children, especially the said Jusepe Calvo," whether "having given birth in September of 1626 she was overcome by an accident of madness and disturbed judgment, due to which she tried various times to kill herself and her children," and whether before and after the murder of her son, Ambrosia "committed many acts of a furious and mad woman not in her right mind." If so, witnesses were instructed to "say what they saw her do, giving clear evidence that she was mad and that they are certain that she was out of her mind."[35] The questions posed to all the witnesses asked them to state whether the information they provided about Ambrosia was publicly and widely known.[36] It was important, to both the defense and the prosecution, to determine whether there was general agreement and recognition within the community about her mental state.

Curiously, each side based its strategy on the same essential question and seeking the same answer: whether Ambrosia was generally known to be a woman of sound judgment. For the defense, arguing that she was sane and mentally stable helped establish that the murder was an exceptional act provoked by her condition following the birth of her third child. The phrasing of the question posed to witnesses is crucial: they meant to suggest that her madness was an "accident" in the Aristotelian sense of an aspect or condition that is not part of the essence of a person. Ambrosia's frenzy, in this view, was a momentary aberration of her behavior and beyond her conscious control, causing actions for which she should not be held responsible. For Lorencio, however, casting Ambrosia as a normally rational person would confirm his argument that she could not have been insane, that the murder was therefore intentional and the result of conscious choice, and that she should bear full responsibility for her actions. In Lorencio's words, "[S]he always was and is a woman of whole [mental] capacity, and therefore cannot be excused of such a grave and atrocious crime."[37] To this end, Lorencio's three witnesses made brief statements that they knew her to be "a woman of good judgment" and "sound reason." At most they expressed doubt over how to explain Ambrosia's behavior. As one put it, "[H]e had never found in her anything of madness or agitation . . . when they say that she cut the throat of her child . . . he does not know whether she was crazy or not."[38] Lorencio's goal was to emphasize her responsibility for the crime. His prosecution followed the direction we might expect from the usual framework of the law regarding infanticide, asking for her to be "condemned and punished with the gravest penalties according to the laws of these realms . . . for her own punishment and as an example to others."[39]

On Ambrosia's side, seven witnesses were questioned, including a doctor who had previously treated Ambrosia, a local priest, neighbors who lived nearby, and a servant who had worked for Lorencio for several months. All of them affirmed that they knew Ambrosia well, and they testified that she was an honorable woman, calm, stable, of sound judgment, and affectionate to her children. These witnesses then gave more extensive statements about Ambrosia's behavior, especially in the days following the birth of her third child in late September of 1626. Diego Díaz, the servant, was in their house when he saw her seize a knife and try to injure herself. The priest testified that Ambrosia had, during one of these moments of madness, called him the devil and said he should keep away from her. (Curiously, even though religious authorities considered diabolical possession to be one of the possible causes of madness, such a possibility was not broached in this case.) Several witnesses said that during these episodes she "went around acting crazy" and "said many nonsensical things," and that at one point she declared that she would leave everything, wandered out of town, and had to be retrieved by her husband. They also described how, following the knife incident witnessed by the servant, she had to be tied to her bed to keep her from hurting herself or her children, as she was acting "under the force of said madness."[40] With each description they explained that it was by these unusual and uncharacteristic moments of disordered speech and behavior that they knew she was not in her right mind.

These accounts emphasized the temporary nature of Ambrosia's actions, that she was normally a person of sound judgment, and that these were momentary episodes when she was not herself. Echoing the words suggested by the defense, several witnesses stated that she suffered from "an accident of madness" and that she was in such a state when she killed Jusepe.[41] Furthermore, they directly related that madness to the condition she was in several days after giving birth to her third child. The label of postpartum depression, of course, is a modern one,[42] but Martín Abad, Ambrosia's legal representative, described her condition as a "frenzy proceeding from a postpartum ailment," and Ambrosia's former servant, Diego Díaz, described her as being "overcome by a madness from said childbirth."[43] The doctor, Luis Alvarez de la Peña, testified that "Ambrosia had given birth a few days earlier, and he saw and knew that due to the said birth she was taken with madness."[44] Alvarez and one of the neighbors noted that her husband, Lorencio, had taken ill at about the same time and that Ambrosia seemed to be even more unhinged by the fear that he would die, even though the doctor assured her that he would recover. The doctor's account paralleled those of the other witnesses in identifying the transient nature of her insanity and its connection to her postpartum condition. The only contribution he made that specifically reflected his medical training was to say that she seemed to suffer "from a kind of madness that is known as mania,"[45] a diagnosis that fit the early modern understanding of the humoral imbalance that manifested as odd laughter, babbling, restless wandering, and nonsensical actions.[46] Given this testimony, Martín Abad asked for Ambrosia to be absolved of Jusepe's murder,

> [B]ecause at the time she is said to have killed her son, she was frantic, insane, and without judgment . . . she even wished and tried to kill herself from the force of the said madness and frenzy . . . and therefore committed no crime and should incur no punishment.[47]

Even though Lorencio insisted on her culpability, in the end, the investigating judge concluded that Ambrosia should be absolved of all criminal responsibility, freed from prison, and allowed to return to her home—adding, rather unrealistically, that her husband Lorencio "should trouble her no more in this matter."[48] Neither of them appears in the archival records again.

The idea of infanticide provoked by madness was not unheard of in early modern Europe, and a small number of other cases demonstrate the possibility of a similar outcome, where even women who were clearly responsible for their children's deaths could be exculpated due to some form of madness, rather than being held to the harsh punishment usually associated with infanticide. In the 30 cases of infanticide in Navarre identified by Mikel Berraondo from the sixteenth and seventeenth centuries, two of them brought up the possibility of what we might now call an insanity defense.[49] María de Cemboráin in 1629 was accused of concealing an unwanted pregnancy and burying her newborn behind the church, while Bernarda Marco in 1677 gave birth to a child, which she then threw out of a window. Both of these cases hew more closely to the more common patterns of infanticide; both were unmarried women dealing with presumably unwanted newborns, and both had concealed their pregnancies. Their investigations, though, proposed the same kinds of questions as in Ambrosia's case, trying to determine whether the women were perceived as not being in their right minds and resting on the judgment of their communities (also small towns). Unlike Ambrosia, both women were described by their neighbors as being consistently mentally unwell and not of sound judgment, though possibly deserving of sympathy.

Even though the prosecuting authorities in Bernarda's case demanded a death sentence, describing her actions as cruel, atrocious, unnatural, and against all divine and human law, she was sentenced to exile instead because of not having been in her right mind. Similarly, although the discussion of sanity played a lesser role in María's case, her sentence was also reduced to two years of exile because of her mental state.[50]

These cases can serve as interesting markers in the chronological evolution of understandings of both madness and infanticide in the early modern period. Concerns about crime, madness, and other forms of moral and social disorder reached their peak in the sixteenth century, but without clear medical or legal guidelines to address them. By the eighteenth century, there was a clear shift toward greater state involvement and authority, with an emphasis on treatment and/or incarceration rather than capital punishment or exile. Many studies of crime have focused on this eighteenth-century development, when Enlightenment legal processes changed in favor of greater lenience, more incorporation of evidence and information about the circumstances of a crime, and an emphasis on incarceration and reform than physical punishment and public retribution. In the aforementioned cases in the Holy Roman Empire, lawyers in the earlier period had reached decisions in cases of infanticide without knowing the name, age, or profession of the accused women. By the eighteenth century, they increasingly came to consider the social environment and individual circumstances of those accused.[51] In general, sentences for infanticide became more lenient and gradually transitioned to imprisonment rather than death or exile, with more sympathy for the plight of unmarried mothers.[52] In Scotland, Deborah Symonds tracks changes from the late seventeenth century, when women indicted for infanticide were likely to be hanged, through the mid-eighteenth century, when banishment was more predominant, to the early nineteenth century, when punishments were reduced to fairly short jail sentences.[53] By the late eighteenth century in Castile, women who found themselves with an unwanted pregnancy were encouraged to leave their children with a parish priest or orphanage without facing any detention or questioning.[54] Courts also came to demand more proof in the determination of infanticide, rather than relying on hearsay or assumptions about the actions of accused women.[55] And yet, with Ambrosia de Alvarado, as early as 1626, in spite of her confession and the grisly conditions of her son's murder, we find a thorough examination of—and sympathy regarding—the circumstances and the personal situation of the accused. Therefore, we might see the seventeenth century as a transitional space, with the greatest flexibility on the part of authorities, in which the perception and judgment of the community could play a significant role.

We should also be cognizant of the influence of recordkeeping on our own perception of how often these disruptive events took place. As I have noted earlier, many scholars argue that infanticide may have been much more common than its appearance in the archives would suggest. One could expect the same to be true for insanity; in cases where a person was not perceived as significantly dangerous or disruptive to their community, there is no reason for episodes of madness to leave any paper trail. For cases of any kind of disorder that were documented, the records scholars have access to are more likely to come from urban centers and higher courts. Even though Ambrosia's case was a dramatic one, it is registered only in the archives of the small town of Loeches; the lives of people such as Ambrosia and her neighbors are far less visible than those of their counterparts in larger cities. Furthermore, if local authorities generally had room to exercise their own judgment in areas that were not clearly defined by medical, religious, or legal institutions, this must have been even more true in rural societies than urban ones.[56] A generalized understanding of Ambrosia's crime is that it was a violation of motherhood and morality, and her husband, Lorencio, perceived it as an offense to his patriarchal authority. Nothing in the investigation, though, suggests that anyone perceived it as scandalous or a threat to the community. Where prescriptive documents about infanticide and madness would suggest that both were treated harshly, the resolution of Ambrosia's trial suggests a degree of flexibility and sympathy that we associate more with later centuries. Her neighbors saw this event as a tragedy, not a crime. What we know about Ambrosia's case does not upend our existing understandings of criminality and mental illness in the early modern period, and her situation was (one hopes) far from common. It should, however, lead us to be more attentive to individual experience, the nature of authority in smaller towns, and the role of communities in shaping attitudes toward justice.[57]

Notes

1 Case against Ambrosia de Alvarado, Archivo Regional de la Comunidad de Madrid, Loeches, 96014.16 [hereafter Alvarado]. The case was investigated by the vicar general, the chief judicial officer of a diocese, in this case the archbishopric of Alcalá de Henares.

2 Especially in the British Isles, infanticide was a recurrent topic in broadsides, ballads, and other forms of literature. See, for example, Deborah A. Symonds, *Weep Not for Me: Women, Ballads, and Infanticide in Early Modern Scotland* (Penn State University Press, 1997); Susan C. Staub, *Nature's Cruel Stepdames: Murderous Women in the Street Literature of Seventeenth-Century England* (Duquesne University Press, 2005); and Keith M. Botelho, "Maternal Memory and Murder in Early-Seventeenth-Century England," *Studies in English Literature 1500–1900* 48 (2008): 111–30.

3 Mikel Berraondo Piudo, "La violencia interpersonal en la Navarra moderna (siglos XVI-XVII)" (Ph.D. dissertation, Universidad de Navarra, 2012), 97.

4 Diana Bullen Presciutti describes frescoes in early modern Rome that represented women committing infanticide as "grievous sinners, presuming to avoid the shame of the world without thinking of God or of their souls, [who] by the counsel of devils throw away their children without baptism." "Dead Infants, Cruel

Mothers, and Heroic Popes: The Visual Rhetoric of Foundling Care at the Hospital of Santo Spirito, Rome," *Renaissance Quarterly* 64 (2011): 772.

5 René Leboutte, "Offense Against Family Order: Infanticide in Belgium from the Fifteenth through the Early Twentieth Centuries," *Journal of the History of Sexuality* 2 (1991): 165.

6 This was not an unusual resolution, at least in the Holy Roman Empire. Of the 76 cases of infanticide documented in the dukedoms of Mecklenburg-Schwerin and Mecklenburg-Strelitz from 1570 to 1650, 73 resulted in death sentences. Günther Häßler and Frank Häßler, "Infanticide in Mecklenburg and Western Pomerania: Documents from Four Centuries (1570–1842)," *History of Psychiatry* 22 (2011): 80, 90.

7 Mikel Berraondo Piudo, "Los hijos como víctimas: el infanticidio en Navarra (siglos XVI-XVII)," *Memoria y Civilización* 16 (2013): 68. *Encubamiento* was included in the thirteenth-century *Siete Partidas*, but there are references to its use as late as 1838. E. Gacto, "Los principios penales en Las Partidas," in *Rudimentos legales* 3 (2000): 39–41.

8 Berraondo, "La violencia interpersonal," 91.

9 For the surprisingly high rate of accidental infant death attributed to smothering by wet-nurses or their husbands, see Christiane Klapisch-Zuber, "La femme et le lignage florentin," in *Persons in Groups: Social Behaviour as Identity Formation in Medieval and Renaissance Europe* (Center for Medieval and Renaissance Studies, 1985), and more recently, Diego Pedrini and Lucia Dubbini, "The Accidental Smothering of Infants Between the Sixteenth and Seventeenth Century through the Case of the Diocese of Jesi," *Annales de Démographie Historique* 2 (2018): 159–77.

10 Häßler and Häßler, "Infanticide in Mecklenburg and Western Pomerania," 83.

11 Rachel E. Bennett, *Capital Punishment and the Criminal Corpse in Scotland, 1740–1834* (Palgrave, 2018), 102.

12 Berraondo, "Los hijos como víctimas," 68.

13 Alfredo Rodríguez González, "El infanticidio en la España Moderna: entre la realidad y el discurso jurídico y moral," *Tiempos Modernos* 36 (2018): 284.

14 Berraondo, "La violencia interpersonal," 91. Häßler and Häßler also note that in the regions of the Holy Roman Empire they analyze, those accused of infanticide very rarely came from bourgeois or aristocratic families. "Infanticide in Mecklenburg and Western Pomerania," 80. Rodríguez González includes an example of a young woman who was absolved of infanticide, probably because of her father's influence. "El infanticidio en la España Moderna," 300.

15 Rodríguez González suggests that ecclesiastical sources such as letters and pastoral visits reveal cases of infanticide that did not reach the courts. "El infanticidio en la España Moderna," 286.

16 Infanticide or infant exposure for the purpose of limiting family size is known to have been common throughout the Roman Empire and in other premodern societies (see, e.g., the work of John C. Caldwell) but is only recently being investigated in early modern Europe. See Gregory Hanlon, "Routine Infanticide in the West 1500–1800," *History Compass* 14 (2016): 536–37; this argument is more developed in the author's new *Death Control in the West: Sex Ratios at Baptism in Italy, France and England* (Routledge, 2022). See also Laura Hynes, "Routine Infanticide by Married Couples? An Assessment of Baptismal Records from Seventeenth Century Parma," *Journal of Early Modern History* 15 (2011): 507–30.

17 Many such practices that do not leave a conventional paper trail may be pursued through literary sources such as folklore. See, for example, Maria Tatar, *The Hard Facts of the Grimms' Fairy Tales*, expanded 2nd ed. (Princeton University Press, 2003).

18 This supports Tomás A. Mantecón Movellán's argument that women had more legal leverage in practice than in theory. *Conflictividad y disciplinamiento social en la Cantabria rural del Antiguo Régimen* (Universidad de Cantabria, 1997), chapter 1.
19 See, among others, Victor Uribe Urán, *Fatal Love: Spousal Killers, Law, and Punishment in the Late Colonial Spanish Atlantic*, chapter 3.
20 Häßler and Häßler, "Infanticide in Mecklenburg and Western Pomerania," 90; on England, J.R. Dickinson and J.A. Sharpe, "Infanticide in Early Modern England: The Court of Great Sessions at Chester, 1650–1800," in *Infanticide: Historical Perspectives on Child Murder and Concealment, 1550–2000*, ed. Mark Jackson (Ashgate, 2002), 35–51.
21 Symonds, *Weep Not for Me*.
22 Rodríguez González, "El infanticidio en la España Moderna," 284.
23 Joanne Ferraro, *Nefarious Crimes, Contested Justice: Illicit Sex and Infanticide in the Republic of Venice, 1557–1789* (Johns Hopkins University Press, 2008), 14.
24 Alvarado, f. 2–3.
25 Carol Thomas Neely, "Recent Work in Renaissance Studies: Psychology—Did Madness Have a Renaissance?" *Renaissance Quarterly* 44 (1991): 778.
26 Elena Carrera, "Understanding Mental Disturbance in 16th- and 17th-Century Spain: Medical Approaches," *Bulletin of Spanish Studies* 87 (2010): 123.
27 Carrera, "Understanding Mental Disturbance in 16th- and 17th-Century Spain," 132–34.
28 Luis Fernando Barrios Flores, "El internamiento psiquiátrico en España: de Valencia a Zaragoza (1409–1808)," *Revista Cubana de Salud Pública* 28 (2002): 2–5.
29 María Tausiet, "Taming Madness: Moral Discourse and Allegory in Counter-Reformation Spain," *History* 94 (2009): 283.
30 For an excellent overview of early modern understandings of madness, see Dale Shuger, *Don Quixote in the Archives: Madness and Literature in Early Modern Spain* (Edinburgh University Press, 2012), chapter 1.
31 Tausiet, "Taming Madness," 280; Elizabeth G. Dickenson and James M. Boyden, "Ambivalence Toward Suicide in Golden Age Spain," in *From Sin to Insanity: Suicide in Early Modern Europe*, ed. Jeffrey R. Watt (Cornell University Press, 2004), 103.
32 Dale Shuger, "Madness on Trial," *Journal of Spanish Cultural Studies* 10 (September 2009): 279.
33 Shuger, "Madness on Trial," 282; see also Cristian Berco, "Determining Insanity in the Inquisition: Sensory Perception and Legal Culture in Seventeenth-Century Lima," *eHumanista* 36 (2017): 52.
34 Alvarado, f. 18.
35 Alvarado, f. 22.
36 "que todo lo dicho es de pública voz y fama," a common legal phrase, f. 22.
37 Alvarado, f. 13.
38 Alvarado, f. 20.
39 Alvarado, f. 11.
40 Alvarado, f. 24–27.
41 "le sobrevino una acidente de locura," f. 23v. The same phrase was used by at least one of the other witnesses.
42 Today we would identify Ambrosia's condition as postpartum depression or possibly postpartum psychosis, a rarer condition that can include hallucinations and delusions, including those that prompt the mother to kill her child. Susan Ayres, "Newfound Religion: Mothers, God, and Infanticide," *The Fordham Urban Law Journal* 33 (2006): 336–37. Descriptions of such symptoms date back to

Hippocrates, but there was no real medical evaluation of them until the nineteenth century, and postpartum psychosis does not currently have its own diagnostic classification in the DSM-V.

43 Alvarado, f. 25 (Díaz), 32 (Abad).
44 Alvarado, f. 12.
45 "con una especie de locura que se dice manya." f. 32v.
46 Carrera, "Understanding Mental Disturbance," 123. Carrera also notes that for medical authors, "mania" was the equivalent of the more popular term "locura," or madness.
47 Alvarado, f. 12. Abad uses the term "frenesí," or frenzy, although none of the witnesses used this word; they all referred to her condition as "locura."
48 Alvarado, f. 38.
49 Berraondo, "Los hijos como víctimas," 63–64.
50 Berraondo, "La violencia Interpersonal," 102–8, 200. For the sentences, see the Archivo General de Navarra, Tribunales Reales, 105802 (Bernarda Marco, 1677) and 268000 (María de Cemboráin, 1629). Cases beyond Spain include those studied by Häßler and Häßler in the Holy Roman Empire, where, of over 70 women found guilty of infanticide, four went unpunished because they were found to be mad or deluded, even though they had confessed to their crime. "Infanticide in Mecklenburg and Western Pomerania," 91.
51 Häßler and Häßler, "Infanticide in Mecklenburg and Western Pomerania," 79.
52 Häßler and Häßler, "Infanticide in Mecklenburg and Western Pomerania," 90.
53 Symonds, *Weep Not for Me*, 94; see also Bennett, *Capital Punishment*, chapter 4.
54 Berraondo, "Los hijos como víctimas," 69. See also Rodríguez González, "El infanticidio," 282–84.
55 Rodríguez González, "El infanticidio," 296.
56 Mantecón Movellán, *Conflictividad y disciplinamiento social*, 16.
57 Support for this approach is well articulated in David S. Nash and Anne-Marie Kilday, "Introduction," *Law, Crime and Deviance Since 1700: Micro-Studies in the History of Crime*, eds. David S. Nash and Anne-Marie (Bloomsbury Academic, 2016).

Selected Bibliography

Berco, Cristian. "Determining Insanity in the Inquisition: Sensory Perception and Legal Culture in Seventeenth-Century Lima." *eHumanista* 36 (2017): 42–61.

Berraondo Piudo, Mikel. "La violencia interpersonal en la Navarra moderna (siglos XVI-XVII)." Ph.D. dissertation, Universidad de Navarra, 2012.

Berraondo Piudo, Mikel. "Los hijos como víctimas: el infanticidio en Navarra (siglos XVI-XVII)." *Memoria y Civilización* 16 (2013): 55–82.

Carrera, Elena. "Understanding Mental Disturbance in 16th- and 17th-century Spain: Medical Approaches." *Bulletin of Spanish Studies* 87 (2010): 107–36.

Ferraro, Joanne. *Nefarious Crimes, Contested Justice: Illicit Sex and Infanticide in the Republic of Venice, 1557–1789*. Johns Hopkins University Press, 2008.

Hanlon, Gregory. "Routine Infanticide in the West 1500–1800." *History Compass* 14 (2016): 535–48.

Häßler, Günther, and Frank Häßler. "Infanticide in Mecklenburg and Western Pomerania: Documents from Four Centuries (1570–1842)." *History of Psychiatry* 22 (2011): 75–92.

Nash, David S., and Anne-Marie Kilday. "Introduction." In *Law, Crime and Deviance Since 1700: Micro-Studies in the History of Crime*, edited by David Nash and Anne-Marie Kilday, 1–15. Bloomsbury Academic, 2016.

Rodríguez González, Alfredo. "El infanticidio en la España Moderna: entre la realidad y el discurso jurídico y moral." *Tiempos Modernos* 36 (2018): 280–301.
Shuger, Dale. *Don Quixote in the Archives: Madness and Literature in Early Modern Spain*. Edinburgh University Press, 2012.
Shuger, Dale. "Madness on Trial." *Journal of Spanish Cultural Studies* 10 (September 2009), 277–97.
Tausiet, María. "Taming Madness: Moral Discourse and Allegory in Counter-Reformation Spain." *History* 94 (2009): 279–93.

9

ON MISCARRIAGE AND ASSAULT IN EARLY MODERN ROME

John Christopoulos

Introduction

Women and their bodies lie at the heart of forensic medicine. In early modern Europe, criminal tribunals frequently investigated cases that centered on women's bodies. They also increasingly relied on midwives as expert witnesses who helped judges assess evidence and adjudicate cases. The largely non-elite women who testified in these trials described violence, interpreted signs of trauma, tracked the progression of symptoms, and assessed the severity of injuries. By doing so, ordinary people made medico-legal arguments to support their cases or to diminish accusations. Though varying in detail and sophistication, their arguments played a crucial role in furthering their legal aims. They also contributed, perhaps unwittingly, to the development of forensic medicine and criminal justice.

In this essay, I will examine three cases of miscarriage caused by assault that were investigated in Rome in the late sixteenth and seventeenth centuries. Through them, I will reflect upon how women's bodies became objects of evidence in the pursuit of justice. By exploring the circumstances that brought non-elite people to court and led them to make medico-legal arguments, these three cases reveal the vital role that ordinary individuals played in shaping the development of forensic medicine.

With a diverse population of over 100,000 people, early modern Rome was a dynamic and chaotic metropolis. Most of its residents were adult men, immigrants, and visitors, some who passed through the city briefly and others who stayed for a lifetime. The site of the headquarters of the Catholic Church, Rome drew elites, including nobles, diplomats, clerics, and professionals vying for influence; artisans eager to hone their skills; and laborers

DOI: 10.4324/9781003486404-13

looking for a living. The marginalized and destitute were also drawn to the Eternal City, hoping for a better life and for solace. Ambition and struggle coexisted, creating a city of stark contrasts.[1]

Violence of every sort and degree of severity was a common part of life in this big city. Romans learned to navigate their streets and piazzas knowing that violence could erupt at any moment. This was especially true for women. Violence against women was common, with single and lower-status working women bearing the brunt of these attacks. In response to violence and disorder, the papacy and Rome's civic authorities increasingly invested in courts and policing, urging people to report violent crime and to settle disputes through official and judicial means rather than personal vendettas. Romans, including non-elite women, became adept at using the courts to seek justice against their assailants. Rome had several tribunals to handle crime, but the Governor's Criminal Tribunal was the main court where most turned for justice. Judges and notaries conducted thorough investigations, questioning witnesses, collecting evidence, and documenting everything. Notaries were supposed to transcribe verbatim the words of witnesses from every corner of society, or at least as close to it as possible. If the case moved forward, the detailed dossiers (*processi*) produced through notaries would be used by lawyers to craft their arguments, shared with expert witnesses for analysis (*consilia*), and scrutinized by judges as they made their decisions.[2]

For historians, trial documents offer a rare and revealing glimpse into both the criminal justice system in action and the intricate fabric of early modern Roman society. Testimonies often went beyond the alleged crimes and can shed light on social structures, customs, and everyday life. Because the depositions were recorded verbatim, they give voice to ordinary individuals whose experiences and thoughts rarely found their way into print. At the same time, the surviving trial records are multilayered sources that require careful analysis. Witnesses who testified in court knew that they were navigating a precarious landscape. They knew that every word they uttered was being recorded for later scrutiny by a judge who could have them tortured to confirm the truth of their statements. What one said in court had consequences and could lead to retribution. Consequently, witnesses often withheld the truth or lied. But, amidst caution and duplicity, many witnesses spoke openly and with candor, recounting their experiences and opinions with the hope that justice would prevail.

Another challenge posed by the surviving records is that their conclusions are frequently missing. Litigants often settled out of court; such resolutions left no official record. Unfortunately, the conclusion of the cases examined in this essay is unknown, leaving us without resolution but not without insight. Despite such challenges, however, historians continue to be drawn to these records because of their ability to illuminate early modern life. Often, these documents offer the only window we possess onto the lives and perspectives of non-elite people.[3]

Despite the pervasive violence in daily life, assaulting a pregnant woman was universally condemned as a grave sin and serious crime. Although Rome's criminal statutes did not explicitly address miscarriage caused by assault, criminal courts treated it as a crime with established procedures for investigating such cases. Cases began with women, their husbands, or kin denouncing their assailants. Judges and notaries questioned witnesses, assessed evidence, and prosecuted assailants, including abusive husbands. The termination of a pregnancy due to violence was generally not classified as homicide unless the woman died as a result of the miscarriage. Women and their families sought financial reparations for the harm suffered and for the loss of offspring, with increased compensation if the woman died from the miscarriage.[4]

Women who brought such cases to court knew that proving the link between assault and miscarriage required more than just personal testimony. Blending personal experience with legal strategy, women and their witnesses described the violence they endured, described in detail the symptoms that followed, and connected these symptoms to the assault. They also knew that they needed the expertise of legally recognized medical professionals. Midwives were essential figures in the investigation of these cases, and this made them vital participants in Rome's criminal justice system. Rome was one of the most medically sophisticated cities of the early modern period, and its medical practitioners regularly served the law and its institutions.[5] Judges relied on the expertise of university-educated physicians, surgeons, and apothecaries in cases of poisoning, murder, and various forms of physical trauma.[6] Midwives, too, were regarded as expert witnesses—the only female experts (*periti*) recognized by law. Their testimony was crucial in cases involving women's health and bodies, including cases of defloration and rape, suspected pregnancy and childbirth, and procured abortion and miscarriage caused by assault. Midwives were called to examine women's bodies and assess evidence. Judges and notaries relied heavily on midwives' testimonies, acknowledging their expertise in these matters. Litigants and witnesses also recognized midwives' authority and understood their role in the legal process. Women strategically sought their support, knowing that a midwife's testimony was needed to turn their trauma into a convincing case.

The trials of miscarriage caused by assault examined here reveal both the harrowing violence and personal trauma faced by three lower-status pregnant women and how their ordeals contributed to the evolving intersection of law and medicine. These trials are more than just individual stories of gendered violence and its consequences; they highlight the critical role that ordinary people and midwives played in shaping criminal justice in early modern Italy. The following section delves into three specific cases, illustrating how law and medicine intertwined in the pursuit of justice and how women's bodies and expertise were central to this process.

Orsolina de Mirandola vs. Germanico Rastello, May 1581

In early modern Rome, conflicts over money and honor were common and often escalated into violence. One such altercation occurred on May 28, 1581.[7] It involved Orsolina de Mirandola, a boarding-house keeper in her mid-forties, and Germanico Rastello, a man of some means but unknown profession. Orsolina claimed that Germanico owed her money on behalf of a former lodger. Recently, Germanico had reassured her that he would settle his friend's debt. A few days later, Orsolina unexpectedly encountered Germanico outside a pharmacy—where she had gone to address her own debts and overdue payments[8]—and she reminded him of his promise and pleaded with him for a speedy payment. Germanico was embarrassed by the loud and public request. Their confrontation quickly escalated. Insults were exchanged, and the argument turned violent. Orsolina reported that Germanico and his servant attacked her with "many blows, kicks, punches, and slaps" and that he drew a dagger, wounding her on the head. She would later tell the judge that if others had not intervened, they might have killed her—perhaps she believed this but such claims were also a common part of assault cases.[9]

This incident, while dramatic, was not uncommon in Rome, where public confrontations over debt often involved heated exchanges and led to violence, even against women. Such displays served to protect the debtor's honor while deflecting creditors. What made Orsolina's case different, however, was not just the assault but its aftermath: a few days later, she suffered a miscarriage of a two-month-developed male fetus.

> I say that from the wounds and the many hits that [Germanico and his servant] gave me, with weapons and without, I was close to dying, and after about four or five days from the beating, I began to urinate a lot of blood and later, when the bleeding stopped, I expelled from my body a dead fetus, which was male according to the midwife and in my opinion also, and, from what I can remember, the fetus was around two months [developed].[10]

She appealed to the court for "justice," asking that Germanico and his servant be punished "as they deserve."[11] Orsolina was seeking both retribution and compensation for the assault and the danger to her life.

To succeed in such lawsuits, women like Orsolina needed to do more than prove that they had been assaulted—they had to convincingly link the assault to their miscarriage. This required a carefully constructed narrative supported by credible witnesses and evidence. Orsolina understood this and, in her deposition, identified witnesses who could corroborate both the assault and its consequences. The judge heard from a variety of witnesses, including Fabio Martini, who was with her during the assault, and several bystanders in the piazza, including the pharmacist (to whom she was in debt) and his apprentice, as well as a tailor and barber whose shops overlooked the piazza. Each witness confirmed that Germanico had initiated the threats, escalated the argument into physical violence, and attacked Orsolina with such force that she bled, a crucial detail that intensified the case.[12]

To establish the link between the assault and her miscarriage, Orsolina relied on the testimonies of those closest to her—her friends, lodgers, and neighbors who tended to her following the assault.[13] Two of her lodgers, Fabio and Paolo, along with her neighbor Angelica, described seeing her stumble home, wounded and battered. They attended to her and observed that she soon began to expel a significant amount of blood. Upon examining a basin used to collect the blood and expulsions, they noticed what appeared to be pieces of flesh ("*un pezzo di carne*," "*certi pezzi di carne*"). Though initially uncertain about what they were seeing in the basin (the midwife told them what it was), the men were not excluded from such matters.[14] Angelica, who also inspected the expulsions, identified the piece of flesh as a fetus: "In my opinion, Orsolina had a miscarriage. But, whether it was male or female, I don't know."[15] To Angelica's untrained eye, the sex of the immature fetus remained unclear. These witnesses painted a vivid picture of Orsolina's condition following the attack, detailing her suffering and the progression of her symptoms leading to the miscarriage. However, their testimonies also revealed that Orsolina's pregnancy, being only two months along, was largely unknown before the miscarriage, which added complexity to the case.

The most authoritative testimony in this case came from Agata, an experienced midwife with nearly 30 years in the profession. Summoned to the judge's office in the Savella prison, Agata's account carried significant weight, not just because of her extensive experience but also because she was the one who verified Orsolina's miscarriage. Agata was not a court-appointed expert witness but rather one of Orsolina's named witnesses. Nevertheless, she made it clear to the judge that she did not know Orsolina personally, suggesting she was less likely to be biased in her favor. Agata approached her testimony with caution, careful not to speculate beyond her observations.

Agata recounted that she had been brought to a woman's home by another woman, neither of whose names she remembered, though she stated she would recognize their faces. Upon arriving, Agata found Orsolina lying in bed, clearly distressed. When asked what had happened, Orsolina told her about the assault and claimed it had led to heavy bleeding and a miscarriage. Orsolina asked Agata to examine a basin that contained her expulsions. With the practiced eye and touch of a seasoned midwife, Agata examined the basin and handled its contents. She identified the small piece of flesh as a fetus. On the basis of its level of formation, she estimated its gestational age to be around two months and confidently judged it to be male.[16] The identification of the fetus' age and sex was significant because, according to contemporary theologians and jurists, a fetus at around two months could be considered "animated" and in possession of a soul, making its termination a potentially graver offense.[17]

What stands out in Agata's testimony is not just what she observed but also the role she played in the legal process. Unlike many other instances where midwives were called to a woman's bedside to assist during a miscarriage and to provide medical intervention and care, Agata's role here appears to have been purely diagnostic. Orsolina did not call for a midwife to help her through the miscarriage or for therapy afterward. Instead, Agata was summoned to confirm that what Orsolina had expelled was indeed a fetus, to determine its sex, and to estimate its developmental stage. Agata's involvement points to Orsolina's legal savvy: she understood the need for a midwife's confirmation to strengthen her case against Germanico. Agata was called to be an expert whose testimony would carry significant weight in court. While Orsolina and her witnesses were convinced that she miscarried, they knew that the court needed a midwife to confirm that the expelled tissue was indeed a fetus.

Witness testimonies, and especially midwife Agata's, made it clear that Germanico's assault likely caused Orsolina's miscarriage. However, Judge Vittutio, tasked with delivering justice, had to determine if Germanico knew Orsolina was pregnant. The uncertainty about whether Orsolina herself knew she was pregnant and the fact that her witnesses were silent on this issue made it harder for the judge to establish intent and gauge the seriousness of the crime, even though he was likely convinced that Germanico caused the miscarriage. Predictably, Germanico's defense challenged Orsolina's account, using his own medico-legal arguments to downplay his responsibility and her credibility.

Judge Vittutio had Germanico arrested and questioned him at the Tor di Nona prison. He started with the standard question posed to all prisoners: did he know why he was in jail? Germanico responded by citing the warrant: Orsolina had accused him of striking her and causing a miscarriage. He sarcastically remarked, "For this reason, I have committed homicide,"[18] exaggerating the charges to make them appear absurd. Germanico denied the accusations and shifted blame onto Orsolina, claiming she confronted him while he was buying chicory in the piazza and demanded money. Although he admitted to threatening her, he insisted she provoked him with insults, calling him a cuckold and slandering his wife. According to Germanico, when her companion Fabio intervened and struck him, he drew a dagger in self-defense, only inflicting a minor wound on Orsolina with its handle. He also claimed that after the incident, he tried to report it but was unable to find any officials. A few days later, he learned that Orsolina had already filed a complaint. Germanico portrayed Orsolina as unstable and himself as the true victim. He argued that he acted in self-defense and minimized the impact of his actions.[19]

Germanico's key strategy was to undermine the credibility of Orsolina's miscarriage. Despite the midwife's and other witnesses' testimonies, Germanico argued that Orsolina could not have miscarried because, at over 45 years of age, she was too old to be pregnant. He also pointed to her lack of other children as evidence suggesting long-standing infertility.[20] In a subsequent interrogation, Germanico introduced additional evidence to support his claim that she did not miscarry because she could not have been pregnant. He claimed that Orsolina was menstruating during their altercation, which he argued explained her bleeding and proved she could not have been pregnant. Germanico named witnesses who could corroborate this assertion: Ludovico Monticuli, a surgeon who apparently tended to Orsolina following their altercation (but who was never called on to testify), allegedly told him that Orsolina refused therapeutic bloodletting because she was menstruating and feared the loss of too much blood; a woman named Dionora allegedly told him that she saw Orsolina removing her menstrual pad after their altercation.[21] Germanico did not perceive any contradiction in asserting that a 45-year-old Orsolina could be both beyond reproductive age and still menstruating. He was adamant that she had fabricated the miscarriage to frame him, attempting to pass off menstruation as a terminated pregnancy.

Judge Vittutio, however, seemed to give little credence to these allegations. He did not ask follow-up questions or summon the witnesses named by Germanico. Instead, the judge had the notary read out all the testimonies he had collected regarding the miscarriage, highlighting midwife Agata's. In his final recorded statement, Germanico rejected these testimonies, asserting, "I understand what has been read to me, and I say that this is not the truth. This was not a miscarriage." While he acknowledged Orsolina's bleeding, he denied it resulted from a miscarriage, claiming, "People who understand this thing much better know that this was not a miscarriage."[22]

Although the outcome of Orsolina's case against Germanico remains unknown, witness testimonies reveal the interplay between medical knowledge and legal strategy as wielded by ordinary people. Supported by eyewitness testimony, Orsolina depicted Germanico as a violent debtor whose actions caused her to miscarry a two-month-developed fetus and endangered her life. By involving the experienced midwife Agata, Orsolina strategically introduced expert testimony into her case. Germanico, in contrast, sought to discredit Orsolina and her witnesses. He questioned her ability to conceive due to her age and claimed she deceitfully presented menstrual blood as evidence of miscarriage. This defense reflected broader societal suspicions about women's honesty in matters of their reproductive health. Germanico's attempt to assert authority over matters typically associated with women—fertility, pregnancy, menstruation, and miscarriage—illustrates how men engaged with and tried to manipulate medico-legal knowledge to defend themselves in court.

Anastasia Fanensi vs. Giuseppe from Velletri and Giacoma Pisaro

A simple request for peace and quiet outside her home nearly cost six-months-pregnant Anastasia Fanensi her life.[23] In late August of 1630, Anastasia confronted a fruit vendor named Giuseppe and a sex worker named Giacoma, who were being loud and raucous outside her home near the Pantheon. She asked them to quiet down and move away. Giuseppe responded with insults, and Giacoma threatened her, saying, "You deserve to be beaten."[24] The situation quickly escalated when Giuseppe charged at Anastasia and punched her in the belly, leading to a life-threatening miscarriage. Anastasia denounced her assailant to the court and demanded justice.

In her deposition, Anastasia carefully detailed the symptoms that followed the attack. She and her neighbor Giulia, who witnessed the assault and tended to Anastasia afterward, both provided a meticulous account of the progression of symptoms that led to the miscarriage. Following the assault, Anastasia was in considerable pain and bedridden. Two days later, she began bleeding, and this lasted for a few days. This was followed by an expulsion of water. Giulia stated that Anastasia went into labor eight days after the assault. Their neighbor, Virginia, came to help as Anastasia delivered a stillborn female fetus. Giulia held the fetus in her hands and told the judge, "We all saw that its shoulders and head were bruised."[25] The women knew that carefully recounting the progression of Anastasia's symptoms leading to the expulsion of the stillborn fetus was necessary for mounting a case against the assailants.

In the aftermath of Anastasia's assault, her friends quickly called Laura Lapidici, a local midwife, to her bedside. It is unclear if Laura and Anastasia knew each other. Laura arrived promptly and found Anastasia bleeding heavily. She provided care, though she did not tell the judge the specifics of her actions. When Laura returned later, she discovered that Anastasia had miscarried. Giulia and Virginia, Anastasia's neighbors, were present, with one of them holding "a dead fetus in her hands." Midwife Laura was careful to note that the miscarriage occurred before her arrival, emphasizing that she did not witness the delivery herself—a deliberate statement that might have been intended to distance Laura from the event. Laura then examined the fetus: she identified it as female, approximately six months developed, and fully formed. She noted that it had bruises on its shoulders and a bump on its head. Recognizing the importance of these observations, Laura said: "I cannot say with certainty if [the bump] was caused by the blows its mother had received because often children are born with some bump on their head." However, she was more confident about the bruising: "The bruise on its shoulders, I am sure, was due to the suffering from the blows its mother had received—as she said—by which the said *creatura* may have died in the womb." Laura concluded her testimony by asserting that her judgment was based on "my experience in the art of midwifery" and affirmed that "this is the truth," a standard legal formula used by midwives when testifying to state their credentials. By invoking her experience, Laura asserted her legal standing as an expert witness whose testimony carried significant weight.[26]

After a two-week pause in the investigation, the judge sought further confirmation about the connection between Anastasia's miscarriage and the assault. He called another midwife, Adriana Basili, to testify as an expert witness. Unlike Laura, who was brought in by Anastasia's friends and had a direct connection to the case, Adriana was court-appointed: she was tasked with providing an objective analysis on the basis of her professional expertise and knowledge rather than her observations of Anastasia's particular case. The judge specifically asked Adriana to clarify what signs a punch to the abdomen would leave on a six-month pregnant woman and her fetus, and whether these signs aligned with the symptoms Anastasia experienced. With over ten years of experience, Adriana testified with confidence: "[W]ithout a doubt," a six-month pregnant woman who suffered a blow to the abdomen—whether by a punch or a fall—would likely have a fetus that suffers trauma, potentially leading to its death. She described the typical progression of symptoms in such cases, noting that while some women miscarry immediately after a blow, others may bleed continuously for several weeks before expelling water and the fetus. She referenced a recent case in which she assisted a woman who had fallen about a month earlier deliver a living *creatura* at five or six months' gestation. It was bruised from the waist down due to the fall. It was baptized but survived for only an hour. Adriana likely mentioned this previous episode in an attempt to establish a pattern of symptoms and outcomes in similar situations. This case helped clarify the link between a traumatic event (a blow to the abdomen), the progression of symptoms over time, and the condition of the fetus. Moreover, by referencing a specific and recent case, Adriana showcased her experience, perhaps hoping to increase the judge's confidence in her testimony and authority.

Laura and Adriana's testimonies reveal the critical role midwives played in early modern Italy's criminal justice system. Laura's account, cautious and grounded in her direct observations, reflects the hands-on expertise of an experienced midwife. Summoned by Anastasia for both care and later testimony, Laura understood that her words could carry significant authority. Her hesitation to definitively link the trauma to the assault highlights the limitations of observational testimony, especially when the observer missed the crucial moment of injury. Still, she found Anastasia's symptoms consistent with her account of assault. In contrast, Adriana, as a court-appointed expert, provided a more authoritative perspective, offering general medical knowledge that could help the judge make a determination. Her testimony was intended to offer a broader understanding of the signs and symptoms associated with miscarriage caused by assault and trauma. The involvement of both midwives reveals the law's reliance on midwives' expert knowledge.

On the basis of the witness testimonies and the midwives' reports, Giuseppe's attack caused Anastasia's miscarriage. As soon as Giuseppe heard about the miscarriage, he fled, and no one knew where he went. His companion Giacoma also disappeared. They evidently realized that Giuseppe's assault caused the miscarriage and feared punishment. Anastasia appears to have waited a few weeks for their return to the neighborhood before eventually pressing charges. Both were condemned in absentia, but it is unknown whether they were ever found or what penalty they might have received.[27] This episode of senseless violence demonstrates how vulnerable pregnant women could be, even right outside their homes. For six-month-pregnant Anastasia, asking for quiet outside her door led to a near-death experience. Her case highlights the precarious position of women and the critical role that midwives played in advocating for them.

Francesca and Bartolomeo Giacobi vs. Guard Magnaguadagno

Violence against pregnant women was not confined to public spaces, like piazzas and streets; it also occurred within Rome's jails—institutions ostensibly meant to uphold public order and discipline deviance. On June 29, 1647, Francesca Giacobi, detained in the Corte Savella jail, was beaten by a guard and suffered a miscarriage. Although the reason for her imprisonment remains unknown, the details of her mistreatment are harrowing. On the night of June 28, Francesca, locked in her cell, began feeling unwell and requested medical help. As her condition worsened, her cries for help escalated into screams. In the middle of the night, a guard named Magnaguadagno, described as a "big, fat man," angrily approached her cell, demanding to know why she was causing a disturbance. When Francesca explained her intense pain, Magnaguadagno mocked her and, despite her protests that she was pregnant, punched her in the belly before locking her back in the cell and threatening her again should she continue to complain. In the early morning of the 29th, she was moved to the public room of the prison to await her husband, Bartolomeo, who was to escort her to the judge to hear her testimony in the case for which she was being detained. Two fellow inmates would later testify to hearing Francesca's cries during the night and to witnessing the guard Magnaguadagno's assault. Francesca, bleeding heavily, miscarried on a mattress in the public room. Another inmate, Livia from Milan, attempted to comfort her by washing her fevered body with vinegar. When her husband, Bartolomeo, arrived, he was horrified to find his wife in this condition. He immediately called for help and transported her to the Consolazione Hospital.[28]

Bartolomeo Giacobi brought the case against the guard Magnaguadagno to the notary Liberato Palenco. Francesca, gravely ill and at risk of dying, gave a brief testimony from her bed at the Consolazione Hospital, recounting the guard's assault and her miscarriage. Understanding the importance of evidence, Bartolomeo collected Francesca's blood and expulsions in a rag before taking her to the hospital. After ensuring her care, he returned to the jail to formally accuse the guard and presented the blood-soaked rags to the notary, stating, "I have brought here the blood she made and also some pieces of flesh, which are in these blood-soaked rags."[29]

Rome's criminal judges and notaries were no strangers to violent crimes and the trauma inflicted on bodies, but one wonders how often they were presented with blood-soaked rags containing tissue. After receiving Bartolomeo's deposition, Palenco summoned two midwives, Ersilia Valeriana and Margarita Gallacina, to examine the evidence. Both midwives were experienced, with Ersilia, the senior of the two, having practiced midwifery in Rome for 34 years. Without providing them with case details, the judge asked them to assess the contents of the bloody package. After carefully handling and examining the objects, both midwives confirmed that the tissue was from a recent miscarriage. While Bartolomeo and the judge noted two pieces of flesh, the midwives focused on the larger piece, determining that it was a fetus about two months developed and likely female. They based this on the level of limb development, explaining that a male fetus would have shown more advanced development. They noted that the blood on the cloth was fresh and without a strong odor, while the fetus, which still had the placenta attached, was starting to decay. This led them to conclude that the miscarriage occurred approximately two hours earlier. To verify the connection between the evidence and Francesca, the judge had the midwives accompany him to the hospital to examine her. Their physical examination confirmed that Francesca had indeed recently miscarried; they noted that her uterus was open and she was still bleeding. The midwives said that she was at risk of dying, likely from blood loss.[30] Unfortunately, the trial documents end abruptly, leaving the outcome of the case and Francesca's fate unknown. It is unclear if the notary ever questioned Magnaguadagno or if justice was served.

Although they are short and fragmentary, the testimonies in the distressing case reveal the critical intersection between material proof and medical expertise in the criminal justice system. Bartolomeo's decision to collect Francesca's blood and tissue reveals that he knew it was necessary to have tangible evidence to substantiate claims of Francesca's miscarriage and trauma caused by the guard's brutal assault. Recognizing that this evidence needed expert interpretation, the judge summoned experienced midwives to examine the blood-soaked rags and later Francesca herself. Midwives Ersilia and Margarita were essential in confirming the miscarriage and trauma

Francesca suffered and thus in legitimizing her account of events and her case against the guard. The court and women like Francesca relied on midwives' expertise in the pursuit of justice.

Francesca's case offers a harrowing glimpse into the brutal conditions of early modern Rome's jails and the vulnerabilities faced by incarcerated women. The guard's treatment of Francesca was likely not an isolated incident but reflective of a broader pattern of abuse within these institutions. The involvement of other inmates, who both witnessed the brutal assault and tried to care for Francesca afterward, highlights a moment of solidarity among prisoners but also their limited ability to intervene against such mistreatment. Although we do not know whether Magnaguadagno was ever questioned or punished, Francesca's case illustrates that even in such dire circumstances, women (and their kin) could sometimes seek redress from the very tribunals meant to discipline them, exposing the systemic violence they endured from those charged with their custody.

Conclusion

Orsolina, Anastasia, and Francesca's cases bring into sharp relief the intersections of gender and violence, law and medicine in early modern Italy. They reveal how non-elite women, often marginalized by both their social status and gender, experienced violence and trauma, and how they navigated the criminal justice system. These women, their kin, and supporters demonstrated remarkable agency and savvy in bringing their terrible ordeals to court, leveraging the limited resources available to them in their pursuit of justice. Despite their lack of formal education, the individuals involved in these trials, as both litigants and witnesses, described experiences of violence, interpreted signs of trauma, tracked symptoms, and evaluated injuries. In doing so, they made medico-legal arguments to advance their cases or defend themselves against accusations. In these cases, we also see how midwives were crucial mediators between the legal and medical worlds. Experienced midwives like Agata, Laura, Adriana, Ersilia, and Margarita were expert interpreters of medical evidence and authoritative voices in the judicial process. Their involvement in these cases was not exceptional: midwives' expertise and authority in matters pertaining to women's health were acknowledged by the law and its institutions and by society at large. These cases reveal that women's experiences and knowledge were not just peripheral but also central to the development of forensic medicine.

Despite the compelling evidence and expert testimonies, the outcomes of these and many other cases of gendered violence and miscarriage caused by assault remain ambiguous or unresolved. Did Orsolina receive compensation from Germanico (or even the debt she was owed)? Although they were condemned in absentia, did the court ever find Giuseppe and Giacoma and punish them accordingly for Anastasia's trauma? Francesca's case, in particular, leaves us with haunting questions. Did the guard Magnaguadagno ever face justice for his terrible abuse of power? How many guards treated women inmates the same way? Perhaps most importantly, did Francesca survive the assault and miscarriage? The trauma that these women faced was not just the product of individual cruelty but rather of broader social structures that seem to have normalized such violence, even as it was prohibited and criminalized. The development of forensic medicine as an increasingly important element of early modern Italian law rested on the bodies and the suffering of women like Orsolina, Anastasia, and Francesca, and on their pursuit of justice.

Notes

1 See the essays in Pamela M. Jones, Barbara Wisch, and Simon Ditchfield, eds., *A Companion to Early Modern Rome, 1492–1692* (Brill, 2019). For the demography of early modern Rome, see Eugenio Sonnino, "The Population in Baroque Rome," in *Rome, Amsterdam: Two Growing Cities in Seventeenth-century Europe,* eds. Peter van Kessel and Elisja Schulte (Amsterdam University Press, 1997), 50–70; and Eugenio Sonnino, ed., *Popolazione e società a Roma dal medioevo all'età contemporanea* (Il Calamo, 1998).

2 On Rome's criminal tribunals, see Irene Fosi, *Papal Justice. Subjects and Courts in the Papal State, 1500–1750*, trans. Thomas V. Cohen (Catholic University of America Press, 2011) and the most recent synthesis with bibliography by Elizabeth S. Cohen and Thomas V. Cohen, "Justice and Crime," in *A Companion to Early Modern Rome, 1492–1692*, eds. Pamela M. Jones, Barbara Wisch, and Simon Ditchfield (Brill, 2019), 115–30.

3 The classic methodological literature on working with early modern trial records is at this point very well known, and the number of studies using trial records is vast and ever growing. For discussion of using this source material in reference to the history of early modern Rome, see the earlier cited works as well as Elizabeth S. Cohen and Thomas V. Cohen, *Words and Deeds in Renaissance Rome: Trials before the Papal Magistrates* (University of Toronto Press, 1993), and most recently Elizabeth S. Cohen, "Writing History from Trials in the Governor's Court in Early Modern Rome. A Brief Guide for New Users," in *Una curiosità generosa. Studi di storia moderna per Irene Fosi*, eds. Giuseppe Mrozek Eliszezynski and Giovanni Pizzorusso (Viella, 2024).

4 Even without specific laws, Roman courts treated cases of miscarriage caused by assault as grave and investigated them thoroughly. Alongside the criminal cases studied here, see the case discussed by Elizabeth S. Cohen in "Miscarriages of Apothecary Justice: Un-Separate Spaces of Work and Family in Early Modern Rome," *Renaissance Studies* 21 (2007): 480–504, where a candy maker pursued reparations after his wife suffered a miscarriage and died following a distressing encounter. For similar investigations in other early modern European contexts, see Ulinka Rublack, "Pregnancy, Childbirth and the Female Body in Early Modern Germany," *Past & Present* 150 (1996): 84–110; Garthine Walker, *Crime, Gender and Social Order in Early Modern England* (Cambridge University Press, 2003), 60–63. For the jurisprudence and prosecution of miscarriage caused by assault in medieval England, see Sara M. Butler, "Abortion by Assault: Violence Against Pregnant Women in Thirteenth-and Fourteenth-Century England," *Journal of Women's History* 17 (2005): 9–31 and "Sara M. Butler, "Abortion Medieval Style? Assaults on Pregnant Women in Later Medieval England," *Women's Studies* 40 (2011): 778–99.

5 Rome boasted a renowned university medical faculty, a robust college of physicians with an increasingly rigorous licensing system for medical practitioners, and numerous hospitals catering to the sick and needy. See Elisa Andretta, *Roma Medica. Anatomie d'un système médical au XVIe siècle* (École française de Rome, 2011).

6 Physicians' expertise extended to civil trials as well, where they played a pivotal role in cases involving marital separations due to infertility and inheritance disputes, as well as contract cases related to cognitive impairment and mental illness, disability and unexpected death, and sometimes to canonization proceedings where they had to assess the bodies and miracles of prospective saints. For an overview of the history of forensic medicine, see Katherine D. Watson, *Forensic Medicine in Western Society: A History* (Routledge, 2011). For the Italian context, Alessandro Pastore, *Il medico in tribunale. La perizia medica nella procedura penale d'antico regime (secoli XVI-XVII)* (Edizioni Casagrande, 2004). The use of medical practitioners as witnesses in court in early modern Rome has received significant attention due to its long history and the influential work of Paolo Zacchia, author of the *Quaestiones Medico-Legales* (1661), a three-volume synthesis of forensic medicine and the leading work on the subject well into the eighteenth century. Silvia De Renzi, "The Risks of Childbirth: Physicians, Finance, and Women's Deaths in the Law Courts of Seventeenth-century Rome," *Bulletin of the History of Medicine* 84 (2010): 549–77; De Renzi, "Witnesses of the Body: Medico-Legal Cases in Seventeenth-Century Rome," *Studies in the History and Philosophy of Science* 33 (2002): 219–42. On Paolo Zacchia, see Alessandro Pastore and Giovanni Rossi, eds., *Paolo Zacchia. Alle origini della medicina legale: 1584–1659* (FrancoAngeli, 2008).

7 Archivio di Stato di Roma (ASR), Tribunale criminale del Governatore (TCG), Processi, 1581, b. 175, fols. 982r–997r.

8 She did not tell the judge anything about this debt other than that the owner of the pharmacy, Petro de Girona, had made a complaint against her to the Vicar's Tribunal.

9 ASR, TCG, Processi, 1581, b. 175, ff. 983r–85r.

10 ASR, TCG, Processi, 1581, b. 175, f. 983r.

11 ASR, TCG, Processi, 1581, b. 175, f. 983r.

12 ASR, TCG, Processi, 1581, b. 175, fols. 985v–86v, 988v–91r.

13 Orsolina testified that three or four physicians also saw the aborted fetus. "Three or four physicians" was quite a lot of medical attention. ASR, TCG, Processi, 1581, b. 175, f. 983r-v.

14 ASR, TCG, Processi, 1581, b. 175, ff. 985r–86r.

15 ASR, TCG, Processi, 1581, b. 175, ff. 986v–87r.

16 ASR, TCG, Processi, 1581, b. 175, f. 988r–v.

17 ASR, TCG, Processi, 1581, b. 175, f. 988r–v. On animation, John Christopoulos, *Abortion in Early Modern Italy* (Harvard University Press, 2021).

18 ASR, TCG, Processi, 1581, b. 175, ff. 991v–92r.

19 ASR, TCG, Processi, 1581, b. 175, ff. 991v–94r.

20 ASR, TCG, Processi, 1581, b. 175, f. 994r.

21 ASR, TCG, Processi, 1581, b. 175, ff. 995r–96r, 988r–v.

22 ASR, TCG, Processi, 1581, b. 175, f. 996v.

23 ASR, TCG, Processi, 1630, b. 257, ff. 1870r–1875r.

24 ASR, TCG, Processi, 1630, b. 257, ff. 1870r–1871r.

25 ASR, TCG, Processi, 1630, b. 257, ff. 1871r–1872r, 1873r–v.

26 ASR, TCG, Processi, 1630, b. 257, ff. 1872r–1873r.

27 On the front page of the trial dossier, the notary wrote "condemned." ASR, TCG, Processi, 1630, b. 257, ff. 1870r.

28 ASR, TCG, processi, 1647, b. 405, ff. 1217r–1225v.

29 ASR, TCG, processi, 1647, b. 405, ff. 1218r–v. 1221r–1222r. See also the testimonies of two incarcerated witnesses, Livia de Rosa from Milan (ff. 1223r–1223bisv) and Erminia Caccilla (ff. 1223bisv–1225v).

30 ASR, TCG, processi, 1647, b. 405, ff. 1219r–1220r, 1222r–v. Also see ff. 1220r–1221r.

Select Bibliography

Andretta, Elisa. *Roma Medica. Anatomie d'un système médical au XVIe siècle.* École française de Rome, 2011.

Butler, Sara M. "Abortion by Assault: Violence Against Pregnant Women in Thirteenth-and Fourteenth-Century England." *Journal of Women's History* 17 (2005): 9–31.

Butler, Sara M. "Abortion Medieval Style? Assaults on Pregnant Women in Later Medieval England." *Women's Studies* 40 (2011): 778–99.

Christopoulos, John. *Abortion in Early Modern Italy.* Harvard University Press, 2021.

Cohen, Elizabeth S., and Thomas V. Cohen. *Words and Deeds in Renaissance Rome: Trials before the Papal Magistrates.* University of Toronto Press, 1993.

Cohen, Elizabeth S. "Miscarriages of Apothecary Justice: Un-Separate Spaces of Work and Family in Early Modern Rome." *Renaissance Studies* 21 (2007): 480–504.

Cohen, Elizabeth S. "Writing History from Trials in the Governor's Court in Early Modern Rome. A Brief Guide for New Users." In *Una curiosità generosa. Studi di storia moderna per Irene Fosi*, edited by Giuseppe Mrozek Eliszezynski and Giovanni Pizzorusso. Viella, 2024.

Cohen, Elizabeth S., and Thomas V. Cohen. "Justice and Crime." In *A Companion to Early Modern Rome, 1492–1692*, edited by Pamela M. Jones, Barbara Wisch, and Simon Ditchfield. Brill, 2019.

De Renzi, Silvia. "Witnesses of the Body: Medico-Legal Cases in Seventeenth-Century Rome," *Studies in the History and Philosophy of Science* 33 (2002): 219–42.

De Renzi, Silvia. "The Risks of Childbirth: Physicians, Finance, and Women's Deaths in the Law Courts of Seventeenth-century Rome." *Bulletin of the History of Medicine* 84 (2010): 549–77.

Fosi, Irene. *Papal Justice. Subjects and Courts in the Papal State, 1500–1750.* Translated by Thomas V. Cohen. Catholic University of America Press, 2011.

Jones, Pamela M., Barbara Wisch, and Simon Ditchfield, eds. *A Companion to Early Modern Rome, 1492–1692.* Brill, 2019.

Pastore, Alessandro. *Il medico in tribunale. La perizia medica nella procedura penale d'antico regime (secoli XVI-XVII).* Bellinzona: Edizioni Casagrande, 2004.

Pastore, Alessandro, and Giovanni Rossi, eds. *Paolo Zacchia. Alle origini della medicina legale:1584–1659.* FrancoAngeli, 2008.

Rublack, Ulinka. "Pregnancy, Childbirth and the Female Body in Early Modern Germany." *Past & Present* 150 (1996): 84–110.

Sonnino, Eugenio. "The Population in Baroque Rome." In *Rome, Amsterdam: Two Growing Cities in Seventeenth-Century Europe*, edited by Peter van Kessel and Elisja Schulte. Amsterdam University Press, 1997.

Sonnino, Eugenio. *Popolazione e società a Roma dal medioevo all'età contemporanea.* Il Calamo, 1998.

Walker, Garthine. *Crime, Gender and Social Order in Early Modern England.* Cambridge University Press, 2003.

Watson, Katherine D. *Forensic Medicine in Western Society: A History.* Routledge, 2011.

PART IV

Special Victims

10

ON CHILDREN IN SPAIN

Lu Ann Homza
William & Mary

Over the last 20 years, scholars of medieval and early modern Europe, as well as the early modern Atlantic, have come to appreciate that all socio-economic classes, educational levels, and sexes understood how to use law courts for their own advantage.[1] Investigators have taught us about feuding, peace-making, slaves' quests to overturn their status, powers of attorney and legal petitions, and judicial marketplaces.[2] In general, current scholars reject the notion that turning to a legal system represented a teleological process of increasing rationality and objectivity.[3] Passions in legal cases were all too obvious; motives for prosecutions, lawsuits, and petitions were all too personal.

We do not yet have enough comparative research into the multiple legal jurisdictions in early modern Spain to compare access to them. Attempts to conduct that research are hampered significantly because of the tremendous range of sources that survive in the various legal systems: numerous tribunals remain uncatalogued, and many trials have been destroyed.[4] Nonetheless, evidence from Navarre suggests that turning to the royal and episcopal courts was routine, despite barriers of distance, weather, poverty, and language.[5] The sources preserved in Pamplona—which number in the thousands—indicate that illiterate Basque speakers valued the judicial systems available to them for their potential to correct physical, financial, social, and familial injuries. If these villagers also enhanced the authority of the state by turning to the courts, there are no signs they cared.

This essay focuses on the legal and communal ramifications of violent crimes against children in Navarre in the early modern period. Its fundamental objective is to investigate where the lines of local involvement might be when Navarrese villagers witnessed or came to know about children's

DOI: 10.4324/9781003486404-15

physical injuries and the children in question were not their own. Recent archival discoveries strongly suggest that *verbal* violence against children did not produce a community reaction, even if the spoken words were death threats. In the village of Olague, 12 miles from Pamplona, adults in 1611 verbally menaced their neighbors' children with the prospect of beatings, drownings, and other forms of brutality in order to coerce those youngsters into false accusations of witchcraft. Calling someone a witch was a dreadful slur; the adults in question here wanted to ruin the honor of their enemies. While grown men and women who uttered public insults could be prosecuted for defamation in Pamplona's royal secular court, a child who defamed others could not be sued for slander. Children were thus the perfect witchcraft accusers because there was no legal remedy to stop them.[6]

We know about the events in Olague because adults there sued each other for libel, and children testified for both plaintiffs and defendants.[7] Boys and girls as young as six told the court that they had publicly relayed to parents, bystanders, and local priests that neighbors had promised to club them to death if they refused to make false accusations of witchcraft. The children remained consistent in their stories; their accounts were backed up by adults who told the secular court under oath that they had conversed with men and women who proposed physically injuring children over questions of witches. The adults who learned about the threats heartily disapproved of the proposed intimidation, but no adult in Olague stepped in to help when the threats were being made. The puzzle here is that public speech acts by anyone of any age were treated with the greatest seriousness in early modern Iberia. Yet when it came to children and verbal menacing, no public outrage or measures ensued.[8]

The fact that Olague's adults did not step in seems to have come from a firmly held but tacit social norm: adults in early modern Navarre generally did not get involved with children who were not their own so long as death was not in play. There were multiple *refranes,* or proverbs, in early modern Spain that warned about strangers' interference in other people's families: for instance, one reads "*entre padres, hijos, y hermanos, nadie meta las manos*," which can be translated as "no one meddles when it comes to parents, children, and siblings."[9] The question here is, did that taboo have limits? In fact, it did. Although archival evidence indicates that a verbal promise or threat of violence against children did not provoke a communal reaction, actual physical violence did, with families and neighbors acting immediately even before they pursued a legal remedy.

There were three legal jurisdictions in Navarre that were deputized to investigate and solve crimes in the early modern period. The secular court system was ultimately overseen by the viceroy's court in Pamplona; the episcopal court system was supervised by Pamplona's bishop; finally, heresy was handled by the inquisitorial court system, which was based in a tribunal in

Logroño that lay outside Navarre itself.[10] These three legal bodies shared certain expectations: they presumed defendants were guilty; they believed a full proof consisted of either a confession or two eyewitnesses to the same event, but they preferred confessions. At the same time, the secular and inquisitorial jurisdictions would engage in torture to move an interrogation forward to a confession, but the episcopal system in Navarre never did so.[11]

As for forensic evidence, it could arise in various ways and take different forms. Witnesses could notice incriminating circumstances, such as engaging in flight or seeking ecclesiastical sanctuary in a local parish church; they also could pay particular attention to the physical setting in which the violence had occurred. Bystanders could conduct investigations on the local level, which might entail searching for bodies or spying on potential malefactors. Residents of villages also might stage experiments to arrive at a conclusion: one particularly dramatic example occurred in 1611, when adults in one Navarrese village, under ecclesiastical supervision, opened a tomb of a dead priest to see if he really had been cannibalized by witches, as village children had claimed.[12]

Unlike the episcopal or inquisitorial forum, there were two levels to the secular legal jurisdiction. The initial one was called the court of "first instance," which took place in villages: there, plaintiffs brought complaints to the local judge and mayor, called the *alcalde*. The alcalde could order village constables to seize and imprison suspects; the alcalde could hear evidence about the alleged crime and seek solutions from the two parties. If no resolution was forthcoming and the misdeeds were serious—murder, attempted murder, infanticide, robbery, and so on—the alcalde could send the case, the prisoner, and the plaintiff to the royal court in Pamplona. The government of Navarre funded secular trials for crimes, although slander and debt cases were exceptions: in the latter, plaintiffs and defendants had to subsidize the taking of witness depositions, and one side could sue the other for costs.

Whether in the court of first instance or in the royal court of Pamplona, and irrespective of the offense under investigation, witnesses in general demonstrated that they made connections between what they had seen or heard or handled and legal evidence that would be valued in a courtroom. Illiterate Basque villagers remembered incriminating behavior; they noticed signs of crimes; they conducted tests to verify their suspicions. Remarkably, their investigative impulses seem to have occurred irrespective of age, sex, occupation, or education. Their use of forensic evidence demonstrates the reach of the law in what Castilian elites always imagined as a liminal space.

These investigative efforts clearly came into play when children were physically harmed. For example, adults in Navarre intervened vigorously in cases of infanticide, including when the dead infant did not belong to their own families. For instance, on the night of June 18, 1606, María de Baztan was seized by the constables of her village, Zabaldika, on suspicion of having killed her child.[13] María had spoken to an older woman, Gracia de Zozaya, earlier in the day and had asked Gracia for burial space for her two-year-old daughter, because "without a doubt she would die soon." The child was alive and in María's arms as the latter made the prediction; Gracia consequently asked how she could know such a thing when the baby was perfectly well.

María left with the baby but returned crying some 40 minutes later, with the now-dead child in her arms. She begged Gracia and other women who by then were present to dress the baby properly for burial. Gracia snatched the child and began to examine her: she was shocked to find the toddler not breathing, with her eyes closed. Gracia and her companions then shouted at María that she had strangled and killed her toddler, who had marks on the front of her neck. María ran away with the body.

From there, Zabaldika's villagers sprang into action. The women informed the parish priest, a messenger was sent to the constable, and the constable and a crowd then began to search for María and the baby. It was late at night; the group carried a torch. They found María in a shed in the woods with the door locked from the inside, a detail that eyewitnesses found incriminating; after breaking in, the constable imprisoned María in a private home with guards. He carried the dead child "in his arms" to his own house; before daybreak, he fetched a local surgeon and made him examine the corpse. The surgeon concluded that the signs on the child's neck had "been made with a violent hand." After María was transferred to Pamplona's royal court, the local constable took the body along as well, "so that the judges there could see the signs on the throat with their own eyes." Pamplona's surgeons agreed that the marks on the child were likely done "with fingernails and the fingers of a hand, pressing and exerting force with the ends of the fingers. If it had been a wound from a poisonous animal, the signs of violence would have been much smaller."[14] María was sentenced to ten years of exile, though the penalty was lifted when her defense lawyer produced two more doctors who swore the child died naturally.[15]

Adults in Navarre demonstrated the same energy when children went missing. For example, in 1559, a three-year-old boy in Obános disappeared. His adult neighbors searched for him all night; the next morning, they found the toddler's body in a well. It turned out that a ten-year-old boy had thrown the child into the well after the latter repeatedly called him crazy.[16] Some astute adults became suspicious when the same ten-year-old declined to go look at the corpse with everyone else and, instead, ran into his house and shut the door. A nine-year-old eyewitness to the crime eventually deposed in court: he, the defendant, and the toddler had been playing at bowling with rocks next to the well, which was open. The eyewitness saw the defendant pick up the toddler in his arms and toss him to his death; the boy had agreed not to say anything so long as he received a copper coin. When the defendant failed to give him the money, the witness told the dead child's parents what had actually occurred.[17] The ten-year-old defendant was sentenced to ten years of exile, though it ultimately was reduced to two.

In March 1596, in the village of Muzqui, a similar tragedy occurred when parents sent their ten-year-old daughter with a slightly older companion to have some wheat milled. The daughter never came home; she was found drowned in a pool of water.[18] The men who recovered her body took care to preserve it, placing it in a nearby church overnight. Immediately the next day, they began to walk around the area, calling out their terrible news. When the parents heard about the corpse, they went running. After seeing their dead child, they instantly suspected the older companion and adjured the village constables to find her. When the parents confronted her, she confessed that she had pushed the younger girl into the water in order to steal the wheat they were carrying. She had hidden the wheat in her father's house, under the bed she shared with four siblings.[19] When the murder suspect was taken to Pamplona, she confessed again in the royal secular court, though her defense lawyer tried to turn the incident into an accident. It had all been a mistake. The two girls were very fond of each other and never quarreled; they were just playing as they walked to the mill, giving each other gentle shoves as children often do.

The prosecution's testimony in the Muzqui case was especially damning because so much forensic effort lay behind it. Men from the village, as well as its surgeon, testified in the royal court about their efforts. One of the village constables told the court,

> When he and the others went to claim the victim, they saw that the pool where they found her did not have lapping water for her to have been able to drown, unless it was due to someone knocking her down and holding her there by her legs. Furthermore, on the banks of the pool they found more than twelve footprints of small, bare feet, where the girls had walked.[20]

The village surgeon also examined the crime scene: he too found the pool to have been too shallow for drowning and noticed the footprints of the barefoot girls on the shore. He told the court that the victim had pooled blood on her back, buttocks, and behind her thighs, as if someone had kneeled on her while she was in the water. He also believed that two large rocks around the pool had been moved, though he couldn't say why or by whom.[21] In the end, the child-killer was sentenced to be paraded around Pamplona naked from the waist up, with a town crier announcing her crime. She then was supposed to receive 100 lashes and be exiled from Navarre for six years.[22] Later, the court changed the period of exile to ten years and annulled the rest of the verdict.

As a final example of missing children and community anxiety over them, we might consider a prosecution from 1627.[23] Here, two *gitanas* were prosecuted for "seizing" [*secuestro*] a four-year-old girl. Her parents had gone to Eneritz in July to celebrate the feast of St. Mary Magdalene; while they were there watching the processions, they told the court of first instance in Puente de la Reina that *gitanas* appeared and stole their daughter. Multiple witnesses, predominantly women, backed up the parents' story by attesting that they had seen the *gitanas* in question with the little girl. Graciana de Labayen, a resident of a neighboring village, said in court that she had seen three *gitanas* on the road walking along with a girl of three to four years of age: the local judge had shown her the two *gitanas* currently in prison, whom she identified; she attested that the third was elderly, with ragged and torn clothing, while the child was wearing a little blue skirt.[24] Another female witness, age 60, told the court that she was a card-maker

> and due to her job, she is always in the street, and while selling fruit with the keen-nosed Agueda de Muniain, both of them saw how the two *gitanas* who currently are in jail were going along the street, and she personally saw a baby who looked like a girl and who would have been about four years in age, and the toddler was following the *gitanas;* and Agueda de Muniain asked the child if she was a *gitana,* and the child said she was, though this witness nevertheless did not think so.[25]

Agueda verified her friend's story: she said the child had golden, reddish hair, and because it seemed to her that she couldn't be a *gitana*, she asked the child and the child replied that she was a *gitana* too, "but she didn't believe it because the child was beautiful."[26]

Men too affirmed the parents' story about their missing child and who was responsible for it. A younger man, a shoemaker, saw the *gitanas* with the girl and told the court that she didn't appear to belong to them. An older agricultural laborer ran into the three *gitanas* with the child while he was working: they asked him for a drink, which he gave to them; he asked them where they had acquired the child because she looked like one of his neighbor's offspring. The *gitanas* allegedly replied, "[T]here are many children in the world who look like one another."[27]

The *gitanas* under arrest in this 1627 case were moved to the royal secular court in Pamplona, where they were tortured but maintained their innocence.[28] It seems likely that they were unjustly accused since the allegedly kidnapped toddler was found dead on the outskirts of Eneritz at the beginning of September, and expert witnesses affirmed in court that she had died through natural causes. She had been stumbled upon by men who instantly recognized her "due to her golden, reddish hair, and her hands, and the rest of her appearance."[29] When the dead child's mother returned to court in September 1627, she explained for the first time how her daughter came to be lost. On that feast day of Mary Magdalene, she went to Eneritz to sell fruit, and she sent the dead girl, Isabel, along with two boys to Eneritz: the children were supposed to go to their aunt's house.[30] After the mother sold the fruit, she too went to the aunt's house, but her daughter wasn't there: she was told the girl and the boys had gone to the market. She and her husband immediately followed and spent the entire day looking for their daughter, to no avail. The following day, she heard about the *gitanas* and pursued them with all diligence. Then, in September, she was told by men whom she knew that they had found the child,

> and she went there in terror, and she recognized her daughter by her hair, hands, shirt, and all the other bodily details . . . and she is certain her daughter died naturally because of the position of her body. She was lying face up in a thicket of trees, with one leg on an oak bush, and the other on the ground . . . and she had been dead a long time.[31]

Nevertheless, the royal court insisted that the *gitanas* had let the child die from neglect and then had hidden her body. The sentence was harsh: 100 lashes, public humiliation, and ten years of exile.[32]

Secular court cases involving dead infants and missing children are suffused with evidence about boundaries, community values, and emotions in early modern Navarre. Everyone believed that a deceased baby was their business; everyone treated missing children as a highly important matter. Adults sought, preserved, and publicized evidence. They noticed physical environments. They talked among themselves and collaborated in efforts to locate the missing. Local judges in courts of first instance held line-ups of imprisoned suspects for potential witnesses. Men and women noticed significant physical or emotional signs of guilt or innocence, and they also had the imagination to put themselves into a parent's grief-filled condition.[33] One of the first female witnesses in the 1627 *gitana* case, Graciana de Labayen, changed her legal deposition just a day after giving her first statement: she told the court that her original testimony was false, that she actually had never seen the *gitanas* or the child. When the court asked whether she had been induced or pressured to retract, she said no: instead, she wanted to discharge her conscience. She had given her first statement after she was "moved to pity by the mother's tears"; she explained that she had been told about the child's disappearance by a neighbor.[34]

In terms of noticing and recalling forensic details, Navarrese villagers were equally sensitive to animal histories, animal personalities, and owner neglect. They recognized patterns of aggressive behavior and failures of human oversight and deposed about both in court. In such cases, they took care to highlight the public environments in which victims had been hurt. For example, Pamplona's main secular archive holds dozens, if not hundreds, of homicide and injury cases in which the youngsters were trampled or kicked by horses or mules. In 1582, a nine-year-old boy died after being hit in the head by a mule's hooves. The mule was owned by Domingo de Ubalde, and it had a reputation for viciousness. Domingo left it in the public street without a guard or any precautions, though he knew "it was male and accustomed to kick people."[35] The witnesses were uniform in their opinion: this mule was "malicious and evil-tempered and prone to kick out at people in the streets." The dead child had done nothing to provoke the animal; two witnesses had seen the tragedy unfold.[36] In other instances—though here, no one charged the animals themselves with malice—thoughtless carriage drivers ran over small children as the former were moving through villages with their goods. Witnesses to these events emphasized how careless the drivers had been around public turns and blind spots.[37]

The processes of learning about, investigating, and deposing about physical harm to children seem to have been a community obligation, and the evidence suggests that child-killers, whether adults or not, incurred legal consequences unless they successfully ran away. If their communities caught them and believed they were guilty, they ultimately could be taken for trial to the royal secular court in Pamplona. Children and adults could be sentenced in some of the same ways, though women were never condemned to the galleys, nor were men under 20 or over 60 or 70. Exile appears to have been the typical punishment for child-killing, though as we will see, its duration varied, and that variation may indicate a judgment about culpability. At the same time, court sentences could become irrelevant if the victim's family did not want to pursue charges.

As for legal arguments, child deaths due to rocks, clubs, or gunpowder could entail assertions about intentions or accidents or both, depending upon the prosecution and the defense's points of view. A prosecutor could voice a motive, which often turned upon a feud between the perpetrator and the parents of the child victim. A defendant, in turn, could maintain that the death was a chance coincidence. The language and verdicts of the royal court do not reveal a stable hierarchy of injury. Most deaths of children were described as involving *agresión* rather than *homicidio*: at first, I thought this linguistic difference might indicate something significant, but that turned out to be a false lead. Here, the term "aggression" means to attack someone in order to harm them: it was applied as well in cases involving the attempted murder of adults by other adults, so there was nothing child-specific about it.

We know that certain conditions, such as debt, were common settings for adult male violence. Perhaps not surprisingly, the parallel of hunger seemed to create possibilities for the violent deaths of children. The female murderer who drowned her friend was so poor that she spent all day, every day, begging for alms: the wheat she stole must have seemed like an irresistible temptation. Significantly, children could also die for encroaching on other people's gardens.

In 1626, in the village of Grez, a boy named Martín Ximénez, aged nine or ten, gathered with a group of young male friends on the feast of Mary Magdalene. That afternoon, the boys went to some small agricultural plots owned by residents of the village; they were particularly focused on the garden behind the house of Pedro de Elduaien, which had plum trees. A girl from the Elduaien house sounded the alarm that boys were entering the property to eat plums. A young brother-in-law of the owner went out to confront the thieves with a stick in his hands, "and as he came upon them, he threw the stick at them, and the weapon reached Martín Ximénez and gave him a great blow behind the left ear."[38] Martin bled profusely; his assailant ran to the house, where he told his relatives that he had done more harm than he had intended.[39] People from the house carried Martín into it, and after some efforts at care, deposited him with his parents. Despite the attention of a surgeon, Martín died 11 days later. The suspect's defense attorney insisted his client had only wanted to frighten the boys; he opined that where there was no motive, there was no crime. The court disagreed. The defendant was sentenced to three years in the galleys, a verdict subsequently altered to six and then eight years of exile.

In 1635, in the village of Esparza, another boy, aged 13, perished after a similar encounter.[40] Again, it occurred on a feast day, this time in honor of St. Lawrence, August 10. The royal prosecutor charged a 58-year-old, Pedro de Suescun, with having struck the adolescent with a stick without provocation; the blow was so ferocious that it broke the child's head open and exposed his brain. As the trial went on, however, the events seemed to have been more complicated. Pedro had found the boy in his garden, gathering fruit; he slapped the boy several times "on account of what he was doing, and because the garden was closed."[41]

At that point, witnesses deposed that Pedro departed. But the child subsequently asked Pedro for the shepherd's crook that he had left in the garden: Pedro flung [*arrojó*] the stick at the boy and hit him in the head "unexpectedly," behind the left ear. Pedro knew he had caused catastrophic physical injury and immediately went running into the parish church for sanctuary. Once in church, Pedro told multiple parishioners and neighbors what he had done, as they later attested in court. When those adults tried to reassure Pedro that the boy would be cured, he replied, "[H]ow is that possible, since I took the stick out of his head myself?" Throughout his conversations in church, "Pedro was crying and very much distressed at having done such a bad thing to the boy."[42] He ultimately fled and was recaptured. Witnesses said that Pedro was quiet and a friend of all his neighbors, whom he was accustomed to aid. His lawyer noted too that where there was no intent, there was no crime, but even though Pedro presented a formal act of pardon, signed by all his victim's siblings, the court ignored it. He was sentenced to five years of exile.[43]

These cases of death by stick offer intricate evidence about community support, private property, and legal culpability within a larger setting of a subsistence economy and hunger. In the first case from 1626, members of the killer's household carried the victim to their own domicile and then to his parents' in an obvious attempt to help. The killer had only intended to frighten the boys; he had no disagreements with the family of his victim; there could be no crime where there was no motive.[44] Yet despite the fact that the dead boy and his crew were physically in someone else's garden in 1626, the court delivered a guilty verdict because it heard additional circumstances that demonstrated overreach as well as purpose. The garden didn't belong to the defendant but to a relative of the defendant. The defendant had told his sister in advance that he was going into the garden to ward off the fruit thieves; she replied that he should be careful; the defendant had borrowed the stick he carried from the local oxherd. Soon, the royal prosecutor and the victim's father were arguing the case was about intent to murder. The children had no way to defend themselves. The victim was seated on a wall of the garden when he was struck; he wasn't even walking among the plum trees or carrying plums. The defendant had opined that the murderous stick was little and thin, but the royal court was in possession of it: in fact, it was very sturdy and long.[45]

In contrast, in the case ten years later, in 1636, the perpetrator made no attempt to deny or shift blame for the death of the adolescent: rather, he told everyone in church what he had done; his emotions and sorrow were physically apparent. Though his garden was private and the door was closed when the offender entered it, the attacker merely slapped the victim and then thought the incident was over. It was only when the victim asked for his own stick—the perpetrator didn't have one—that the adult threw the object and the injury occurred. (Coincidentally, this child victim was also an oxherd, so we can presume the stick was substantial.) It seems as if personal responsibility voiced to a wide audience, no premeditation, and throwing back the victim's own weapon made a difference here in terms of the lesser sentence, five years of exile rather than eight. Once again, the royal court and its witnesses understood how to notice and relay forensic and circumstantial evidence.

Similar signs of community involvement and forensic attention occurred in 1714, when a four-year-old boy was killed by a gun.[46] The shooter was Pedro Bandera, whose age at the start of the trial was given as eight or ten but then changed later on the same folio to 17 or 18.[47] Two witnesses attested that at 9:00 at night, they saw their local priest return from hunting with his shotgun. In the local cemetery, the priest handed the gun to Pedro so that Pedro could take it to the priest's house. As Pedro walked away, the same witnesses saw Pedro play at threatening boys and girls on the street by raising the gun to his face and pretending to fire it. Pedro had scarcely left the sight of the witnesses when they heard a shot; though they went running, they could not locate him. They did find a dead child who had a penetrating wound that ran from his chin down his right side.

Action was swift. The village mayor instantly dispatched residents to search for the suspect; they investigated houses as well as "other suspicious places." When Pedro's aunt found him, he was striking himself in the head. When she asked him what had happened, he replied that he had been imagining himself firing the gun, and it went off. The local priest confirmed his gun had been loaded. When the mayor and other residents examined the gun, they found it had been discharged; the safety mechanism was not engaged. The conclusion from the village was that the shotgun had certainly been fired after the priest had deployed it while hunting. This case ends without any evidence of a trial or verdict in Pamplona, but it demonstrates proof of neighborly concern and forensic efforts where children's deaths were concerned.

Finally, historians have described competitive settings for "male sociability and honor"—namely, gambling and sports—as flashpoints for adult violence.[48] I haven't ever come across legal sources that feature children as gamblers, but they could certainly suffer when adults played with rocks. In 1576, some older boys and male adults from Fitero decided to entertain themselves by "playing the pebble" [*jugar* or *tirar al canto*], which involved throwing a rock at a target to see who could come closest to it.[49] Out of consideration and good breeding, they invited a stranger, Pedro de Villalba, to throw the pebble first, and Pedro accepted.[50] In a loud voice that could be heard by everyone, he said, "[G]entlemen, don't mess around. The pebble is large and I am a poor wretch." When Pedro threw his rock, it struck nine-year-old Bernardo de Aguijo in the head. Blood flowed from the wound; the court used the standard phrase that the rock had "cut skin and flesh" and noted that Bernardo was in a very bad way. Bernardo soon died.

The royal prosecutor argued that Pedro de Villalba had sustained many arguments with Bernardo's father and was determined to avenge himself by attacking the son.[51] The defendant and his witnesses responded that on the day of the tragedy, everyone had been happy and in a good mood. Pedro deposed that he didn't even know the child's family, so vengeance was out of the question. Witnesses said that throwing rocks was a common pastime; the child happened to be crossing where he had no business being, given that everyone should have known that the game was in progress. The child died "because of how the rock fell."[52] Pedro himself couldn't see the child as he was throwing; the fact that the rock hit the child was accidental and unexpected, and it was really the child's fault. Plus, the child's family didn't want to go to court. Ultimately, Pedro was sentenced to five years of exile, which, as we have seen, was on the low end of sentencing and may have reflected an awareness of the possibility of accidental death.

The game of throwing a bar could be just as risky as hurling rocks, though by the eighteenth century, the court in Pamplona had created a category of crime called "accidental aggression."[53] In 1761, a four-year-old boy was injured in the head when Domingo Sánchez's pass went through a window of a neighboring house. The boy fell to the ground from the blow; the local surgeon gave exact measurements of the wound to the court and noted the boy was improving. The defendant, Domingo, admitted he was responsible for the accident in front of everyone and told the court it was done without malice. He also explained in detail to the court how his throw had gone wrong. Domingo said he had clenched his throwing hand more than was necessary. As a result, the throw did not go in the correct direction but rather swerved toward the child's house. The bar hit the kitchen window and, as it fell, struck the child's head.[54] No one had been warned that the child was in the window, nor was the throw intended in any way to cause harm to anyone. It was pure misfortune because he had closed his fist too tightly on the bar. Domingo was condemned only to costs; by the eighteenth century, the royal judges had mitigated their punishments and perhaps increased their sensitivity to inadvertent consequences, especially since this child recovered.

In 1611, children in Olague were not necessarily voicing far-fetched scenarios when they insisted adult neighbors had threatened to hurt them with sticks and stones. Such attacks not only occurred but also offer insights into what onlookers and the court expected in terms of forensic proof. Ownership of the weapon, the size of the weapon, the physical details of the setting, the emotions or lack thereof of the attacker, not to mention the actual outcome of the assault: all these aspects mattered. As for the degree of community interest in and responsibility for injured youngsters, these legal cases help to clarify which lines could be crossed and when. Purposeful or accidental physical injuries that resulted in death or harm to children did indeed allow and even call for the meddling of bystanders. Although early modern Spain had no criminal category for child abuse, child deaths absolutely garnered the interest of both villagers and the secular court, even if verbal threats against children did not.

Notes

1 For the use of the secular and episcopal legal jurisdictions by illiterate Basque speakers, Lu Ann Homza, "When Witches Litigate: New Evidence from Early Modern Navarre," *The Journal of Modern History* 91 (2019): 245–75; Amanda L. Scott, "Bullfighting, the Basque Clergy, and Tridentine Reform," *Renaissance Quarterly* 73 (2020): 489–526.

2 As a sample, see Stuart Carroll, "The Peace in the Feud in Sixteenth- and Seventeenth-Century France," *Past & Present* 178 (2003): 74–115; Scott Taylor,

Honor and Violence in Golden-Age Spain (Yale University Press, 2008); Nancy E. van Deusen, *Global Indios: the Indigenous Struggle for Justice in Sixteenth-Century Spain* (Duke University Press, 2015): Michelle A. McKinley, *Fractional Freedoms: Slavery, Intimacy, and Legal Mobilization in Colonial Lima, 1600–1700* (Cambridge University Press, 2016); José Carlos de la Puente Luna, *Andean Cosmopolitans: Seeking Justice and Reward at the Spanish Royal Court* (University of Texas Press, 2018); Chloe L. Ireton, "Black Africans' Freedom Litigation Suits to Define Just War and Just Slavery in the Early Spanish Empire," *Renaissance Quarterly* 73 (2020): 1277–319; Adrian Masters, *We, the King: Creating Royal Legislation in the Sixteenth-Century Spanish New World* (Cambridge University Press, 2023).

3 Daniel Lord Smail, *The Consumption of Justice: Emotions, Publicity, and Legal Culture in Marseilles, 1264–1423* (Cornell University Press, 2003). For an effort to include Latin America in the Enlightenment, which highlights links between the use of the law and modernity, see Bianca Premo, *The Enlightenment on Trial: Ordinary Litigants and Colonialism in the Spanish Empire* (Oxford University Press, 2017).

4 For example, the inquisition tribunal in Logroño, which oversaw Navarre, was destroyed by Napoleon's troops when they invaded Spain in 1808.

5 For the overwhelming presence of Basque in early modern Navarre, see Peio Monteano Sorbet, *El iceberg Navarro: Euskera y castellano en la Navarra del siglo XVI* (Pamiela, 2017).

6 Homza, *Village Infernos.*

7 For the Olague cases, Homza, *Village Infernos*, 72–77, 109–21, and Homza, *The Child Witches of Olague*, Magic in History Series (Penn State University Press, 2024).

8 Significantly, one father in Olague took six weeks to confront the female neighbor who had pressured his young son into naming his parents as witches. Homza, *The Child Witches of Olague*, chapter 2.

9 Margarita Torremocha Hernández, *Violencia familiar y doméstica ante los tribunales, XVI-XIX: Entre padres, hijos, y hermanos, nadie meta las manos* (Silex, 2021). Other variations of this sentiment include "Entre marido y muger, nadie se debe meter" and "La pintura y la pelea, desde lejos me la otea." Also see Edward Behrend-Martínez, "The Castigation and Abuse of Children in Early Modern Spain," in *The Formation of the Child in Early Modern Spain*, ed. Grace E. Coolidge (Ashgate, 2014).

10 For the secular jurisdiction, Juan José Martinena Ruiz, *Guía del archivo general de Navarra (Fuentes para la historia de Navarra)* (Gobierno de Navarra, 1997); for the episcopal jurisdiction, José Luis Sales Tirapu, *Catálogo del archivo diocesano de Pamplona* (Gobierno de Navarra), whose volumes run from 1988 to the present; for the Spanish Inquisition tribunal that oversaw Navarre, Marina Torres Arce, *La inquisición en su entorno: Servidores del Santo Oficio de Logroño en el reino de Felipe V* (Universidad de Cantabria, 2001).

11 Such hesitancy over torture was not necessarily true for the episcopal legal jurisdiction in Aragón.

12 Homza, *Village Infernos*. The priest's body was intact, which convinced Olague's villagers that the children had been lying about that particular detail. None of the surviving evidence indicates that Olague's adults moved from the discrepancy over the priest's corpse to doubt about the reality of witchcraft.

13 Archivo Real y General de Navarra, Tribunal Real [AGN], 013570. Significantly, some members of María's adult family, including her husband, had been expelled by Zabaldika's residents for their offensive and insulting behavior. María stayed in the village with no visible means of support; she had another young child in addition to the one she allegedly murdered.

14 AGN, 013570, 2r–2v.
15 AGN, 013570, f. 30r.
16 AGN, 096974.
17 AGN, 096974, f. 84r–v. The child-murderer tried to tell the court that he had seen the toddler walking around the edge of the well, holding onto a branch of a fig tree; when the branch broke, the baby fell in. The defendant asserted that his father had promised to go to the victim's parents to break the news; he also affirmed that his younger sister, age eight or nine, did go to the victim's home but found the door locked "from the outside."
18 AGN, 012643.
19 AGN, 012643, ff. 3r–4r.
20 AGN, 012643, f. 16r. The men used a highly specific term for the pool that contained the victim, describing it as a *pozanco* which signifies "a pool that stays on the banks of rivers when water has receded after a flood."
21 AGN, 012643, ff. 17v–18r.
22 AGN, 012643, f. 26r.
23 AGN, 015103.
24 Graciana told the court that "she saw three *gitanas* in the road, two of whom are in prison and have been shown to her by the lord judge" [". . . y en el camino vio tres gitanas que son las does les que esta en el carcel quien le han sido mostradas por el senor alcalde."] AGN, 015103, f. 1v.
25 AGN, 015103, f. 2v.
26 AGN, 015103, f. 3r–v.
27 AGN, 015103, ff. 4v., 39v.
28 AGN, 015103, ff. 45r, 46r–47r. The royal prosecutor in Pamplona urged the torture be applied quickly, for fear "the *gitanas*' collaborators would have more time to hide the kidnapped girl."
29 AGN, 015103, f. 71r.
30 I am presuming that the boys involved here were the dead child's brothers, though the manuscript does not clarify this detail.
31 AGN, 015103, f. 71r–v. On f. 70r–v, a surgeon from Anorbe testified that he did not find any injury on the dead girl, and her body was very much consumed, leaving only "skin and bones." Her body was damp and "was stuck in the dirt, a bit less than three fingers deep"; nevertheless, he "knew from her hair and her dress" who she was.
32 AGN, 015103, f. 78r.
33 The same phenomenon is a real possibility in the witch hunt of 1608–1614, though my sources do not explicitly reveal it: Homza, *Village Infernos*. Of course, an adult's conviction that a false accusation of witchcraft had occurred could produce the opposite reaction: Homza, *The Child Witches of Olague*.
34 AGN, 015103, ff. 4r, 5r.
35 AGN, 282231, f. 1r–v.
36 AGN, 282231, ff. 2v, 3r, 6r. The case ends without a verdict.
37 AGN, 283667 (1597); AGN, 284895 (1608). Dogs and their owners also could be blamed for injuries. In a quite remarkable case, villagers from Adoáin took a fellow resident and shepherd to royal court because he would not or could not control his mastiff: the dog was supposed to guard the flock but instead "went into the road and did much harm to people, and put them in danger of their lives, and attacked more than eight of them": AGN, 031204 (1654), f. 1r. The owner of the dog protested that his neighbors were simply jealous of his dog's superior abilities.
38 AGN, 15112, f. 1r.
39 AGN, 15112, f. 3v.

40 AGN, 102263.
41 AGN, 102263, f. 17v. This trial and the previous one raise the question of whether gardens owned by private people might have been opened to the wider community on certain days of the year or whether villagers expected as much.
42 AGN, 102263, f. 17r.
43 AGN, 102263, ff. 9r, 61r–v. Stuart Carroll, "Revenge and Reconciliation in Early Modern Italy," *Past & Present* 233 (2016): 101–42; Taylor, *Honor and Violence*, also discusses peace accords.
44 AGN, 102263, f. 22r.
45 AGN, 102263, f. 58r.
46 AGN, 125926.
47 AGN, 125926, compare f. 1r to f. 1v.
48 Scott Taylor, *Honor and Violence*; Colin Rose, *A Renaissance of Violence: Homicide in Early Modern Italy* (Cambridge University Press, 2019), 15, 17, 115–16, 177.
49 AGN, 294617.
50 AGN, 294617, ff. 21v–22r.
51 AGN, 294617, f. 29r.
52 AGN, 294617, f. 34r.
53 AGN, 302811.
54 AGN, 302811, f. 6v.

Select Bibliography

Behrend-Martínez, Edward. "The Castigation and Abuse of Children in Early Modern Spain." In *The Formation of the Child in Early Modern Spain*, edited by Grace E. Coolidge. Ashgate, 2014.

Carroll, Stuart. "The Peace in the Feud in Sixteenth- and Seventeenth-Century France." *Past & Present* 178 (2003): 74–115.

Carroll, Stuart. "Revenge and Reconciliation in Early Modern Italy." *Past & Present* 233 (2016): 101–42.

de la Puente Luna, José Carlos. *Andean Cosmopolitans: Seeking Justice and Reward at the Spanish Royal Court*. University of Texas Press, 2018.

Homza, Lu Ann. "When Witches Litigate: New Evidence from Early Modern Navarre." *The Journal of Modern History* 91 (2019): 245–75.

Homza, Lu Ann. *The Child Witches of Olague*. Magic in History Series. Penn State University Press, 2024.

Ireton, Chloe L. "Black Africans' Freedom Litigation Suits to Define Just War and Just Slavery in the Early Spanish Empire." *Renaissance Quarterly* 73 (2020): 1277–319.

Martinena Ruiz, Juan José. *Guía del archivo general de Navarra (Fuentes para la historia de Navarra)*. Gobierno de Navarra, 1997.

Masters, Adrian. *We, the King: Creating Royal Legislation in the Sixteenth-Century Spanish New World*. Cambridge University Press, 2023.

McKinley, Michelle A. *Fractional Freedoms: Slavery, Intimacy, and Legal Mobilization in Colonial Lima, 1600–1700*. Cambridge University Press, 2016.

Monteano Sorbet, Peio. *El iceberg Navarro: Euskera y castellano en la Navarra del siglo XVI*. Pamiela, 2017.

Premo, Bianca. *The Enlightenment on Trial: Ordinary Litigants and Colonialism in the Spanish Empire*. Oxford University Press, 2017.

Rose, Colin. *A Renaissance of Violence: Homicide in Early Modern Italy*. Cambridge University Press, 2019.

Sales Tirapu, José Luis. *Catálogo del archivo diocesano de Pamplona.* Gobierno de Navarra, 1988.
Scott, Amanda L. "Bullfighting, the Basque Clergy, and Tridentine Reform." *Renaissance Quarterly* 73 (2020): 489–526.
Smail, Daniel Lord. *The Consumption of Justice: Emotions, Publicity, and Legal Culture in Marseilles, 1264–1423.* Cornell University Press, 2003.
Taylor, Scott. *Honor and Violence in Golden-Age Spain.* Yale University Press, 2008.
Torremocha Hernández, Margarita. *Violencia familiar y doméstica ante los tribunales, XVI-XIX: Entre padres, hijos, y hermanos, nadie meta las manos.* Silex, 2021.
Torres Arce, Marina. *La inquisición en su entorno: Servidores del Santo Oficio de Logroño en el reino de Felipe V.* Universidad de Cantabria, 2001.
van Deusen, Nancy E. *Global Indios: The Indigenous Struggle for Justice in Sixteenth-Century Spain.* Duke University Press, 2015.

11
ON SEX CRIMES IN ITALY

Celeste I. McNamara

Sexual crimes are notoriously difficult to prosecute and often underreported. Stigma, honor culture, and patriarchal tendencies to disbelieve or blame victims prevent many from speaking up, and those same cultural forces work against those who do, who often find themselves struggling to prove their assault when typically the only eyewitnesses were victim and perpetrator. This is true today and was equally true for early modern Europeans. However, in eighteenth-century Venice, there were more than 150 cases prosecuted that by modern standards would be defined as rape and that by their own definitions were occasionally labeled *stupro* (rape) but more commonly "defloration," "seduction" (often "under pretense of marriage" or breach of promise), or "violation," and attempted versions of these same crimes. While this is surely a fraction of the actual instances of sexual violence, it is a sizeable sample with which to investigate how these crimes were prosecuted.

Venetian courts saw a substantial number of these cases because judges proved reasonably sympathetic to victims. Eighteenth-century Venice had numerous courts, ecclesiastical and secular, policing the illicit sexuality of its residents. The judges were Venetian noblemen, keen to preserve the stability and supposed tranquility of Venice, and sex crimes were deeply disruptive to communities. The vast majority of defloration and rape cases were handled by the Esecutori contro la Bestemmia, or the Executors against Blasphemy, a secular court established by the powerful Council of Ten in 1537 to prosecute crimes against public morality,[1] but these cases could also be found in the criminal courts of the Signori di Notte (Lords of the Night),[2] and the Quarantia Criminale (the Forty), prosecuted by the Avogaria di Comùne (public prosecutors).[3]

DOI: 10.4324/9781003486404-16

Although there were some differences in how these courts operated, their basic trial structure was fairly standard. In cases of sexual assault, they typically received denunciations from victims or their families, interviewed the complainant to determine if the case had merit, and then investigated and interviewed witnesses. Physical evidence was usually collected immediately after the complainant's testimony, while she was still present in court. Witnesses gave sworn testimony if possible, but the court also accepted unsworn testimony from children or from witnesses with only hearsay evidence; unsworn testimony had less weight but was still acceptable and usable. All witnesses had their testimonies repeated back to them; any corrections were made in the margins, and then witnesses signed or drew a cross to ratify their testimony and indicate that they accepted the court's requirement of secrecy. If the judges continued to see merit in the case, they either summoned the accused to appear "voluntarily" or issued a warrant for his arrest. If he appeared or was arrested, he was typically imprisoned for the remainder of the trial. He was interrogated, presented with official charges and a summary of the evidence thus far, and invited to make his defense with the help of a lawyer. This defense could present challenges to the evidence already collected, undermine the reliability of the complainant, and/or present exculpatory evidence or claims. The court heard his defense and interrogated witnesses he named, and then the judges—nobles who did not necessarily have any legal training[4]—voted on whether to convict or acquit, and in guilty verdicts proposed and voted on the sentence.

In cases of sexual assault, determining if a crime had occurred (and precisely how to define it) required three types of evidence: the victim's own account of the crime, accounts from family and neighbors, and physical evidence garnered through examination of the victim's body by expert witnesses. This chapter will examine the use of physical evidence in two broad types of sexual assault cases with female victims: defloration of adult women (mostly with promise of marriage), and defloration or attempted defloration of girls under 14. Defloration under pretense of marriage was a social nuisance; premarital sex was acceptable so long as marriage was on the horizon, so the real problem in most cases was the man either lying about his freedom or willingness to marry or changing his mind. The sexual abuse of minors, on the other hand, was considered a horrifying violation,[5] as reflected by the language of both witnesses and judges. Both types of cases had high rates of conviction or other resolution in favor of the victim, but there are significant differences in the compensation received by victims, and minimal differences in the punitive sentencing. In this chapter, I argue that the forensic evidence presented in these cases both demonstrates the perceived challenges of reading bodily evidence of sexual assault in the eighteenth century and helps to explain why a crime that Venetians clearly considered heinous was nevertheless punished roughly commensurately with one considered merely bad behavior.

Prosecuting Sexual Assault

Although both categories of crime under examination here were labeled as "defloration," they were prosecuted differently depending on the age of the victim. In most cases with adult victims, the allegation included a promise of marriage, and the crime was the taking of the woman's virginity under false pretenses. She thus needed to prove three things: that she had been a virgin of good moral standing prior to her relationship with the accused, that he had taken her virginity, and that he had promised marriage, either before or during the initial sexual encounter. Most of the victims described their initial sexual encounter as forced, typically in terms that we would define as intimate partner or date rape; as one woman put it, he came "with force, and with beautiful words."[6] Regardless of how we might understand the often formulaic framing of these encounters as forced,[7] this detail seems to have been largely irrelevant to the judges; at most it reinforced other claims of the victim's own upstanding morality. Much more important were claims of pain and of bleeding, both taken as signs the hymen was broken during the encounter. Whether or not she had been raped, the judges only wanted confirmation that the sexual encounter she described had been her first and that he had promised marriage.

In cases with victims under 14, the victims were assumed to be virgins before the alleged assault, and there was no expectation of a marriage promise. Girls and their families therefore only had to prove defloration or attempted defloration and convince the judges that the accused was the responsible party. Unlike other European jurisdictions, Venetian courts were flexible in the prosecution of child rapists; whereas elsewhere full penetration had to be proven (but then often carried a death sentence) or a new trial for assault had to be initiated after acquittal for defloration, in Venice a trial could easily be shifted from defloration to attempted defloration depending on the forensic evidence (and death sentences were never applied).[8] Defloration was still the more serious offense; however, so precise expert witness testimony was necessary.

Forensic evidence, in the form of physical examinations by expert witnesses, is found in both types of trials, though there are some differences in the choice of experts, the testimony they were asked to provide, and the impact of that testimony. In cases with adult victims, two licensed public midwives[9] were asked to examine the woman for signs of defloration and sometimes pregnancy. Occasionally, they were also asked about venereal disease.[10] In cases with child victims, there was less consistency. In the average case, the court summoned three experts, most commonly two midwives and a surgeon or doctor, but could rely on anywhere between one and six experts. Typically, midwives were asked to testify to defloration and vaginal trauma, while male medical practitioners were asked about venereal disease, though both men and women testified to all the above.[11] The need for additional expert witnesses, as well as the tendency to get male medical practitioners involved, suggests both the greater difficulty in "reading" a body that was not fully developed and the evidentiary difficulty in "proving" loss of virginity. It may also relate to the difficulty of trusting child witnesses, who could not give sworn testimony and who may not have been trusted to know their own bodies or understand sexual assault.

More rarely, forensic evidence could also be found in defenses. In cases where venereal disease was alleged, men sometimes presented written testimony from a doctor or surgeon to certify they showed no signs of disease.[12] However, the court found this unconvincing; in all such cases, the court also solicited the expert opinion of both doctors and midwives, who confirmed to the judges that one could be infected with venereal disease and transmit it to another person without showing external signs of infection.[13] Without a more sophisticated means of diagnosis, the men could not actually prove they were disease-free. The judges were aware, in other words, of both the value and the limitation of expert witnesses' testimonies and had clear ideas of what they could or could not read on the bodies of men, women, and girls.

Expert Witnesses in Venetian Defloration Cases

In 93 cases of simple defloration or seduction under pretense of marriage that I have examined (dating from 1700 to 1796), only 11 lack expert testimony from midwives.[14] Unlike in France, Venetian courts did not hire permanent expert witnesses;[15] instead, they seem to have drawn from the long list of licensed public midwives somewhat at random. Only two registers of public midwives remain, from 1786 to 1787 and 1790; there were 85 midwives in 1787 and 98 in 1790.[16] Over the course of the entire century, the courts called 54 different midwives to examine adult women alleging defloration. Thirty-two were called only once, and another 14 were called five times or fewer. The remaining eight were much more regular attendees at trials; one was called to examine 21 different women! There is no clear indication why certain midwives were chosen or why some were summoned repeatedly and others only once; while they tend to cluster somewhat in the middle of the city, they come from all six *sestieri* (neighborhoods) of Venice, and although the frequently summoned midwives come from parishes near San Marco, they are not necessarily those closest to the courts, which met in the Ducal Palace.[17]

Regardless of which midwives were chosen, their task was always the same. A notary explained to the midwife what information the court sought, then sent her into a separate room where the victim was waiting to perform the examination in private. She then returned and provided her testimony under oath. As this was done without supervision, it is impossible to say how much of the midwives' testimonies are on the basis of physical examinations and how much came from something the victim said to them, but they always stated that their testimony came from their expertise. The midwives examined the woman separately, but their testimonies are remarkably consistent. In every case, they both confirmed defloration, which required a complete rupture of the hymen. Midwives unanimously confirmed 29 pregnancies and provided estimated progress for 29 of them. Most were in the second or third trimester, and the midwives' estimate never deviated by more than a month. They confirmed another 19 recent births. This means that 58% of women who approached the courts did so with a baby or in the knowledge that one would soon come, consistent with research on seduction cases that finds women typically turned to the courts at crisis points, when other modes of resolution such as community pressure had failed.[18]

Midwives could also provide other information to the court. In 25 cases, one or both midwives elaborated on their expert observations. Many of these observations related to either the timing of the defloration or the frequency of sexual encounters, both of which could have significant bearing on the woman's case. Usually, the midwives' testimonies supported the woman's story, but if they testified that she had been deflowered long ago and she claimed a recent crime, or if she said they had only had sex once and the midwives judged her "much used" ("molte volte adoperata"), this could be a problem for her.[19] This was the case for Elena Nichizola, a servant, who in 1796 accused a fellow servant, Zuanne Folin, of deflowering her under pretense of marriage.[20] According to Elena's testimony, Zuanne began courting her 14 months earlier. Thrice he found her alone at home and attempted to rape her (while promising marriage). She escaped and threatened to tell her father, though it seems she never followed through. About a month before she appeared in court, Zuanne took her to the area of San Francesco della Vigna, a relatively remote spot about a 20-minute walk from her home, where he pushed her into some vegetation and raped her. Soon after, in spite of his marriage promises, he began to speak badly about her around town. She first sought the help of her sister and then her parish priest, who told her to go to the court. As she explained to the judges, Zuanne Folin was her "betrayer, having taken [her] honor," and she had "also lost [her] health" as he had infected her with venereal disease.[21]

Unfortunately for Elena, however, the two midwives who examined her at the court's request agreed that she was "entirely deflowered a long time ago" and that she had a "very deep ulcer," suggesting that the infection was not recent either.[22] Their examinations took place a week after the initial complaint, roughly five weeks after the alleged rape. Both were experienced expert witnesses, called in eight and nine cases, respectively. The final note in the trial dossier, immediately after the midwives' testimonies, indicates that the case was dropped due to insufficient evidence; even if Elena's story about Zuanne raping her was true, it seems she was not a virgin, which released him of any promise and destroyed her claim.

For the most part, midwives' expert testimonies in defloration and seduction cases involving adult women were straightforward and backed up women's stories. Whether or not they played a major role in the court's decision is impossible to say, but of the 66 cases where some resolution is noted, 43 ended in guilty verdicts, and another ten ended with some resolution outside of court (typically the accused married or dowered the victim without a court order, and she dropped the case). Only five were absolved, seven cases were dropped before sentencing (possibly outside resolutions that were not noted), and one case was suspended pending further evidence. In other words, 80% of cases were resolved in favor of victims, who all had the testimony of expert witnesses on their side, and as Elena Nichizola's case demonstrates, contradictory evidence could derail a case.

Expert Witnesses in Child Rape Cases

In the 36 cases of eighteenth-century child abuse, all but three contain testimonies by medical professionals.[23] Twenty-nine cases contain testimony by 39 different midwives, and 24 cases contain testimony by 24 surgeons and seven doctors. Thus in the vast majority of these cases judges sought expert testimony from both male and female medical professionals, in contrast to cases with adult women, where surgeons and doctors were only called as expert witnesses once to identify an alleged abortifacient.[24] The choice of midwives seems as random as in cases with adult victims; they came from all six *sestieri*, and only nine of 35 living in Venice were summoned more than once. The most called-upon midwife in both types of cases was Elisabetta Rosetti of San Paternian, who examined 21 women and six children. Thirteen midwives were asked to examine children but not women, but the remaining 21 had appeared in court at least once to examine an adult victim too. The selection of doctors and surgeons is equally opaque; they too came from every *sestiere*. Most were asked only once; four testified twice, and only the surgeon of the prison infirmary (an obvious choice for convenience) was a frequent witness, appearing in six trials.

Cases involving child victims often required more—and more detailed—expert testimony because the evidence was seen as more ambiguous.

Male and female experts explained to judges precisely what they saw that led them to nuanced conclusions. The greater ambiguity of children's bodies also meant that the experts were more likely to disagree at least a bit on what they saw. Complete disagreement is rare, but there were a number of cases where experts disagreed on whether or not a child was infected with venereal disease or just suffering from sexual trauma, or where they disagreed about whether the child was fully or partially deflowered. As this could change the nature of the crime, the question of full or partial defloration was critical; however, the judges seem to have considered it sufficient that even one expert testify to defloration. At least one expert testified to defloration in 12 of 29 cases; in 17 others, they testified about either partial laceration of the hymen or other signs of trauma consistent with sexual abuse but not with full penetration.

Although there is a general assumption that judges had a hierarchy of expert witnesses (doctors, surgeons, midwives),[25] the Venetian cases do not entirely support this. The preference to call male medical professionals in addition to (or sometimes instead of) midwives does suggest that they were granted a certain level of respect or prominence and that their expertise was particularly sought to diagnose venereal disease.[26] Yet in all but one case, male practitioners either confirmed midwives' testimonies or at most added further details (mostly in cases where midwives did not offer testimony on possible infection). Moreover, that one case suggests that the courts trusted midwives and took their testimony seriously, even while they also wanted male expert witnesses.[27]

In this case, a widow named Serena complained to the court that her seven-year-old daughter Teresa had been deflowered by her uncle.[28] After the death of her husband, Serena and Teresa took refuge with her brother-in-law Zuanne Baldan, and after Serena remarried, she left Teresa behind.[29] Recently, she had returned to Venice to visit her daughter and found her in a sorry state. She told the court that Teresa looked only five due to malnutrition, and the child explained that she was only allowed to eat once a day and that her uncle beat her. Serena noticed Teresa walking strangely, one of the common ways in which child sexual abuse was discovered,[30] and she examined the girl's genitals and found them swollen and red. When she pressed Teresa for answers, the girl told her that her uncle had raped her with a candelabra. Serena took her to a surgeon, who prescribed medication and told her to report it to the courts. When the court interviewed Teresa, she confirmed the story in childish terms, telling the judges "[O]ne evening he put a candelabra between my legs and with it he hurt me a lot and I thought I would die, but my mother is now healing me."[31]

After confirming that Teresa had not made her first communion (rendering the legal standing of her testimony dubious),[32] the court ordered her examined by two midwives. Both told the courts, "I judge, from the experience that I have, that she was not ever touched." The swelling and redness she exhibited, they argued, resulted from "a natural great heat."[33] The court did not ask any men to examine Teresa, but they did take testimony from the surgeon who had treated Teresa before, who told the court he had found the child swollen and with some hard spots on her genitals. He had asked Serena what had happened, and she had told him what Zuanne did with a candelabra. As he testified, he had no way of knowing if this was the truth, but he did offer his expert opinion that the girl had been penetrated by something other than a penis, and he seemed to accept that she had been violated somehow.[34]

The court also interviewed neighbors and the local priest and found Zuanne was a very disliked man. Although reputation was at best circumstantial evidence, the court did consider it, and a poor reputation, or *fama,* could be very detrimental to a defendant. Zuanne had apparently cast his (well-respected and liked) wife from the house after quarrels and mistreated her during pregnancy. He did not feed his niece enough. One witness offered hearsay evidence about the sexual abuse, but no one had direct evidence, as was common in cases of child abuse. The testimony did not prove that Zuanne had raped his niece, but neither did it exculpate him; he was abusive and mean and did not take proper care of the child. This plus Serena's and the surgeon's testimony could easily have convinced the judges that Zuanne was guilty of far worse behavior; other cases ended in conviction on similar levels of evidence. But they had to reconcile that with the testimony of the midwives that the child's condition could have natural causes.

At this point, the judges had to decide whether to arrest Zuanne Baldan and interrogate him and found themselves deadlocked. In five rounds of voting, they could not agree. At this point, they could have dismissed the case or suspended it pending further evidence, as they typically did when deadlocked, but instead they agreed by a three-to-one vote to summon Zuanne to be "seriously warned" and to require him to deposit ten ducats to be paid out to Teresa as "compensation for the harms suffered."[35] Such an outcome is very unusual; only two cases ended in absolution, one was suspended, one was dropped, and six are now incomplete, while 26 ended in guilty verdicts. It seems in this case that while the evidence pointed toward sexual abuse, the midwives' testimonies had enough weight to cause significant doubt to two judges, but yet they were sufficiently convinced of Zuanne's abuse of the girl that they would not completely let the case go.

Beyond the evidence provided by this case, we can also see that the courts valued midwives' testimonies through the simple fact that they kept requesting them. Although the courts could have relied solely on doctors and surgeons to provide expert testimony on both defloration and venereal disease, and indeed the testimonies across professions rarely contradicted one another, rendering the repetition of it seemingly unnecessary, they kept summoning in—and paying—two midwives per case.

Impact of Expert Testimony

Where we can best see the impact of expert testimony and forensic evidence in cases of sexual violence, however, is in the sentencing. When men were found guilty of either seduction/defloration of a woman or defloration/attempted defloration of a child, they received a sentence of banishment (if they fled trial), galley or military service, or prison. In addition, they often faced a financial penalty, such as a dowry for the victim or sometimes paying for other expenses such as medical bills, and typically the sentence could not be completed without payment of this amount even if they served their time. In cases of seduction under pretense of marriage, men were typically offered a chance to marry or dower the woman quickly and thus avoid the rest of the sentence, an option that at least some clearly took; the same was not offered in cases of child abuse.[36]

As shown in Tables 11.1 and 11.2, the difference in prison, galley/military, and banishment is fairly small, with child rapists being punished slightly more

TABLE 11.1 Sentences in months, monetary penalties in ducats, for cases with adult victims (total of 46 cases)

	Prison	*Galley/ Military*	*Banishment*	*Dowry*	*Other Payment*
Avg	32.4	36	71	163.3	20
Med	24	36	60	150	20
Min	4	36	12	40	20
Max	84	36	180	500	20
Count	24	2	39	39	2

TABLE 11.2 Sentences in months, monetary penalties in ducats, for cases with child victims (total of 27 cases)

	Prison	*Galley/ Military*	*Banishment*	*Dowry*	*Other Payment*
Avg	42.3	57	126.5	122	76.25
Med	24	48	120	150	40
Min	6	18	24	50	25
Max	240	120	240	200	200
Count	19	8	13	9	4

harshly (but considering elsewhere in Europe defloration of a child was punishable by death, these sentences are not especially harsh). While elsewhere in Europe historians have found that courts struggled to sentence child rapists due to the difficulty of proving defloration, this was not a problem in Venice. They did not need to absolve the man and bring new charges for assault or attempted rape, as was the case in England.[37] Venice's more flexible judiciary system meant that if they could not prove defloration, they simply shifted the proceeding to attempted defloration without interruption. Moreover, they were not hamstrung by sentencing limits or requirements. But while they differed little in custodial/banishment sentences, there was a larger difference in the provision of dowries. In contrast to adults, 85% of whom received a dowry, girls were much less likely to receive any money, and when they did, they often received less. Only 33% of girls received a dowry, and only 48% received money at all (dowry or other payment, typically for medical bills). The victimization of girls, then, was generally less costly to the perpetrator than the seduction of women.

The awarding of a dowry was the court's recognition that the victim's marriage prospects were damaged, and thus she would require a higher-than-average dowry in order to marry. The damage to women's prospects seems clear, and when dowries weren't awarded, there were often hints of why in the case; the lack of a viable proposal, for example.[38] For child victims, however, the picture was murkier. What exactly damaged prospects? In the 27 cases with guilty verdicts, the judges obviously felt satisfied that a crime had taken place. Charges were frequently posted publicly, and even cases that proceeded more quietly must have sparked rumors, as neighbors were summoned to testify, so girls and their families surely suffered reputational damage just like adult women. Moreover, of the 24 cases with forensic evidence and guilty verdicts, 15 children were found infected with venereal disease; one can only imagine this too would damage their future prospects. But in most cases with dowry awards, the deciding factor appears to have been defloration. Intact or lacerated hymens meant no reckonable damages to marriage prospects in 92% of cases, while in 73% of cases, even one expert witness testifying to defloration meant that a dowry was awarded.[39]

Thus, while expert witness testimony in cases with adult victims seems fairly straightforward, it was much more significant and potentially fraught in cases with child victims. Adult victims simply had to worry that the midwives would see a dramatic contradiction of their story written on their bodies, which rarely happened, whether because they told the truth or because midwives and victims had the opportunity to collude. But with child victims, although parents and guardians invariably claimed defloration in their complaints (probably aware that this was both a more serious crime and could result in much-needed financial assistance), midwives, surgeons, and doctors gave varied testimony which the judges took seriously.

The differences in numbers and choice of expert witnesses, length and variation in testimonies, and trial outcomes all point to a greater difficulty in reading the evidence of sexual violence on a child's body. Their small and underdeveloped bodies, as well as the trauma they experienced, made the tasks of midwives, surgeons, and doctors much harder than when the victim was a fully mature woman who—even if the first sexual encounter had been forced—was often in a consensual relationship with the accused at or before the time of trial. At the same time, the ambiguity of children's bodies made expert testimony much more significant; while any reasonable testimony of sexual violence was likely to lead to a conviction, only certification of defloration had a good chance of leading to critical financial support that might help the victim someday marry, the presumed end goal for nearly all women.

Notes

1 See Renzo DeRosas, "Moralità e giustizia a Venezia nell '500-'600. Gli esecutori contro la bestemmia," in *Stato, societa, giustizia*, ed. Gaetano Cozzi (Jouvance, 1980), 431–528.

2 See Sergio Baldan, "I Signori di Notte al Criminal. Un'antica magistratura veneziana nel secondo Settecento," *Studi Veneziani* 49 (2005): 191–273.

3 On the justice system more broadly and these bodies specifically, see James Shaw, *The Justice of Venice: Authorities and Liberties in the Urban Economy, 1550–1700* (Oxford University Press, 2006).

4 Shaw, 12. The Esecutori contro la Bestemmia (henceforth ECLB) had three or four judges, the Signori di Notte (SNC) had six, the Quarantia (QC) had forty, and there were three Avogadori (AC).

5 Joanne Ferraro, "Youth in Peril in Early Modern Venice," *Journal of Social History* 49 (2016): 769.

6 ASVe, ECLB, b. 8, "Contro Giacomo Michielini," fol. 1v. The allegation of force in seduction cases varied across Europe. It was never mentioned in Navarre; see Abigail Dyer, "Seduction by Promise of Marriage: Law, Sex, and Culture in Seventeenth-Century Spain," *Sixteenth Century Journal* 34 (2003): 445. It was neither expected nor unusual in Florence, Rome, and the Basque region; see Georgia Arrivo, "Raccontare lo stupro: Strategie narrative e modelli giudiziari nei processi fiorentini di fine Settecento," in *Corpi e storia: Donne e uomini dal mondo antico all'età contemporanea*, eds. Nadia Filippini, Tiziana Plebani, and Anna Scattigno (Viella, 2002), 80–81; Elizabeth Cohen, "La verginità perduta: autorappresentazione di giovani donne nella Roma barocca," trans. Marina Bocconcelli, *Quaderni storici* 23 (1988): 185–86; Renato Barahona, *Sex Crimes, Honour, and the Law in Early Modern Spain: Vizcaya, 1528–1735* (University of Toronto Press, 2003), 60. It was common in England and France; see Katie Barclay, "From Rape to Marriage: Questions of Consent in Eighteenth-Century Britain," in *Interpreting Sexual Violence, 1660–1800*, ed. Anne Greenfield (Routledge, 2012), 35, 38; Julie Hardwick, *Sex in an Old Regime City: Young Workers and Intimacy in France, 1660–1789* (Oxford University Press, 2020), 23.

7 Because these cases are often formulaic across Europe, scholars differ in how they understand women's stories, particularly as they often still sought to marry men who they claimed raped them. I, alongside other feminist historians, consider this to be a demonstration that sexual violence was common enough that this became the expected and plausible narrative, which also means that it is likely many women experienced the violence they testified to suffering. As Katie Barclay has

argued, this also suggests that sexual violence was a culturally acceptable part of courtship, "such that many women did not believe it should operate against future marriage." Barclay, "From Rape to Marriage," 44.

8 The general consensus among scholars of early modern European child abuse is that it was taken seriously and punished severely when defloration could be proven; see William Naphy, "'Under-Age' Sexual Activity in Reformation Geneva," in *Children and Sexuality*, ed. George Rousseau (Palgrave Macmillan, 2007), 120; Martin Ingram, "Child Sexual Abuse in Early Modern England," in *Negotiating Power in Early Modern Society: Order, Hierarchy, and Subordination in Britain and Ireland*, eds. Michael Braddick and John Walter (Cambridge University Press, 2001), 83; Julie Gammon, "'A Denial of Innocence': Female Juveniles Victims of Rape and the English Legal System in the Eighteenth Century," in *Childhood in Question*, eds. Anthony Fletcher and Stephen Hussey (Manchester University Press, 1999), 76; Garthine Walker, "Sexual Violence and Rape in Europe, 1500–1750," in *The Routledge History of Sex and the Body, 1500 to the Present*, eds. Sarah Toulalan and Kate Fisher (London: Routledge, 2013), 436. However, there was also widespread doubt that it was possible to penetrate young children. See Satu Lidman, "Intersections of Rape Crime and Child Protection in Early Modern Courts," in *Interpersonal Violence: Differences and Connections*, eds. Marita Husso, Tuija Virkki, Marianne Notko, Helena Hirvonen, and Jari Eilola (Routledge, 2017), 21; Sarah Toulalan, "'Unripe' Bodies: Children and Sex in Early Modern England," in *Bodies, Sex and Desire from the Renaissance to the Present*, eds. Kate Fisher and Sarah Toulalan (Palgrave Macmillan, 2011), 140; Garthine Walker, "Rape, Acquittal and Culpability in Popular Crime Reports in England, c.1670-c.1750," *Past & Present* 220 (2013): 130.

9 From 1624, Venice provided official licenses to midwives, and from 1719, midwives were expected to prove literacy and attendance at obligatory anatomy sessions to receive this license. Nadia Filippini, "The Church, the State and Childbirth: The Midwife in Italy during the Eighteenth Century," in *The Art of Midwifery*, ed. Hilary Marland (Routledge, 2005), 162.

10 The use of midwives as expert witnesses to testify about virginity, pregnancy, and venereal disease is common across much of late medieval and early modern Europe (in many places surgeons and doctors were also consulted). As training and standards for midwives improved over the seventeenth and eighteenth centuries, their expertise gained further recognition in court. See Erwin Ackerknecht, "Midwives as Experts in Court," *Bull. N. Y. Acad. Med.* 52 (1976): 1224–28; Hiram Kümper, "Learned Men and Skillful Matrons: Medical Expertise and the Forensics of Rape in the Middle Ages," in *Medicine and the Law in the Middle Ages*, eds. Wendy Turner and Sara Butler (Brill, 2014), 88–108; Cathy McClive, "Blood and Expertise: The Trials of the Female Medical Expert in the Ancien-Régime Courtroom," *Bulletin of the History of Medicine* 82 (2008): 86–108; Kirsi Vainio-Korhonen, "Midwives as Expert Witnesses in the 18th-Century Finnish Courts of Justice," *Scandinavian Journal of History* 45 (2020): 433–56.

11 On midwives as experts in ECLB cases, see also Alessandro Pastore, *Il medico in tribunale. La perizia medica nella procedura penale d'antico regime (secoli XVI-XVIII)* (Edizioni Casagrande, 1998), 161–73.

12 For an example, see ASVe, ECLB, b. 40, "Contro Magno Quinto," testimony of surgeon Pietro Vacrini, n.p.

13 For an example, see ASVe, ECLB, b. 18, "Contro Girolamo Tergo," testimonies of surgeons Antonio Pulisan and Gaetano Sartori, n.p.

14 There are a total of 117 cases/fragments of cases; the remaining cases are too fragmentary to be able to get much from them. The cases I have examined are

found in the ASVe, ECLB, bb. 7–53; SNC, bb. 3–15; QC, bb. 72, 142; and AC, bb. 4153–637. In the cases where midwives were not consulted, it is usually clear why: the case wasn't really about sexual assault, the dossier is incomplete (and thus the trial may have contained expert witness testimony that is now lost), or the trial is dropped before such evidence is collected. In ASVe, ECLB, b. 47, "Contro Anzolo Fanolo," a surgeon submitted a report, which the court may have felt obviated the need for midwives' examinations.

15 McClive, "Blood and Expertise," 87–88.

16 ASVe, Provveditori alla Sanità, b. 584, "1786 Registro delle Publiche Comare" and "1790 Registro Comare."

17 In eighteenth-century Paris, according to Christelle Rabier, proximity to the courts was the key factor in the summoning of surgeons to provide expert testimony. In Venice, it seems the courts tended toward reasonable proximity but did not simply grab the closest midwife they could find as needed. Christelle Rabier, "Écrire l'expertise, traduire l'expérience. Les rapports des chirurgiens parisiens au xviiie siècle," *Rives méditerranéennes: Expériences du corps, récits de soi, constructions du savoir* 44 (2013): 43.

18 In Florence, for example, pregnancy was the precipitating crisis in 90% of cases. Arrivo, "Raccontare lo stupro," 74, 81. In Pamplona, by comparison, only 18% were pregnant. Dyer, "Seduction by Promise of Marriage," 440.

19 For an example of this sort of testimony (though in this case confirming, rather than challenging, the victim's story), see ASVe, ECLB, b. 42, "Contro Isidoro Piazza," Testimony of Paulina Clera.

20 ASVe, ECLB, b. 53, "Contro Zuanne Folin."

21 ASVe, ECLB, b. 53, Testimony of Elena Nichizola, n.p. When discussing venereal disease, witnesses used a variety of terms interchangeably, and it is never clear exactly which disease the victim had. Mal francese, mal celtico, and gonorrhea did not necessarily map onto specific conditions consistently.

22 ASVe, ECLB, b. 53, Testimony of Anna Miotto pubblica ostetrica, fol. 6r; Elena Lucatello agreed (fol. 6v.).

23 The cases are in ASVe, ECLB, bb. 8–53; and AC, bb. 4192–584. Of the three missing forensic testimonies, one contains no forensic testimony without any clear reason; one is missing 300 folios, so it may well have included forensics; and the final one alleges inappropriate behavior and emotional seduction but not defloration, rendering forensic testimony unnecessary.

24 The surgeon and doctor employed in the prison infirmary and two apothecaries were asked for their opinion on the nature of the substance in ASVe, ECLB, b. 22, "Contro Piero Cavazan."

25 Diego Carnevale, "Visum et Repertum: Medical Doctrine and Criminal Procedures in France and Naples (17th-18th Centuries)," in *The Body of Evidence: Corpses and Proofs in Early Modern European Medicine*, ed. Francesco Paolo de Ceglia (Brill, 2020), 258; Olivia Weisser, "Poxed and Ravished: Venereal Disease in Early Modern Rape Trials," *History Workshop Journal* 91 (2021): 14–15.

26 This seems to align with how Venetians sought treatment for venereal disease (more often from surgeons than midwives), which is at least partly due to the ban on midwives prescribing any medication taken by mouth. Nadia Filippini, "Levatrici e ostetricanti a Venezia tra Sette e Ottocento," *Quaderni storici* 20 (1985): 158.

27 Gianni Buganza, "Stupro e ostetricia: documenti giudiziari, consulenza medica e pratiche peritali nella Padova penale del secondo Settecento," *Studi Veneziani* LXIV (2011): 269.

28 ASVe, ECLB, b. 26, "Contro Zuanne Baldan."

29 This was a common practice in early modern Italy, where children were understood to be part of the patrilineal bloodline. Christiane Klapisch-Zuber, "La 'Mère cruelle'. Maternité, veuvage et dot dans la Florence des XIVe-XVe siècles," *Annales. Histoire, Sciences Sociales* 38, no. 5 (1983): 1102.
30 Ingram, "Child Sexual Abuse," 70; Lidman, "Intersections of Rape Crime and Child Protection in Early Modern Courts," 22; Weisser, "Poxed and Ravished," 55.
31 ASVe, ECLB, b. 26, "Contro Zuanne Baldan," Testimony of Teresa Baldan.
32 The age of minority for girls in Venice was 14 from 1586, and children under seven were not considered responsible for their actions as they did not properly know right from wrong. Ferraro, "Youth in Peril," 764. Most European legal systems did not allow minors to offer sworn testimony, and some would not accept testimony at all from children under seven. Gammon, "A Denial of Innocence," 85.
33 ASVe, ECLB, b. 26, "Contro Zuanne Baldan," Testimony of Gerolema Valentini, public midwife of San Martin. Cattarina Saveri, the other midwife, provided a nearly identical testimony but referred to it as a "calor eccessivo naturale."
34 ASVe, ECLB, b. 26, Testimony of Tommaso Doglioni, surgeon.
35 ASVe, ECLB, b. 26, Vote of 24 September 1756.
36 Several trials contain either copies of the marriage register or a receipt for the payment of the dowry, dated within the time limit, as an indication that the sentence was not served. Occasionally there are also petitions from men who fled and who also missed the deadline, requesting clemency if they paid or married immediately.
37 Gammon, "A Denial of Innocence," 76.
38 This was true of three cases; in another the judges offered the man only the option of marriage, so the issue of her prospects was still "solved." See ASVE, ECLB, b. 25, "Contro Giovan Maria and Tomaso Rossetti;" b. 44, "Contro Domenico Ferrarese;" b. 48, "Contro Don Francesco Marotta;" and AC, bb. 4424 and 4631, "Contro Antonio Corradin."
39 It is not entirely clear why three deflowered girls were not awarded dowries, though in two cases there was some doubt about the guilt of the accused. In ASVe, ECLB, b. 34, "Contro Anastasio Valanza," the accused presented evidence that he did not have the *morbo gallico*, which the victim did, and also managed to cast doubt on the honor of the victim's family; he received the lightest sentence of six months in prison. In ASVe, ECLB, b. 37, "Contro Antonio Pasquati," the judges were split in their vote to convict, two to one. However, in the third case, ASVe, ECLB, b. 45, "Contro Gasparo Bagozzi," the evidence seemed clear and the judges were unanimous.

Select Bibliography

Arrivo, Georgia. "Raccontare lo stupro: Strategie narrative e modelli giudiziari nei processi fiorentini di fine Settecento." In *Corpi e storia: Donne e uomini dal mondo antico all'età contemporanea*, edited by Nadia Filippini, Tiziana Plebani, and Anna Scattigno. Viella, 2002.

Buganza, Gianni. "Stupro e ostetricia: documenti giudiziari, consulenza medica e pratiche peritali nella Padova penale del secondo Settecento." *Studi Veneziani* 64 (2011): 247–90.

Dyer, Abigail. "Seduction by Promise of Marriage: Law, Sex, and Culture in Seventeenth-Century Spain." *Sixteenth Century Journal* 34 (2003): 439–55.

Filippini, Nadia. "Levatrici e ostetricanti a Venezia tra Sette e Ottocento." *Quaderni storici* 20 (1985): 149–80.

Gammon, Julie. "'A Denial of Innocence': Female Juveniles Victims of Rape and the English Legal System in the Eighteenth Century." In *Childhood in Question: Children, Parents, and the State*, edited by Anthony Fletcher and Stephen Hussey. Manchester University Press, 1999.

Ingram, Martin. "Child Sexual Abuse in Early Modern England." In *Negotiating Power in Early Modern Society: Order, Hierarchy, and Subordination in Britain and Ireland*, edited by Michael Braddick and John Walter. Cambridge University Press, 2001.

Lidman, Satu. "Intersections of Rape Crime and Child Protection in Early Modern Courts." In *Interpersonal Violence: Differences and Connections*, edited by Marita Husso, Tuija Virkki, Marianne Notko, Helena Hirvonen, and Jari Eilola. Routledge, 2017.

McClive, Cathy. "Blood and Expertise: The Trials of the Female Medical Expert in the Ancient-Régime Courtroom." *Bulletin of the History of Medicine* 82 (2008): 86–108.

Pastore, Alessandro. *Il medico in tribunale. La perizia medica nella procedura penale d'antico regime (secoli XVI-XVIII)*. Edizioni Casagrande, 1998.

Toulalan, Sarah. "'Unripe' Bodies: Children and Sex in Early Modern England." In *Bodies, Sex and Desire from the Renaissance to the Present*, edited by Kate Fisher and Sarah Toulalan. Palgrave Macmillan, 2011.

Vainio-Korhonen, Kirsi. "Midwives as Expert Witnesses in the 18th-Century Finnish Courts of Justice." *Scandinavian Journal of History* 45 (2020): 433–56.

Walker, Garthine. "Sexual Violence and Rape in Europe, 1500–1750." In *The Routledge History of Sex and the Body, 1500 to the Present*, edited by Sarah Toulalan and Kate Fisher. Routledge, 2013.

Weisser, Olivia. "Poxed and Ravished: Venereal Disease in Early Modern Rape Trials." *History Workshop Journal* 91 (2021): 51–70.

12

ON THE BLIND AND DISABLED IN SPAIN

Amanda L. Scott

In 1598, in the village of Tiebas just outside Pamplona, Martín de Guerrendiaín went to the shrine of Santa Catalina to pray. Martín suffered from frantic fits and periods of dizziness, which caused him to black out and sometimes do things he would not remember. Later, he would tell authorities that this illness ran in his family and that his father had suffered from it as well. This evening, Martín walked from his nearby village of Guerrendiaín and decided to take refuge in the shrine, which was one of the only places he felt calm. He wanted to have a mass said for himself and the soul of his father, and he had brought money for this purpose, but he couldn't find the priest, so he put the money on the altar and sat down to wait. He soon fell asleep. When he woke, he went out of the church to pee, and on his way back in, he encountered a figure in the darkness. One of Martín's fits came just right then, and he became convinced that this shadowy figure was the Devil, come to steal the alms. In his altered mental state, he stabbed the figure and then headed to a different (Devil-free) church, still hoping he might be able to have a mass said. But upon arriving at the church of San Juan, Martín was arrested: a local blind man, Juan de Ciurriz, had just been stabbed, and Martín was the prime suspect.[1]

When Martín was later deposed in Pamplona, he insisted that he had stabbed the Devil, though he also explained that he couldn't think clearly when he was suffering from one of his fits and that he had been very confused about who the shadowy figure might have been. Juan de Ciurriz died shortly thereafter, but his testimony was similarly complicated: upon his deathbed, he testified that he had been *told* he had been stabbed by Martín, though he had of course not been able to see his attacker. There were no other

DOI: 10.4324/9781003486404-17

witnesses, and authorities decided to take Juan's second-hand hearsay as first-hand eyewitness testimony.[2]

Juan's brutal murder and Martín's alleged mental illness provide an entrance into the ways in which early modern courts evaluated evidence provided by victims who could not offer standard testimony about serious crimes in which they had been involved. In particular, such cases show how the sympathies of justices and court personnel could tip the balance in the favor of more vulnerable individuals, allowing for the admission of evidence that would usually not be considered or ordering additional stages or alterations of testimony. Early modern Navarrese authorities treated blind and disabled defendants and plaintiffs differently but appear to have been much more lenient in admitting alternative evidence and testimony for victims of crimes over perpetrators. Varying ability to offer standard testimony provoked flexibility among court officials, though there were limits.

The cases under consideration here suggest that what was actually written down by administrators handling violent crimes may not always capture the entire picture about how varied circumstances affected how complicated evidence was admitted and weighed. Certain kinds of illnesses and disabilities surface more easily in the Navarrese court records but were certainly just as present in other jurisdictions as well. As disability scholars remind us, early modern people navigated a range of different abilities, many of which carried different social and cultural meanings than they do today.[3] These scholars identify a social construction of disability, or that physical impairment is not necessarily the same as disability: that is to say, that in a world in which many people navigated various illnesses, mutilations, and accidents, what we might consider a disability today did not necessarily impair someone's day-to-day functioning in the past. This differs from a cultural construction of disability, which sees both impairment and disability as culturally constructed throughout history.[4] Both these models are critical for understanding how defendants, witnesses, and authorities identified and debated impairment in a legal context, for they underscore the extent to which disability was constantly negotiated, constructed, challenged, and reconstructed.

Across both civil and criminal records, references to blind deponents, plaintiffs, and victims are far more common than those of deaf individuals. Mental illness, desperation (depression), epilepsy, and intellectual delay are also frequently mentioned and are fairly consistently defined, at least by early modern standards. Many of these refer to horrific crimes, such as the home invasion and rape of a blind 15-year-old girl in 1561 or the sodomy and rape of a blind pilgrim in a hospital in Gipuzkoa; others are simple assaults and robberies. Given early modern pressures of survival to adapt and push through significant pain or physical impediment, blindness and physical disability tend to surface as identifiers in early modern trials, serving as part of a complex corpus of methods to place a person. Similarly, these identifiers tend to be binary—all or nothing—disabilities rather than a spectrum as we are more familiar with today. The blind were totally blind, the disabled were totally missing a limb, and the mentally ill were catastrophically and dangerously so. Nuances—such as the passing fits described by Martín de Guerrendiaín—were harder to prove, and courts looked at these skeptically. Still, their handling and sentencing of allegedly disabled individuals exposed recognition of their physical limitations.

Unusually diligent record keeping in the royal court of Pamplona allows for an unparalleled view into how criminal law played out procedurally and how it was experienced by ordinary defendants, both navigating disabilities and not. There were various moments in which defendants and their lawyers could submit new evidence, challenge admitted evidence, and, importantly, provide open-ended depositions or challenge opposing testimony. Importantly, unlike many other jurisdictions in Spain and Europe, Navarre preserved *all* intra-trial material. Other jurisdictions routinely threw out the ephemera of multiple intra-trial petitions and motions by attorneys to speed along the trial, as well as much of the intra-trial witness depositions. Instead, they summarized everything at the end of the trial with a short summary of what had happened and the sentence. In contrast, Navarre filed everything into tidy dossiers.

The royal court of Pamplona served as a court of second instance and appellate court—and often a court of first instance as well—meaning that multiple stages of criminal procedure were preserved in individual trial dossiers. In cases of recidivism, later trials were often combined with earlier investigations, allowing us to see how justices followed up with (or failed to make good on) threats to accelerate punishment in cases of non-compliance. In other jurisdictions, what we often view as complete judicial records are actually only part of what was once a more extensive legal dossier, we rarely are rewarded with insights into not only how a trial unfurled but also the degree to which attorneys and other administrators took interest in the trial. In Navarre, we can see how administrators went above and beyond (or shirked their duties), and most importantly, we can learn a lot about their legal strategies surrounding the production, presentation, and challenge of physical and verbal evidence. We know these things because they tell us through repeated petitions and motions; then, as today, legal process was slow and bureaucratic.

There were two primary ways that defendants found themselves in the royal prison and facing a criminal trial in Pamplona. People accused of crimes in and around Pamplona were tried in the first instance at the royal court, but if they were from outside Pamplona's immediate jurisdiction, they usually were first charged in a court of first instance in their local village or wherever they had been arrested. Some localities were ill-equipped to hold defendants, notorious for botching investigations, or otherwise unwilling to go through with the expense and difficulty of trying some defendants locally; in these cases, the accused were transferred to Pamplona directly. There were no firm and fast rules about why someone might be tried locally or at the central level, but most accused of serious crimes (e.g., banditry, forgery and smuggling, capital crimes, and many vagrants) were immediately sent to Pamplona.

Regardless of these two paths, most cases (like today) began with an official criminal complaint, which could originate with a victim, a magistrate, or the court's attorney (the *fiscal*). This complaint laid out the basis for why someone should be detained and launched an initial investigation into a sometimes vaguely articulated crime or suspected crimes. Often detention and a preliminary interview with the accused followed: defendants were usually asked in broad terms to state why they had been arrested and what they had done, as well as to identify themselves with age, name, profession, and marital and residential status. Upon being admitted to the prison, they were also physically examined, and physical features such as beards, moles, relative height, complexion, and visible impairments were recorded. Whether they had nice clothes or were dressed in rags might also be noted. Given the open-ended nature of these depositions, this part of the investigation often produced extensive and vivid life stories, though defendants rarely immediately confessed to any specific crime (though they might accidentally include incriminating information, nonetheless). On the basis of these initial depositions, the court determined whether defendants were poor enough to merit free public representation (a *procurador de pobres*) or in the case of disabled or adolescent defendants, a free special court-appointed advocate (a *curador*). These attorneys were usually one and the same, and though they could eventually be promoted as *fiscals* or judges, they clearly specialized and could become quite good at representing special-needs cases. This promotion track helps us make sense of another feature of early modern Spanish courts: both defense and prosecuting attorneys were part of the court staff and likely discussed their cases off the record. Early modern courts did not have rules about revealing evidence to opposing counsel, but opposing counsel nonetheless collaborated, for better or worse for defendants.[5]

At the next stage, under the supervision of the *fiscal* and his junior associates, witnesses who could speak to the crime were deposed and then later asked to ratify their statements. From this information, the *fiscal* drew up a list of charges—which actually looked like questions—to ask existing or new witnesses. These charges could include character statements about family, behavior, or religion. A notary who had investigated the physical scene of the crime also submitted his observations, and in cases of bodily harm, physicians might also be consulted. Defendants might also be examined for physical mutilation (suggesting a previous criminal record) or even circumcision (usually in cases involving some aspect of alleged apostasy or even espionage). The defense attorney drew up a list of his own, and both attorneys collected statements from their witnesses, including from the defendant. Following this, the court usually recommended an initial sentence, which was almost always immediately appealed. Importantly, the justices themselves were most likely not present to hear any statement or interact directly with the defendant, victim, or witnesses and instead drew their conclusions from summaries and impressions communicated to them by their assistants.

Following this initial sentence, more evidence could be submitted, and it was usually here that physical evidence that did not appear in descriptive terms in the witness statements appeared. Witnesses who had been hard to track down or were too far away to have been contacted at the first stage were included now; the defense and prosecution might also submit physical evidence like licenses, residence permits, and letters from other cities that might help prove various points in their cases. Similarly, some more enthusiastic defense attorneys also constructed blind criminal line-ups, rounding up similar-looking people and asking victims or accusers to pick defendants out of the lineup. They also might use the open courtyard of the prison for a similar purpose, where prisoners were free to wander about, with or without look-alikes or planted decoys intended to confuse and cast doubt upon accusers' testimonies.

Depending on how this secondary stage of evidence played out, as well as if there had been contradictions in the witnesses' and defendants' statements, the court might also recommend one or more sessions of torture. Torture—under the euphemism of "being put to the question"—was not intended to produce new evidence per se, but rather reconcile inconsistencies or perceived omissions in what the defendant had told the court. Under pressure of the rack, rope burn (tightly looped ropes that were pulled to cause abrasions), or waterboarding, defendants were "admonished" repeatedly to examine their own consciences and to tell the court the truth. A notary was present at all sessions and dutifully recorded all utterances, exhortations for the Virgin Mary to intercede, and, of course, any confessions (or lack thereof). Like other witness testimony, after sessions of torture, defendants were required to ratify what they had said, now in the absence of torture.

Depending on what came of this second stage of evidence presentation and production, the court then moved on to recommend a final sentence. Either side could challenge the sentence, and it was often amended: more or fewer years of exile and galley service might be amended, and fines might be added or removed. Court costs, either the responsibility of the guilty party or absorbed by the court itself in cases of abject poverty, were also assigned and tallied at this stage. In some cases—and always under the direction and recommendation of their attorney—defendants could continue to appeal the case further, leading to additional witnesses, more petitions, and more costs.

Since Navarre maintained some of its ancient privileges and autonomy, all appeals were handled internally and by the same justices, as opposed to other jurisdictions in Spain that then transferred cases to chancery courts at hubs like Valladolid or Granada.

Sprinkled among these various stages were additional levels of legal ephemera, including petitions from defendants to be placed on the prison food docket (prisoners were expected to feed themselves, but if they were too poor, the court provided what was probably terrible food), to receive firewood to warm their cells, to simply be released, or to blame other people. Defense attorneys and *fiscals* also stepped in repeatedly to demand that evidence be dismissed, certain witnesses be stricken, or to expedite the trial toward conclusion. These intra-trial petitions—though usually short and direct—provide invaluable insights into the experiences of passing through the court system and how defendants interacted with their appointed attorneys. Some lawyers seem to have specialized in certain kinds of defendants, and their cases reveal how they honed sophisticated legal strategies over their careers. For instance, Juan Pérez de Dindart—who often represented children, sex workers, Romani, and, importantly, mentally ill and disabled defendants in the 1580s and 1590s, and who also represented Martín Guerrendiaín, whom we met at the beginning of this essay—routinely constructed criminal line-ups, demanded extra time (and funds) to contact more witnesses, and relied upon other prisoners as sources of information about his clients' illnesses and disabilities while in prison. He corresponded with peers in other legal jurisdictions and spent time getting to know his clients while they waited in prison. His case records—like those of his colleagues—evoke a complex European legal world in which justices and counselors were approaching trials and investigations with open minds, creativity, and, above all, a keen interest in proof and evidence.[6]

In this context of rich record keeping, we catch glimpses of blind, deaf, and physically and mentally impaired individuals slipping in and out of trials that were directly about them, as well as about the people around them. Mental illness (as in the case of Martín de Guerrendiaín) was frequently at the center of criminal trials, with doctors, court personnel, other prisoners, and family members weighing in about its severity and the degree to which it affected daily life or implicated someone in a crime. In another case handled by our ever-suffering public defender, Juan Pérez de Dindart, a severely intellectually delayed French teenager, Bernart de Urt, was being held in Pamplona in 1589 for several alleged murders and assaults in the mountain villages along the border. Bernart also suffered from an unhealed broken leg, and the difficulty of waiting in the prison, the isolation, and the confusion of navigating a hostile and unfamiliar set of circumstances pushed Bernart over the edge, and he stopped speaking, dressing, and feeding himself. Despite his experience, Dindart made little headway in communicating with his charge.

He eventually turned to the other prisoners, who had taken over the role of taking care of Bernart each day, carrying him out into the courtyard for air and making sure he ate, "otherwise he would just sit huddled in the corner by himself." In fact, the other prisoners were some of Bernart's *only* character witnesses and provided critical information about how Bernart's disabilities (including his overall physical weakness and smallness) would have made it impossible for him to have committed any of the violent assaults for which he was accused. In one of Dindart's most notable successes, he eventually got Bernart's capital sentence overturned after stalling for weeks waiting on witnesses to appear to populate a blind criminal line-up.[7]

One of the primary questions that Bernart's case hinged upon was whether his disabilities were "genuine," something that also came up in cases of blindness or mental illness: the *fiscal* alleged that Bernart was "faking" his intellectual disability and that he was actually a different person altogether who was fully capable physically and intellectually of planning and executing the crimes. Justices, prison personnel, attorneys, other prisoners, and witnesses also debated what constituted mental illness, particularly those illnesses that caused erratic and violent behavior, which could often be concealed behind claims of amnesia.[8] As in the case of Martín de Guerrendiaín, courts drew upon a range of witnesses, present and past, to provide physical as well as historical evidence about severity, cause, and precedent. And in 1648, when the mayor of Corella went mad, stabbed a servant, ran out into the street naked, and then barricaded himself in his house with a sword, his family and the other members of the city council debated his mental illness on the basis of past vs. current actions: in fact, even the *fiscal* raised a long history of strange behavior going back as far as 12 years, including attacking a visiting archdeacon from Tarazona and chasing a chaplain with a sword through the streets and into a vineyard "for no cause or reason." Indeed, it seemed that everyone agreed that the mayor had a history of mental illness, but the current case hinged more upon whether the more recent stabbing could also be attributed to the same illness or if he had been lucid when it occurred (it is not clear why the town had elected him as mayor, knowing about these episodes).[9]

Some of the more complex cases involving uncertain mental or physical ability or impairment also reveal a striking collaboration between separate jurisdictions, each of which brought their distinctive expertise to bear in reconstructing and examining the physical evidence of suspected crimes. In 1636, a mysterious priest-pilgrim turned up in Sangüesa; he was clearly French, but none of his backstory or travel itinerary added up, and the townspeople arrested him and contacted both the diocesan and municipal authorities. Apparently suffering from epilepsy and amnesia, Don Pierre de Praxelier was unable to offer much in the way of his own defense. The bishop's court took the case—on the grounds that he might be a priest—but they relied also on secular expertise, methods, and personnel in their investigation. An assistant *fiscal* from Pamplona consulted on the case, particularly in the construction of a blind criminal lineup, and doctors, other prisoners, and prison officials offered testimony about the epileptic fits and Don Pierre's overall health while waiting in prison.[10] In another case handled by the diocesan court in 1621 in Ochagavía, church court officials likewise collaborated with their secular peers in collecting, evaluating, and, in this case, even reconstructing evidence: townsperson Martín Belza had been found dead in his house, and it was uncertain whether he had died of foul play or of suicide (the diocesan authorities were more interested in the latter, as it would mean Martín could not be buried in the church cemetery; the secular authorities were interested in the case as a potential capital crime). In this case, which very much resembled a scene out of Umberto Eco's novel, *The Name of the Rose,* authorities first sealed off Martín's house—presumably to preserve evidence—and then proceeded to carefully examine details such as whether the windows were latched from the inside and whether the front door was locked. Martín's body was examined, but the physical crime scene was ultimately more important. Finding Martín's body inside a locked house, with the key to the front door in his pocket, turned out to be just as important to the final decision as other ancillary evidence about Martín's deep depression in the days leading up to his death; Martín's death was ruled a suicide, to the dismay of his family.[11] These cases show both secular and ecclesiastical jurisdictions challenging the existence of disabilities that they could not see and looking for material evidence to prove the degree to which such conditions might impede (or indeed, halt) everyday functions.

Physical pain was also litigated to an extent, at least insofar as it could explain behavior or unemployment, but courts typically relied upon medics to determine whether the pain was felt in the way that a prisoner said it was. When a group of teens and 20-somethings were arrested in Sangüesa for vagrancy in 1582, Juan Pérez de Dindart helped the court understand that many of the youths had ailments or impediments: at least in the case of Juan Iñigo, who was identified as suffering from "a heart condition as well as a withered hand" (possibly polio), the justices handed down a modified and more lenient sentence. Physical deformities or amputations were clearer, and authorities could easily point to these as impediments.

And in 1613, a group of pilgrims traveling from Constantinople were arrested in Pamplona on charges of vagrancy and falsifying certain gruesome injuries to elicit charity. Remon Ribas of Bordeaux, Diego Julian of Lias, and Nicolas Berri of Cambray told the court that they had only recently been released from the Turkish galleys in Constantinople; indeed, they were wearing the "habits of captives" and provided a letter from the French consul of Constantinople certifying their former captivity. Yet the court was more interested in what evidence their physical bodies could tell them: Diego was "covered in tattoos," in a pattern of triangles that the court had never seen and which they assumed must indicate that he had previously been arrested and sentenced in some exotic locale. Remon Ribas "was badly burned from a navigation accident," and after ordering a thorough examination, the *fiscal* alleged that these burns "were not very bad" and that either Remon had added to them to provoke more sympathy or had even "done them to himself." Remon, for his part, told the court that the burns caused excruciating pain, preventing him from working. Because of his impediments, he didn't feel safe traveling alone and had agreed to travel with the other two Frenchmen so they could help take care of him (they would in turn be able to gather more alms due to the visual shock value of Remon's scars and his story). Despite the *fiscal's* attempt to discredit Remon's pain and suffering, the justices were convinced by the medical examination of Remon's wounds and released the entire group without any penalties.[12]

Blindness, however, was somewhat more slippery, perhaps reflecting recognition of progressive impairment (and underscoring disability scholars' reminders to treat disability as a social and cultural construct). Deponents and plaintiffs are frequently described as "alleging blindness" and were pushed by the courts to essentially prove their blindness (or sight). For instance, in 1604, the soldier Andrés de Corcuero alleged blindness amidst a different trial. He had been attacked by a dog while on military duty, which had ripped his face open and damaged his eyes.[13] In 1606, the notary Remon de Yriarte did not allege blindness, but rather sightedness, despite the fact that all his clients were certain that he was blind because he was unable to read back his documents to them. His claims to the contrary fell apart when he was asked to sign a paper and could not find the place to put his hand without the help of an assistant.[14] And in 1618, the *serora* Catalina de Imbulzqueta was forced to prove her blindness as part of a lawsuit over a donkey. Catalina claimed she was totally blind, while her opponent claimed that she was anything but and never had been blind, based primarily upon the fact that she was frequently seen walking around town without "tripping or having any falls." Townspeople testified about her mobility, and doctors were called to evaluate her for cataracts, which they did not find.[15] Ultimately, Catalina's self-identification of blindness was personal: in subjecting her to these humiliating examinations, the court produced little other than a fascinating portrait of litigated disability for future historians.

Within these self-reported descriptions, we catch glimpses of not only how blind individuals moved throughout their communities but also the degree to which blindness was normalized and treated as secondary by the courts. Justices and lawyers for the most part did not argue that blindness merited special treatment under law, while at the same time, they readily made accommodation for the unique kind of evidence that blind deponents and victims could provide. In particular, when blind victims of assault and robbery were deposed about their attacks, they relied heavily upon details that they had been provided by others who were present at the time. This was very much the case with Juan de Ciurriz, who testified about having been told he had been stabbed by Martín de Guerrendiaín, even though no one had seen Martín stab anyone. In other cases, much of the information the blind were able to provide was irrelevant to the crime or the prosecution. Still, victims may have thought it was important to include them in order to show the courts that they paid close attention to detail, thus helping bulk up the rest of their testimony, which could be quite slim.

Yet, in cases where there was no other corroborating evidence and the only description came third-hand from a blind person, this kind of hearsay was strikingly unprecedented. For instance, Francisco Cuellar, blind organist of the Pamplona parish of San Llorente, was attacked and robbed in the street on the way to a musical gig in 1571; he went into notable detail about the torches that his handler had been carrying the night of his attack, stating repeatedly "that he stayed close to the torch." In his deposition, Francisco also self-described himself as "totally blind since birth" and was completely dependent upon friends or family to lead him throughout the streets each day to work and church. He was also unable to tell the court who had attacked him, or much else about the attack, other than a sequence of events leading up to his instruments being stolen. In the end, it appears that the city watch had orchestrated this attack and that Francisco had been tricked into thinking he was being brought to a gig, only to be robbed by the police themselves.[16]

The courts also considered hearsay from the blind alongside testimony from the sighted. Some years later, another blind musician was also attacked at night and robbed; he too provided an array of irrelevant details and described the attack according to what he had been told about it. Fausto de Recalde was an organist, and like Francisco, he frequently took on additional work playing private performances (suggesting both their relative poverty and their fame throughout the city). One evening, Fausto was interrupted at dinner by "a man who told him his name was Don Joseph de Salcedo" and who was interested in contracting Fausto's musical services to entertain several priests who were visiting from out of town. Fausto went into unusual detail in his deposition, explaining that his man had described himself physically to Fausto, telling him how they had previously met and that they had previously spoken. Fausto was uncertain about this (and did not recognize Don Joseph) but relayed this evidence to the court: because Don Joseph had described himself, Fausto was able to relay a relatively complete physical description. Apart from this, much of his deposition was unusually circumspect and unusual for the kinds of evidence typically solicited by the Pamplona royal court. It emphasizes not only that he perceived the situation somewhat differently due to his blindness but also that the court was willing to be flexible about the type of evidence they admitted in this situation: blind deponents and victims were not only allowed to use hearsay evidence but also were evidently encouraged to do so in order to fill in gaps that might not exist with other types of depositions.

Though wary, Fausto decided to follow Don Joseph back to where the other priests were waiting. Fausto rarely went anywhere by himself, he told the court, and in this particular case, his 12-year-old sister, Felicia de Recalde, came too, as did two other friends, who joined Fausto along the way. Together, the group headed through the streets of Pamplona. Like Francisco, who was careful to mention that his group carried torches, Fausto curiously made a point to mention that his companions "told him that the moon was very bright" that evening. In fact, he mentioned this detail repeatedly, including "that it was bright, and you could see around you like it was day, according to the others," but with very little other context—perhaps he thought that light was an important factor in the events that would soon unfold, perhaps he wanted to emphasize that his seeing companions should have been aware of what had happened, or, as I think is most likely, he wanted to emphasize that he was aware of the situation and had taken careful note about contextual details.[17] Either way, the brightness of the moon seems to have ultimately been unrelated: like Francisco's attack, this too was a setup. Some other local youths had tricked Fausto out of his house, with plans to attack him in the street. As an unknown, Don Joseph seems to have been complicit, possibly not even a priest, and maybe one of the youths pretending to be a cleric interested in hiring Fausto for the evening.

Fausto was unable to identify Don Joseph by his voice and remained uncertain about who he was and was possibly further thrown off by the elaborate physical description that the priest had given him. The youth who attacked him, however, was familiar, and Fausto identified him as Joan de Lassa, primarily by his voice: "he knew him by the things that he then said" (Fausto's companions later corroborated this identification, and indeed, only Joan de Lassa was ultimately charged in the attack). Most of Fausto's description of the events revolved around aural evidence: he described the sound of Joan running toward him, and he described the sound of Joan's sword as he slashed at his companions. He also provided and an unusually detailed narration of all the specific things that Joan and the others had shouted at each other, fleshing out this attack with what would have probably been several minutes of dialog. Ultimately, in addition to having his instruments broken, Fausto's face was slashed open, and he was also stabbed in the face, leading to significant blood loss. Joan de Lassa would have likely been identified and prosecuted on Fausto's companions' testimony alone, but it is important that the court eagerly collected and considered Fausto's unique testimony about Joan's voice as well. Joan was ultimately charged with a special kind of assault called "half homicide," or assault with bloodshed, and with the perceived intention to kill.

The death of Juan de Ciurriz (whom we met at the opening of this chapter) at the hands of Martín de Guerrendiaín raises many of these same problems, evoking a legal milieu in which attorneys and justices had broad leeway in defining disability and modifying how evidence was admitted and handled to fit unique situations. Shortly after Juan was stabbed, other townspeople found him lying on the ground near the church. They fashioned a bed of sorts and carried Juan into the cemetery (rather than a morbid act, this was probably a practical consideration; cemeteries were often sheltered areas that were used for communal gatherings rather than just to bury the dead). A surgeon was called, who, after Juan's death, became the primary witness about the medical nature of the assault: Martín de Villava noted that

> [H]e examined Juan's body and found that he had two penetrating wounds, one on his right side towards the back, which entered in [to a depth] that it reached the mouth of the stomach [the cardia] and that the other had shattered [his rib] on the other side . . . both appeared to be made with a dagger.[18]

The surgeon was also a critical witness in solidifying Juan de Ciurriz's second-hand eyewitness testimony as primary witness testimony, particularly regarding the identity of his assailant: Martín de Villava testified that Juan had told him that he (Juan) had been told that Martín de Guerrendiaín "had stabbed him, before fleeing on the *camino real*."[19] Martín was the first witness to have heard this and helped flesh out the timeline of hearsay that informed Juan's testimony. Other witnesses filled in the timeline of events leading up to the crime, and importantly, the development and severity of Juan's blindness: Teresa de Irauziz testified that Juan had been blind for 20 years, as well as how, when the villagers had arrived to tend to Juan, they had carefully closed up the church to preserve the scene. Later, they had captured Martín de Guerrendiaín and tied him up.[20] Juan de Essaín likewise provided evidence about Juan's blindness, stating that "he knew the blindman very well and knew that he would walk from place to place with a stick as his guide." He further added that after the attack, Juan had been so disoriented that he seemed to have also walked into a wall, leading to a different head wound.[21] María de Sarassarena concurred that Juan's blindness was such that he couldn't get around without his stick and that she saw him walking, with his stick, each morning to church.[22]

Yet despite the evidence indicating that Juan was in poor shape to have identified Martín de Guerrendiaín without help—given his blindness, as well as his disorientation following the attack—Martín's attorney (Juan Pérez de Dindart) chose not to try to discredit Juan's identification of Martín as his attacker; both the prosecution and the defense were satisfied to take Juan's second-stage hearsay testimony as a first-stage eye-witness account. Instead, Dindart built his case around the uncertainty that Martín was aware of his actions at the time of his crime or that he was fully in control of himself at all. Among the statements that Dindart wanted his witnesses to speak to, primarily he wanted to show the court that Martín was in a disordered state of mind at the time of the murder: he had spent the night in the church (unusual), and he had left his horse outside without unpacking it (evidence that he was not thinking clearly). These "were acts and things that a crazy person [*un loco*] would do," Dindart declared, and moreover, they are not singular episodes, "but he frequently does and has done these things." Martín and Juan were not enemies in any way "and Martín had no reason to want to kill him, and thus if he did kill him, he would have only done so if he were out of his mind."[23]

Witnesses were remarkably unwilling to testify, and other than the priest who confirmed that Martín spent an unusual amount of time in church (perhaps signifying mental distress), neither the prosecution nor the defense was able to find other townspeople to testify, other than those who had first tended to Juan.[24] Instead, Dindart fell back on one of his other strategies and turned to other prisoners in Pamplona's royal prison who had been interacting with Martín since his arrest. These fellow prisoners—much like those of Bernart de Urt, whom we met earlier—were perhaps even more intimately familiar with Martín's illness than were even his neighbors. For days, they had been suffering alongside him and were witness to various disturbing outbursts that left no doubt that Martín was not in control of his faculties and was possibly even unaware that he had been imprisoned. Tomás de Eraso, for instance, testified that Martín had started dancing when they tried to put him in handcuffs. When he was put to bed, he wouldn't stop playing with his hands and feet; he also talked in his sleep. Another prisoner, Juan de Toloseta, concurred and stated that Martín was clearly a man "without natural reason" and that whenever they tried to restrain him, "he went crazy . . . and started jumping around and exerting himself so much that he got so sweaty that it looked like he had fallen into a well." He was also hitting himself and talking to people who weren't there and hallucinating: another witness recalled seeing him in the prison chapel sitting in front of an image of the Virgin Mary and then shouting about things coming out of holes in the walls.[25]

Despite the likelihood that Martín was currently—and had previously been—out of his mind, the court handed down an initial sentence recommending that Martín be found guilty of murder and sentenced to the galleys for five years. Immediately, Dindart and the *fiscal* appealed. The prosecution wanted a more severe sentence—a capital punishment ideally—while Dindart took advantage of the appeal to finally coerce some more witnesses into testifying. Juan's family even came forward and told the court that they did not want to see Martín punished; they too believed that he was mentally ill and had not understood what he was doing.[26] The extra time also allowed the prosecution to gather evidence about whether the illness ran in the

Martín family; the *fiscal,* of course, wanted to prove that there was no family history, and he found several witnesses who were able to state that they had known Martín's father to be a "man of reason."[27] While this was going on, Martín's behavior deteriorated further, and other prisoners provided updates that Martín had begun "painting" figures on the wall of his cell, "using only his nose," after which he would forget that he had made them, and become frightened and "say that [the figures] were trying to drown him."[28]

The appeal could have gone either way at this point, but a couple of weeks into the appeal, Dindart submitted an emergency petition: there had been an accident, and he needed a medic to come examine Martín. Martín had apparently an extremely violent fit: naked, he had lost control of his limbs and had either fallen down the stairs or had jumped. Dindart wanted the medic not only to treat his injuries but also to determine if this could finally be the evidence that the court needed that Martín was indeed unwell.[29]

When he finally arrived, the medic agreed with Dindart that Martín was unwell and diagnosed him with "mania." He described the brain—allocating certain parts to imagination, reason, and memory—and explained that these parts were not working right for Martín and that the part in charge of memory in particular "had been damaged." Whether this was from the fall or from before was not clear, and neither was what the court thought of this new evidence: like so many cases from this period, there was no sentence, indicating that the court either dismissed the case or, more likely, that Martín had simply died before the justices could evaluate the new evidence. Ultimately, it does not matter: from our perspective, 400 years later, what matters most is how the court proceeded with and controlled evidence provided by and about mentally ill and disabled individuals.

Violent crimes involving people who were not able to provide standard forms of evidence, or otherwise not participate in standard patterns of investigation and deposition, offer important perspectives into early modern legal flexibility, creativity, and empathy. Active and enthusiastic defense attorneys like Dindart—exceptional as he may be—also underscore the ways in which trials could proceed in ways that were crafted and calibrated to individual circumstances and needs. Moreover, cases involving more than one form of disability, as did that of Martín Guerrendiaín and Juan de Ciurruz, push us to consider not only how courts handled disabled victims of crimes but also intersecting forms of impairment and community support. Disability was litigated and mediated at all levels of this process, exactly underscoring the need to think about ability as a social and cultural historical construct, just as scholars of disability have called for.

Cases of assault, robbery, and murders are strikingly common in the Navarrese records for the sixteenth and seventeenth centuries: between 1570 and 1670, there are 175 cases of highway robbery, 819 cases of assault resulting in death, and 2,296 cases of assault resulting in injury, and these extant records are only between a third and two-thirds of the cases there originally were but have now been lost. Though there is some overlap between these cases, this means that the court was handling approximately one of these cases per week, at least (they were also processing over one person per day for robbery and/or vagrancy; the court was exceedingly busy and records are prolific). Importantly, cases involving blind and/or disabled defendants or plaintiffs are small among this vast number. Still, amidst the sheer mountains of paperwork, procedural motions, and witness depositions being produced, the cases of blind and disabled individuals serve as reminders that the courts were capable of proceeding slowly and deliberately. They were not simply churning out sentences but were highly engaged and interested in investigating circumstances and sifting through evidence. In a notable number of cases, they created elaborate criminal lineups or mocked-up travel routes to test witness statements. Then, like today, numerous factors determined whether individuals received better legal aid and treatment, including family connections, money, or sympathy rather than revulsion over their particular physical maladies. However, in focusing on cases involving the intersections of blind and disabled victims of crimes and zeroing in on what might otherwise seem like throwaway statements and irrelevant details about light or sound, we can sense in a different way how the courts could slow down and listen. And if we listen carefully to what they heard and were asking, we too can gain insight into the flexibility of courts in responding to non-standard testimony and diverse experience in the early modern period.

Notes

1 Archivo General de Navarra, Tribunal Real [hereafter, AGN], 40186, ff. 1r, 2v, 5r.
2 AGN, 40186, ff. 6r–v, 65r.
3 In her study of amputations and prosthetics, Heidi Hausse uses the term "the malleable body" to emphasize how fluid pre-modern experiences of impairment might be. *The Malleable Body: Surgeons, Artisans, and Amputees in Early Modern Germany* (Manchester University Press, 2023), 3.
4 Susan Burch and Michael Rembis, eds., *Disability Histories* (University of Illinois Press, 2018); and Michael Rembis, Catherine Kudlick, and Kim E. Nielsen, eds. *The Oxford Handbook of Disability History* (Oxford University Press, 2018).
5 On the professional culture of practitioners of the law in Castile, see Richard Kagan, *Lawsuits and Litigants in Castile, 1500–1700* (University of North Carolina Press, 1981), 243–44.
6 In looking for some commonalities in criminal law during the early modern period and also seeking a model that is not predicated on modern ideas about the purpose of criminal justice, Bruce Lenman and Geoffrey Parker observe a gap between popular attitudes and the formal law of the state; most people were "reluctant prosecutors." But because cases could not be proved without witnesses, the community played an important role, which was mediated and helped along by authorities. "The State, the Community and the Criminal Law in Early Modern Europe," in *Crime and the Law: The Social History of Crime in Western Europe*

since 1500, eds. V.A.C. Gatrell, Bruce Lenman, and Geoffrey Parker (Europa, 1980), 11–48.
7 AGN, 11755, ff. 115r, 117r, 128r, 127v, 128r, 129r.
8 A classic case of mental illness being debated in a legal setting is Sara T. Nalle, *Mad for God: Bartolomé Sánchez, the Secret Messiah of Cardenete* (Virginia University Press, 2001). On perceptions of mental illness more broadly, see David Lederer, *Madness, Religion, and the State in Early Modern Europe* (Cambridge University Press, 2006).
9 AGN, 16089, ff. 5r, 21r–27v, 29r.
10 Amanda L. Scott, "Hot on the Trail: Pilgrimage and Crime in Early Modern Spain," *The Journal of Social History* 57 (2023): 24–48.
11 Or rather, "an act of desperation at the persuasion of devils." Archivo Diocesano de Pamplona, C/646, N.2, f. 2v.
12 AGN, 297203, ff. 1r–3r, 8r–v, 9r, 17r–18r, 21r.
13 AGN, 284465.
14 AGN, 200711.
15 AGN, 177623.
16 AGN, 10923, ff.3r, 3v–5r, 7r, 10r, 23r.
17 Elizabeth Bearden cautions us to be careful with narratives of "compensation" or overcoming. Focusing on the goal to move past disability and more resemble people living without disabilities casts disability more like a personal fault. *Monstrous Kinds: Body, Space, and Narrative in Renaissance Representations of Disability* (University of Michigan Press, 2019), 8–9.
18 AGN, 40186, f. 6r.
19 AGN, 40186, f. 6r.
20 AGN, 40186, ff. 7v–9v.
21 AGN, 40186, f. 10r.
22 AGN, 40186, f. 14r.
23 AGN, 40186, f. 65r.
24 AGN, 40186, f. 80r.
25 AGN, 40186, ff. 86v–87r, 88v.
26 AGN, 40186, ff. 99r–v.
27 AGN, 40186, ff. 110r–v, 111r.
28 AGN, 40186, ff. 104v, 105v, 106r–v.
29 AGN, 40186, f. 114r.

Select Bibliography

Bearden, Elizabeth. *Monstrous Kinds: Body, Space, and Narrative in Renaissance Representations of Disability*. University of Michigan Press, 2019.

Burch, Susan, and Michael Rembis, eds. *Disability Histories*. University of Illinois Press, 2018.

Eyler, Joshua R., ed. *Disability in the Middle Ages: Reconsiderations and Reverberations*. Routledge, 2010.

Gatrell, V.A.C., Bruce Lenman, and Geoffrey Parker *Crime and the Law: The Social History of Crime in Western Europe since 1500*. Europa Publications, 1980.

Hausse, Heidi. *The Malleable Body: Surgeons, Artisans, and Amputees in Early Modern Germany*. Manchester University Press, 2023.

Kagan, Richard. *Lawsuits and Litigants in Castile, 1500–1700*. University of North Carolina Press, 1981.

Lederer, David. *Madness, Religion, and the State in Early Modern Europe*. Cambridge University Press, 2006.

Nalle, Sara T. *Mad for God: Bartolomé Sánchez, the Secret Messiah of Cardenete.* Virginia University Press, 2001.
Rembis, Michael, Catherine Kudlick, and Kim E. Nielsen, eds. *The Oxford Handbook of Disability History.* Oxford University Press, 2018.
Scott, Amanda L. "Hot on the Trail: Pilgrimage and Crime in Early Modern Spain." *The Journal of Social History* 57 (2023): 24–48.

13

ON THE UNDEAD

Francesco Paolo de Ceglia

Introduction: A Medical Nightmare

The nightmare took shape in the late autumn of 1731, when Lieutenant-Colonel Schnepper, commander of the Habsburg militia in the Serbian district of Jagodina, was asked to investigate a series of suspicious deaths that had recently occurred in Medvegja, a village on the border of territories recently taken from the Ottoman Empire. Judging the problem to be a common epidemic, Schnepper sent a small commission there, which included a *Contagion-Medicus,* that is, a specialist in infections and quarantines, whose name was Glaser. Glaser arrived in Medvegja on December 12. Although he found some general malnutrition resulting from the fasts that the Orthodox tradition imposed on the faithful during the Advent season, he uncovered no evidence of "any disease or contagious situation."

Nevertheless, Glaser had to report a problem. Thirteen people in Medvegja had died in the previous six weeks, and almost all of them had complained of side twinges, tightness in the chest, and exhaustion before they expired. Glaser did not know what the exact cause of these deaths might be, but the villagers did: no ordinary circumstances had caused "all these funerals, so quickly, one after the other"; rather, so-called vampires or bloodsuckers were to blame.[1]

In the presence of local authorities, Glaser tried to explain that it was all superstition and that the dead did not return, but he wasted his breath. Villagers were terrified and furious; some threatened to leave the village. They demanded that the authorities proceed with the "execution of those so-called vampires." What should be done?

DOI: 10.4324/9781003486404-18

This essay delves into the events of 1731–2 from the perspective of both forensic medicine and the imagery involved in recognizing and annihilating the walking dead in the Balkans. It then compares the 1731–2 episode with the events of 1755, when vampire phobia was ended by legislative action. Significantly, medicine not only created but also reduced the fear of vampires when it was invoked by political authorities.

The Stigmas of Solitude

In December 1731, everyone in Medvegja was particularly angry with two women who had died only seven weeks earlier: the two females allegedly "had been vampirised [*vervampyret*] while alive, and after their deaths had themselves become vampires and were said to vampirise others." The older one, named Miliza, had come from the Ottoman areas six years earlier. When she was alive, "she told her neighbors that in Turkish territory she had eaten two sheep killed by vampires, and consequently, after her death she too was thought to have become a vampire." The other woman, who was younger and known as Stanno (or Stana, according to a different report), had died in childbirth along with her baby. She

> had told her neighbors that when she was still in Turkish territory, where vampires ruled, she had once rubbed herself with the blood of a vampire in order to protect herself from them. Thus it was said that after her death she too would become a vampire.[2]

The tropes were always the same, more or less. A small town on the edge of the Habsburg dominions experienced a moment of crisis, such as the sudden death of several members of the community. Responsibility for the crisis was attributed to individuals who supposedly knew the traditions of Turkish infidels and who, in turn, became responsible for their own posthumous abnormalities, whether real or presumed.[3] Medvegja had an exceptionally mixed population: some families had lived there for a long time, but the village also housed refugees from the Ottoman Empire and representatives of the Habsburg militia. It was not an environment that lacked social conflict.[4] It consequently matters that the alleged vampires in December 1731 were two women who lived in a certain degree of marginality vis-à-vis the larger community. What made that marginality all the greater was the fact that, so far as we can tell, they lived alone. Miliza and Stanno rose from the dead first and foremost due to loneliness, that is, because they lacked families willing to claim their decomposed bodies.

Glaser was not a surgeon, but urged on by the crowd, he found the two dead women almost intact. [In fact, they were not; see later.] The first, the elder, was described as possessing "a thin and dry constitution," which indicates she was perhaps ill or experienced difficulty in obtaining food. Yet villagers insisted she had put on weight after being buried. Modern historians of medicine would propose that her corpse was in an "emphysematous phase," meaning that she had air spaces or pockets in tissues and organs that typically were not filled with air. For the locals in 1731, however, a skinny corpse getting fat could only mean that it was sucking the energy, strength, and very life of villagers from a distance. The second corpse was in good condition, "as was the first, and so was the premature baby. Since this child had not yet been baptized, they had not laid him in the cemetery but behind a fence near where the mother had lived." There was no mention of a father.

Four other dead individuals were more or less intact, like the women, while nature had taken its course in the remaining cases, including the wife and small child of the local *hadnack* or lieutenant. It is hard to establish the extent to which the certification of the more or less advanced decomposition of a body corresponded to the recording of empirical evidence or was the result of prejudices, narratives, pressures, external influences, and negotiations. Glaser did not have very much to say on the causes of the phenomena, but he did point out that the locals "respectfully request that, after an expert's report, an execution [of the vampires] be granted by the exalted authority in order to avoid this evil. I considered it expedient to try and calm these individuals."[5]

The report that Glaser cobbled together has been described as "rather confusing but discreetly disturbing." It did not exhibit any clear-cut position, but it did seem to give credence to village rumors: at one point, Glaser noted, "I can't blame these people."[6] This was not what Lieutenant-Colonel Schnezzer was expecting to read and, realizing the thorniness of the matter, he forwarded Glaser's report to the High Command in Belgrade, which in turn acted swiftly on what appeared to be a highly serious matter. The order immediately went out for military surgeon Johann Flückinger to go to Medvegja in the company of a handful of officers, two of them surgeons like himself. Flückinger arrived there with his colleagues on January 7, 1732. His objective was not simply to look, as Glaser had done, but to penetrate the corpses with his surgical instruments in order to uncover the possible curse they bore. He sought evidence of the devil's kiss, and he would find it, sure as his name was Flückinger.

Finding the Arch-Vampire, or Patient Zero

Waiting in the village were the dead. They were unburied, as if to demonstrate how easy it was for them to return from that underworld into which the living had too hastily forced them. Meanwhile, Flückinger wondered how all this could have happened. He tried to put the facts in order, to tie up the threads of events, and to identify a root cause. So, who exactly had introduced the infection?

Voices quickly came to him, albeit from the living, of course. They relayed an ugly story about Arnold Paole, who had died falling out of a hay wagon some five years earlier and had returned shortly afterwards to torment the living. Whether or not Arnold Paole was his real name is doubtful, since *Arnaut* was the nickname the Turks gave to the Albanians; very likely, he could have been known as Paul the Albanian, and because he probably hailed from territory under Ottoman control, he may have seemed to have embodied all of its danger.[7] His body had been found in an almost incorruptible state; villagers cut off his head and, before consigning him to the purifying flames, pierced his heart, whereupon a hissing sound was perfectly audible. Locals took that hiss as a sign that his evil residual life was imprisoned in his flesh.

By the time Flückinger arrived, though, nothing remained of Arnold Paole: even his ashes had been scattered. His story also was rather old and thus not a likely cause of what had been taking place over the last months. Nonetheless, the idea of a single culprit seemed more convincing and simpler than the notion of two independent vectors (Miliza and Stanno) to the point that villagers suddenly remembered that four people had died immediately after him and hence, because of him. The connection seemed logical. Yet if the same tale had also been told to Glaser, there probably would have been a trace of it in his writing—and instead, nothing. The discrepancy reveals how village versions of the facts were nourished by events, real or presumed, forgotten or considered secondary, but then subjected to incessant narrative re-elaboration.

Arnold Paole was thus identifiable as "patient zero": he had started everything in Medvegja. Of course, he could also be designated as "zero" because nothing of him remained. On that missing body—as if it were a blank canvas—a thousand portraits could be painted and endless stories told. However, it was now necessary to fill the five-year time gap: how could someone who had already died twice and been dead for quite a few years continue to cut lives short? The rogue, it was explained, had attacked not only human beings but also animals; when the latter had been eaten, they had transmitted their vampiric charge to some of the villagers. The problem was solved: the link between past and present was finally established.

Vampire Autopsies

Glaser was a physician and could only carry out a superficial reconnaissance. Not so Flückinger, who proceeded by performing autopsies on the vampires. The first to be examined was the body of Stanno, who was most certainly thought to have been a vampire, since, the surgeon pointed out, "[W]e found her body mostly intact and uncorrupted." Flückinger seemed sure of this lack of decomposition, although he also described the poor woman's uterus as "in a state of complete putrefaction," and reported that "the skin of the hands and feet, with the old nails, had fallen off spontaneously, showing underneath a fresh, living skin with new nails": in other words, there was no tissue reformation, as he judged, but rather a common post-mortem exfoliation of the epidermis.[8] Stanno had died in the prime of life and in childbirth. In some ways, she was a perfect candidate to remain there, trapped between the two worlds of the living and the dead. Conversely, not much could be understood about the child, who had been "half-eaten by dogs, due to a botched burial."

Still, it was Miliza who played the key role in Flückinger's interpretation, not because of her bodily remains but because she could be declared the link between the episodes of five years earlier and the recent ones. Villagers opined, "[I]t was she who had given rise to the present vampires, since she had eaten the flesh of the sheep that had been killed by the previous vampire."[9] That "previous vampire" was Arnold Paole.

Flückinger's investigation was hasty—13 corpses examined in the space of a winter afternoon—and fairly unsystematic. He was not interested in or even capable of investigating the real causes of death, which might perhaps have shed light on the dynamics of preservation. Nothing is known of the weather conditions during those weeks that villagers had expired, except that there had been abundant rainfall. Whether the soil had affected decomposition at least occurred to Flückinger since he expressly emphasized that the alleged vampires and the other corpses had been deposited in similar types of earth. He did not want to play the fool.

On the contrary, in comparison with Glaser, who had found himself catapulted into the situation unexpectedly, Flückinger had enough time to draw up a more assertive report in which, without mincing words, he would finally speak of bodies "in a vampiric condition" [*im Vampyr-Stande*]. He said it himself, without feeling the need to hide behind the words of the villagers. One had to take responsibility. And Flückinger was convinced: vampires did indeed exist. Even his autopsies had proved it.

Therefore, from the standpoint of public order, the "executions" demanded by the villagers were justified, and they were carried out by the local Roma community. "After the examination had been carried out, the heads of the vampires were cut off by the local gypsies and then burnt together with the bodies"; the ashes were then thrown into the Morava River. (The decomposed bodies, on the other hand, were placed back in their respective graves.[10]) That it was precisely the Roma community that was chosen to celebrate this heinous ritual seems to have derived from a real, almost professional, specialization in this type of cleansing, developed within the Roma groups scattered across the Balkans.[11] The situation in Medvegja had finally been resolved; one could breathe a sigh of relief. The vampires would no longer bother anyone.

The Year of the Vampires

When Flückinger's report reached Vienna, it caused an uproar in diplomatic circles by alerting authorities that the dead were strangely rising on the borders of the Habsburg Monarchy.[12] Then, no one knows how, the same report reached The Hague, Holland, where the editors of the *Glaneur historique*, a cultural journal published in French so as to reach the whole of Europe, decided to publish it in March 1732 in an article entitled "Scientific question on a kind of duly attested prodigy." The adverb "duly," with its peremptory tone, implied that the fact of vampires was certain. What was needed now were explanations.[13]

The report's effects were far-reaching. As Lutheran deacon Michael Ranfft noted, "These facts threw everyone into amazement." Soon, the news that the dead could come back to haunt the living monopolized conversation:

> Wherever people met, no matter whether they were people of the upper or lower classes, they talked about it. Even the ladies began to discuss it. . . . At the last Easter fair in Leipzig one could not enter a bookshop without seeing something about bloodsuckers.[14]

It was 1732: the so-called year of the vampires had begun.

Consequently, vampires leaped from one page to the next, creating a huge wave of fake news that fed on factoids: false facts (almost always the same) or even true ones, but reported in such a way that they gave rise to inconsistent conclusions. Such ambiguity might have been indebted to the literary nature of the publications in play; they were journals whose authors had little access to new information from the field and who instead indulged in erudite reflection. It was the era of "according to me," though at a high level. This paved the way for what historian Richard Sugg, by amusingly putting the words *vampire* and *entertainment* together, has christened "vampotainment."[15]

The Heart of Darkness of Europe

At the same time, the dead's desire to return among the living, which Latin texts called *magia posthuma*, was a terrifying possibility. This was similar to a problem that arose in the context of witchcraft: if the witch was not reduced to ashes, a worse future evil would occur. It was easy for all who died after her and were buried in the same cemetery to become specters [*spectra*] like her, as experiences in many places testified:

> The common man believes that the first spectra [*Gespenst*] blew [*anzublaßen*] on the other dead bodies that were buried later: I quote the words

> as I heard them. And that because of such a blowing [*afflatus*] they must all wander about [*circumcursitare*]. We have heard that the innocent dead children also wander (which is astonishing), which is why their corpses must also be burnt.[16]

In fact, this hideous chain reaction had been occurring in Silesia and Moravia several decades before the events in Medvegja.[17] Between these two regions, dozens of bodies at a time were exhumed, drawn, quartered, decapitated, and consigned to the purifying flames. In many instances, children's bodies were subjected to the same rituals: due to the incompleteness of their life course, even baptized children were felt to be peculiarly prone to return.[18]

It was enough to bury someone accused of *magia*, or suicide, or suspicious behavior for them to exercise their posthumous contagion by becoming the arch-vampire of small chthonic communities. Once introduced into the cemetery, the arch-vampire would take to "blowing" his own posthumous magic underground, and the innocent would be transformed into spiteful revenants: to ascertain their presence, ashes would be scattered around their graves; the next day the footprints of little running feet were thought to be seen on them.[19]

Upon digging in the cemetery, a not-so-decomposed corpse was always found to blame in one way or another. A neutralization ritual was then performed, and the matter could be considered closed there. If, however, the general situation did not improve, fear was inflamed by the possibility that the cause might be more extensive than anticipated. If apparitions and misfortunes did not abate, someone buried was still blowing their posthumous magic.

The consequences here are easy to imagine. The proliferation of posthumous magic carriers—all of whom needed to be exhumed—transformed cemeteries into veritable open-air construction sites. Families inevitably clashed over who should be dug up, not least because of the infamy that would fall on other relatives, whether living or dead. Everyone pushed for the malefactor to be identified as someone who had expired after the loved ones they wished to safeguard. There were also those who—whether because of alleged revenants or local abuse—gathered their despair into a bundle and set off, even without a destination:[20]

> They forced daughters (a horrible thing) to drag their mothers' bodies, to hand them over to the executioner. . . . Poor sick people, women about to give birth, flee, finding death along the way, content at least to avoid infamy after death. These inhabitants, in perpetual fear, are ready to move elsewhere. In a word: everything is disorder.[21]

Clearly, it became necessary to set up a broader organizational process aimed at the recovery, that is, the production, of undecomposed corpses.

In Search of Signs

Pulled from the grave and awaiting the decisions to be made, the more or less undecomposed body was guarded by armed men, who would intervene at the first suspicious manifestation of life. Frequently, a stone was placed in the presumed undead's mouth, which was tightened with a rag or a rope. In some cases, the coffin or the corpse itself was then hung so that it did not touch the ground, perhaps because it was thought that it would draw strength from the earth.[22]

At first, there were no experts on the "signs" of posthumous magic that were supposed to be seen on the bodies of those unearthed. One clue was certainly a lack of decomposition, but must that state be total or partial? With a noxious odor or without? People in charge proceeded by trial and error, but they took as a model the identification of stigmata, which ordinary witches retained on their bodies as a sign of their pact with the devil. In identifying the particular stigma, however, people's imagination could be very lively. In an episode in Breslau, for example, "a magical mark is observed on the big toe of the right foot, a growth in the shape of a rose."[23] At the same time, our surgeon Flückinger noticed "on her right side, below the ear, a blue mark injected with blood, the length of a finger," in the body of "Stanoika, the 20-year-old wife of a brigand," who allegedly had been suffocated in her sleep by a vampire named Miloe.[24]

At first, gravediggers were called upon to conduct the investigations. No one knew better than the rituals that had to be observed around the living dead, when the latter would hurl curses at anyone who discovered their hiding places. Furthermore, gravediggers knew how to distinguish failure to decompose from putrefaction, and they might also be able to discern something on the corpse that resembled a sign of the devil, such as a wart or an irregularly shaped mole. Gravediggers traditionally had been socially marginalized. But from the second half of the seventeenth century, with the explosion of the vampires' "collective return" in Moravia and Silesia, they became experts to whom the fate of the community could be entrusted. It was then that specialized gravediggers from the epicenter of the purported undead acquired an unprecedented visibility. In other words, they became professionalized, which allowed them a certain social ascendancy.

These new professionals were in high demand, as were executioners, and their fees rose accordingly.[25] The purported vampire's family suffered in turn since they had to pay for every expense, even if they risked financial ruin.[26] Family members often were forced to take an active part in the exhumation procedures, if nothing else, dragging their loved ones with long ropes out of the cemetery to hand them over to the executioner. As for the community's trust in the gravedigger professionals, the latter explained their gifts in a variety of ways. When one was asked how he was able to identify the graves that needed to be exhumed, "he replied that he had a plant that enabled him to recognize all the suspicious graves when he ate it. But he could still recognize them without eating it, when he arrived at the cemetery."[27] Magic or hallucinatory effects? Who can say? Some people who were called upon to handle cases of posthumous magic were deeply frightened; they consequently decided to use long hooks to proceed with their observations without even taking the corpse out of the grave. Such became common practice.[28] And yet the protocol could change. At times, the expert gravediggers were replaced or flanked by health workers such as barber-dentist-leechers, who were able to make incisions in suspicious bodies to ascertain whether blood would flow out. Nothing very scientific, in truth, as those with a university education would note with reproach: "two butcher-physicians, who have never seen a desiccated corpse; who knew nothing about the structure of the human body, as they themselves confessed to the commissioners, are the witnesses who pass the fiery sentence."[29]

To be fair, in some of the thornier cases, such as that of Liebe (today Město Libavá) in the 1720s, surgeons and doctors were consulted, and they even proposed establishing an observation crypt where suspicious corpses could be placed.[30] But such consultations and recommendations were the exception rather than the norm: instead, generalized disinterment was institutionalized, and a sort of "vampire factory" was created, with dozens of corpses unearthed at a time. Exhumations nearly became the order of the day.[31] In the aforementioned village of Liebe, which experienced numerous waves of panic, the bodies of 13 adults (11 women and two men) and 60 children were unearthed and destroyed in 1726–7 alone.[32] Yet the more they dug, the more undecomposed corpses they found and the more terror spread. The situation was clearly out of control. The question is simple: how did we get here?

The Vampire: From Criminal to "Demon Saint"

Let us proceed step by step. Until roughly the middle of the seventeenth century, when speaking of the walking dead in these Hapsburg borderlands, one did not so much call them "witch" or *Hexe*, or, as some would later do in a highly refined legal Latin, *Maevia*. Rather, they were labeled as "spirit," *Geist*, or "spectre," *Gespenst*. The elimination of the undead corpse required the permission of the civil authorities, whether local or conceivably the Court of Appeal in Prague. Permission was also sought from the church because of the sacrilege involved in disinterring a properly buried body. But as long as the area remained under the influence of the Protestant Reformation, the rather isolated parish ministers, faced with angry mobs, had no possibility of opposing those mobs' demands, whether they agreed or not. In short, the revenant was treated as a criminal and dealt with by secular justice.[33]

While the local political and administrative apparatus was not particularly strong, it was the church that bore the greatest responsibility in the building of the "vampire factory." By the start of the eighteenth century, Silesia and

Moravia were Catholic: though they had flirted with Lutheranism, they had been slowly and forcibly brought back to the Roman faith. With a renewed Catholicism, the church had become an instrument that the Habsburg Monarchy used to bring order to lands perceived as ethnically heterogeneous.[34] Catholic clergy were supposed to help local secular administrators by bringing order to life in the more peripheral, mountainous, and "pagan" areas, which were exactly the same areas where the undead manifested themselves most vividly.[35]

While Lutheran pastors had not been able to do much, it was also true that their denomination did not aspire, unlike the Catholic one, to manage relations with the afterlife, which God would take care of directly. Luther himself had said repeatedly, "Let the dead bury their own dead" (Mt 8:22; Lk 9:60).[36] Once re-established, however, Catholic bishops and Catholic religious orders took control and refused to retreat in matters that fell under their jurisdiction, such as cemeteries and relations with the world of the dead.

And yet, Catholicism did not make the eradication of the undead easier or faster for local communities, which desperately wanted to get rid of revenant bodies. The church had already symbolically recaptured the cemetery; now, it updated the permissions it had to give for exhumations, whereby it turned matters into actual trials. As the procedures for recognizing the undead became more complicated, so too did the centrality of decision-making come to rest on bishops and related authorities, as well religious-chivalric organizations, such as the Teutonic Order. While these trials might have echoed early modern prosecutions of stereotypical witches, here, there was no defendant able to admit his crimes: the vampire witch was dead and could not be subjected to torture in order to extract a confession. This obstacle led to new legal emphases on the basis of cross-examinations of witnesses and cadaveric inspections. The process increasingly looked like a tragic parody of a saint's canonization, in which the same sort of incorruption was sought but turned toward proof of vampirism. Thus, what had been a cursory assessment of alleged undecomposition turned into a longer, complicated procedure of grueling inspections and interrogations. Villagers knew that from the moment a suspicious corpse was interred, it could blow its posthumous magic on whoever was also consigned to the earth; they began to live as if they existed in a bubble of despair. Each time they had to wait for permission to burn, as the suspicious bodies piled up. Then, with the fires, came a modicum of relief . . . until the next emergency, when they had to start all over again.

When Europe Discovered the "Vampire Factory"

The *casus belli* erupted in 1755, in Frei Hermersdorf, between Moravia and Silesia, which today is Svobodné Heřmanice, in the Czech Republic. Here are the facts. It seems that during her lifetime, Rosina Polackin—or rather

Wolackin, as manuscript records seem to attest—worked as a healer.[37] It was her familiarity with arcane forces that caused villagers to view her with suspicion. Thus, when she died on December 22, 1754, she was soon accused of being a potential vampire. The villagers did not want her in the local cemetery, but the family insisted, and in the end, they won. Rosina was consequently buried in consecrated ground.[38]

People protested that burial because they said they had seen Rosina at night. They also affirmed that she was performing strange and frightening phenomena that only someone animated by posthumous magic could have achieved. Thus, on January 19, 1755, Rosina was exhumed by the exasperated villagers, who found she was more or less undecomposed. They in turn filed a plea for cleansing, which the Catholic bishopric of Olomouc approved on January 30. Rosina had been dead for slightly more than a month; on January 31, she was consigned to the flames.

In truth, although only Rosina's name appeared in the chronicles, a total of 19 corpses were incinerated at that time.[39] As in previous cases, the episode would have passed in silence if the newspapers had not begun to decry the events. The stories were not carried in the Austrian periodicals, which could not write too freely, but they appeared instead in publications from Austria's lifelong frenemies, the Prussians. Frederick II of Prussia—who had already waged two wars against Maria Theresa of Habsburg with the intention of taking Silesia from her and who was about to start a third—took the opportunity to launch a media attack on her. He endorsed the idea that these barbaric events resulted directly from the dogmatism of Catholics and the inability of the Austrian sovereign to handle the situation. As a demonstration that newspapers in the eighteenth century strongly fueled public debate and affected monarchical decisions, one article about the events in Medvegja opened the European debate about vampires, and then another one, about the events in Frei Hermersdorf, would shut it down.

Conclusion: Science in the Service of Politics

Inquiries on the vampire situation in Habsburg dominions had already begun.[40] Nevertheless, decisions could no longer be postponed: if the aim this time was to take legislative measures, then evidence had to be collected, scrutinized, and presented in an uncontroversial manner. Maria Theresa did not delay. On February 8, 1755, she commissioned the best that the Habsburg scientific community had to offer for an investigation: the famous Dutchman Gerard van Swieten, who was her primary physician and the de facto plenipotentiary minister of health. Swieten did not go to the scene in person, but he had assistants who did: Johann Lorenz Gasser, professor of anatomy in Vienna, and Christian Franz Xaver Wabst, proto-medical officer of the Imperial-Royal Army.[41]

Once Gasser and Wabst reached the places concerned, they immediately realized what needed to be affirmed. The lack of decomposition in the corpses was due to natural causes; the greater than normal deaths were due to some epidemic. They believed panic had done the rest. They sent their materials to van Swieten, who examined them and then drew up a comprehensive document to be submitted to the monarch.

Notes on the Silesian Vampirism of the Year 1755 was the title of the report that van Swieten, with the full weight of his authority, drafted for Maria Theresa. It was on the basis of his collaborators' findings, and it took the shape of a recommendation to the monarch. The text, originally written in French and soon translated into other languages, must have been ready between the end of February and the beginning of March. Its exact date of composition is not precisely known. van Swieten pointed out that, Prussian assertions notwithstanding, the Catholics had nothing to do with the superstitions about posthumous magic; rather, "it [was] most probable that the schismatic Greeks are its main authors."[42] That interpretation was forced: while the influence of Slavic culture was undeniable, the blame could not be placed (directly) on the Orthodox Church. However, van Swieten, as a partisan, wanted to ensure the triumph "of Holy Roman Catholicism," as it was called, and he had to protect, on the one hand, Her Majesty, and, on the other, the Pope.[43]

Upon questioning the witnesses to the undead, it turned out that no one had actually ever seen a corpse rise and show up at their relatives' houses. Even the alleged *poltergeist* events were, on closer inspection, very natural phenomena. Some witnesses charged that an animal had appeared out of nowhere, but

> Did the devil then need to animate a human corpse to appear as such a figure? . . . A dog, or especially a cat, if they are black and seen at night, are always taken for the devil or for a spectre, wandering around or inside a cemetery.[44]

Van Swieten then asked pragmatically who had dared to ascertain that the alleged vampires were not corrupt. The answer was straightforward: namely, ignoramuses, that is, two surgeons or, rather, barber-dentists who had never participated in an anatomical dissection. He added that "[I]t is true that the Commissioners of Olmouc did not always use surgeons to examine the facts, but they sometimes sent only spiritual commissioners." Yet it did not take long to realize that in winter, after only a month, a body could still look intact: "[A]natomists keep corpses in the open air in the winter season for six weeks or even two months without putrefaction. It should also be noted that this winter was harsher than usual."[45]

The story had to be told in full, and van Swieten did not shy away from quickly unraveling the web of facts that had brought Rosina's case to international attention. Rather than acting as a diabolical perpetrator, that poor woman was the latest proven victim of the belief in posthumous magic. Furthermore, the last wave of panic about a dead person's return had taken shape a good 18 months before Rosina's death. It had been another woman named Marianna Saligerin who had died.[46] While still alive, Marianna had been credited with a certain ability to cure people, proving that it was sometimes the practice of certain "magic" in life that led people to think that the practitioner would continue to act with his or her magic posthumously. Mariana had tried to do some witchcraft, but for van Swieten, that was just a pathetic strategy of self-promotion, as she attempted to cloak the remedies she sold with "mystery." In some cases, Marianna had then predicted the day of her "patients' recovery and guessed right: but, come on, do we still believe in these stories?"

In fact, van Swieten tried to downplay the most uncomfortable rumors about the healer. Recently scrutinized archival documents reveal that Marianna exercised her role as a practitioner of magic not only in the therapeutic sphere but also in the realm of clairvoyance. Though van Swieten did not tell this story, a couple in Mariana's village once lost their money, and she helped them find it. This was perhaps because she also possessed a kind of mirror with which, when a theft occurred, she could spot the culprit. It was reported that on that particular occasion, she discovered the thief, but he did not confess. He later fell ill and died, which was treated as further evidence of Marianna's powers.[47]

Still, despite such incidents, the woman had passed away with the comfort of the sacraments, van Swieten recalled, and had been buried in consecrated ground. This, however, had not been enough: the villagers had complained of unidentifiable *infestationes nocturnae*. Other members of the community had also died, but no one knew how. Old men, women, and children had begun to move to a neighboring village, leaving Frei Hermersdorf with only strong, young men who could counter the attacks.

A petition was then sent to the Episcopal Consistory in Olomouc, which sent first one and then another commission to Frei Hermersdorf to investigate. They exhumed and inspected the bodies that had been buried since Marianna's internment, which amounted to some 30 bodies in all. Nineteen of those corpses had been found without signs of rot, including the earliest, Marianna, and the last of the series, Rosina. Witnesses had presented Rosina herself as a healer and therefore someone destined to return after death, but in fact, she was the last victim of Marianna's alleged posthumous magic. Put another way, Rosina was the last to have had the misfortune of dying during those 18 months of terror, of being exhumed and found insufficiently decayed. Had she not been a healer, it would have been the same. In any case, the 19 corpses ultimately were set on fire on January 31 and burned to ash.

Van Swieten had every strategic reason to belittle the professionalism of the surgeon-barbers who had conducted the inspection. But what also made an impression upon him was the profoundly cursory way in which so-called experts were confirming the existence of posthumous magic, as the manuscripts relayed. In the cemeteries, the inspectors would apparently make incisions on corpses using long irons. They then would note if anything came out that could be interpreted as blood. What undoubtedly also astonished van Swieten was that, in contrast to the "incorruption" or "un-decomposition" referred to in the reports, in practice, the bodies examined and confirmed to be affected by posthumous magic were judged as such when only a portion of their bodies was intact. The records, for example, contain minimal expressions such as "intact thighs" or "well-preserved left arm."[48] In other words, individuals were accused of vampirism only for having a leg or arm that had not yet been completely skeletonized. This was sheer madness. Even considering the pressure from the inhabitants of the localities involved, the Olomouc Episcopal Consistory was responsible for this folly, which now was in full view for all of Europe.

Thus, without delay, and on the strength of van Swieten's *Notes on Vampirism*, Maria Theresa crafted her own reaction. In her *rescript* of March 1, 1755, she explained that she was perplexed by visions "presented by dreams and imagination." Of course, she was not in a position to argue that vampirism and other magical phenomena could not occur in principle, but there was one thing she certainly could do: remove from ecclesiastical authorities the jurisdiction and competence to investigate magic. Henceforth, investigations into vampirism as well as "spirits, witchcraft, disinterment or . . . someone who claims to be possessed" would belong to the civil authority, which would have to carry out the appropriate investigations with the help of a "reasonable medical expert," that is, a true *physicus* who had studied at university, not a mere barber-surgeon.[49]

Medicine, with its "imperialist" approach, had "monstrified" beings that only existed in the beliefs of subjugated peoples. Medicine had spread fear in Western Europe; its practitioners and theorists would continue to talk about the possibility that vampires were real for more than 20 years. Yet with Maria Theresa's backing, medicine was being named as the dispenser of certainties. In this respect, one cannot but agree with Nick Groom that "geopolitics was both the cause and the solution of the problem."[50]

Marie Theresa's *Rescript* concluded, "Therefore, from case to case, news will be given to us." In what Gábor Klaniczay has called "an early manifestation of so-called enlightened absolutism," decisions were taken away from the bishops of more or less peripheral dioceses and entrusted instead to the centripetalism of Vienna.[51] Out with the local conventions: now, centralized and secular legal jurisdiction was extolled. That jurisdiction clearly stated that if one came across strange apparitions, the investigation should be handled by the civil authority, supported by doctors, and the documents should be taken to court. And no vampire would ever have the courage to disturb Maria Theresa's peaceful nights.[52]

Notes

1 (S.N.) Glaser, Bericht (1731), in *Mortuus non mordet. Dokumente zum Vampirismus 1869–1791*, ed. Klaus Hamberger (Turia & Kant, 1992), 46–49, in particular 46.
2 Hamberger, *Mortuus non mordet*, 48.
3 On the Turkish vampire, Salim Fikret Kirgi, *Osmanli Vampirleri: Söylenceler*, Etkiler, Tepkiler (İletişim Yayınları, 2018). For a more accessible reading, we recommend the earlier work by the same author, from which this volume originated, Fikret Kirgi, "An Early Modern Horror Story: The Folk Beliefs in Vampire-like Supernatural Beings in the Ottoman Empire and the Consequent Responses in the Sixteenth and Seventeenth Centuries" (MA thesis, Central European University, Budapest, 2017).
4 Thomas M. Bohn, *The Vampire: Origins of a European Myth* (2016), trans. Francis Ipgrave (Berghahn, 2019), 84.
5 Glaser, Bericht, 49.
6 Antoine Faivre, "Du vampire villageois aux discours des clercs (Genèse d'un imaginaire à l'aube des Lumières)," in *Les vampires, Colloque de Cerisy* (Albin Michel, 1993), 45–74, in particular 49.
7 Bohn, *The Vampire*, 87–88.
8 Paul Barber, *Vampires, Burial, and Death: Folklore and Reality* (Yale University Press, 1990), 153–76.
9 J. Flückinger, [n.n.] Siegele, and J. F. Baumgarten, "Visum et repertum" in *Mortuus non mordet*, ed. Hamberger (1732), 49–54, in particular 52.
10 Flückinger, Siegele, and Baumgarten, "Visum et repertum," 53.
11 T. Vukanović, "The Vampire (in the Belief and Customs of the Gipsies in the Province of Kosovo-Metohija, Stari Ras and Novopazarski Sandžak, Yugoslavia)," *Journal of the Gipsy Lore Society* 36 (1957): 125–33; 37 (1958): 21–31, 111–18; 38 (1959): 44–55.
12 Faivre, "Du vampire villageois," 50–51, 64–65.
13 Anon. [J.B. de la Varenne], "Question physique sur une espèce de prodige dûment attesté," in *Le Glaneur historique, moral, littéraire, galant, et calottin*, 3 March 1732, n.p.
14 M.M. Ranfft, *Tractat von dem Kauen und Schmatzen der Todten in Gräbern, worin die wahre Beschaffenheit derer Hungarischen Vampyrs und Blut-Sauger gezeigt, auch alle von dieser Materie bißher zum Vorschein gekommene Schrifften recensiret werden* (Teubner, 1734), 179.
15 Richard Sugg, *The Real Vampires: Death, Terror, and The Supernatural* (Amberly Publishing, 2019), 27.
16 K.F. Schertz, *Magia posthuma . . .* (Olomouc, Rosenburg, 1704 or 1706), § 19, n.p.
17 Ferdinand Bischof and Christian Ritter d'Elvert, "Zur Geschichte des Glaubens an Zauberer, Hexen und Vampyre," in *Mähren und Österreich: Schlesien . . .* (Robrer, 1859), 154–56.
18 Daniel Wojtucki, '"Wampiryczne dzieci'—ofiary wierzeń w magia posthuma na Morawach w XVIII w.," in *Klio. Czasopismo poświęcone dziejom Polski i powszechnym* 53 (2020): 211–46.

19 Klaus Berger, "Zum Hexen- und Vampyrglauben in Nordmahren," in *Zeitschrift des Vereines für die Geschichte Mährens und Schlesiens* 8 (1904): 201–24, in particular 217–19.
20 Friedrich Lucae, *Schlesiens curiose Denckwürdigkeiten, oder vollkommene Chronica Von Ober- und Nieder-Schlesien* (Knoch, 1689), 2233.
21 Gerhard. van Swieten, "Considerazione intorno alla pretesa magia postuma" (1755), in van Swieten, *Vampyrismus*, ed. P. Violante (Flaccovio, 1988), 16, notes * and ** added by Giuseppe Valeriano Vannetti.
22 Wojtucki, "Wampiryczne dzieci," 222.
23 M. Weinrich, "Proœmium," in *Strix sive de ludificatione daemonum dialogi tres*, ed. G. Pico della Mirandola (Strasbourg: n.e., 1612), 1–60, in particular 10; H. More, *An Antidote against Atheism . . .* (Flesher, 1655), 209–13, in particular 212–13. Stephen Gordon, "Emotional Practice and Bodily Performance in Early Modern Vampire Literature," in *Preternature. Critical and Historical Studies on the Preternatural* 6 (2017): 93–124.
24 Flückinger, Siegele, and Baumgarten, "Visum et repertum," 53.
25 On this subject, the scholarly community owes much to the seminal archival research of historian Jan Bombera, who showed how this professionalization corresponded, especially after the first decade of the eighteenth century, to an increase in fees.
26 Jan Bombera, "Posmrtná magie na Libavsku," in *Z dob prvních letů na Koštěti*, eds. R. Zuber and J. Bombera (Moravská expedice, 2000), 38–55. M. Slezáková, *Soumrak pověrčivosti—Poslední velký případ vampyrismu na Moravsko-Slezském pomezí* (Masaryk University, 2013).
27 Claude Lecouteux, *Histoire des vampires. Autopsie d'un mythe* (Editions Imago, 2014), 116.
28 A. Schmidt, "Ein Dokument zur Geschichte der schlesischen Hexenprozesse," in *Zeitschrift für Geschichte und Kulturgeschichte Österreichische Schlesiens*, vol. 2 (1906–1907), 193–94.
29 Van Swieten, "Considerazione intorno alla pretesa magia postuma," 15.
30 Ádám Mézes, "Doubt and Diagnosis: Medical Experts and the Returning Dead of the Southern Habsburg Borderland (1718–1766)" (Ph.D. dissertation, Central European University, Budapest, 2020), 236–42.
31 Van Swieten, "Considerazione intorno alla pretesa magia postuma," 15–16.
32 Jan Bombera, "O posmrtné magii na libavském panství v 18. Století" (1984), *Okresní archív v Olomouci* (1985): 79–93.
33 For the reconstruction of the normative dimension of witchcraft trials and those associated with them, see P. Kreuz, "Witch Hunts in Eastern Central Europe," in *The Routledge History of Witchcraft*, ed. Johannes Dillinger (Routledge, 2019), 171–87. Daniel Wojtucki, *Publiczne miejsca straceń na Dolnym Śląsku od XV do połowy XIX wieku* (Fundacja Zamek Chudów, 2009).
34 Mézes, "Doubt and Diagnosis," 397–455.
35 Norbert Conrads, *Schlesien in der Frühmoderne: Zur politischen und geistigen Kultur eines habsburgischen Landes* (Böhlau, 2009), 1–175; T. Parma, "'Bishops Are not Necessary for Reform.' Religious Orders in the Catholic Reconquista of Bohemia and Moravia: Two Case Studies," in *Papacy, Religious Orders, and International Politics in the Sixteenth and Seventeenth Centuries*, ed. Massimo Carlo Giannini (Viella, 2013), 165–82.
36 Martin Luther, *Ob man vor dem Sterben fliehen möge* (1527), in *Werke. . .* (Böhlau, 1901), vol. 23, 323–86. Cfr. Craig M. Koslofsky, *The Reformation of the Dead: Death and Ritual in Early Modern Germany, 1450–1700* (Palgrave Macmillan, 2000); Thomas W. Laqueur, *The Work of the Dead: A Cultural History of Mortal Remains* (Princeton University Press, 2015), 99–106.
37 Mézes, "Doubt and Diagnosis," 406.
38 Bohn, *The Vampire*, 105.

39 Wojtucki, *Magia Posthuma*, 421–41.
40 See the excellent enquiry by Georg Tallar, *Visum Repertum Anatomico-Chyrurgicum* (Mößle, 1784). Ádám Mézes, "Vampire Contagion as a Forensic Fact: The Vampires of Medveđa in 1732," in *Historical Studies on Central Europe*, vol. 1 (2021), 149–76.
41 Gábor Klaniczay, "Gerard van Swieten und die Anfänge des Kampfes gegen Aberglauben in der Habsburg-Monarchie," in *Acta Historica Academiae Scientiarum Hungaricae* 34 (1988): 225–47; S. Horn, "'damit sy in ain rechte erfahrenheit der practighen khummen.'—Der praktische Unterricht für akademische Ärzte vor den Reformen durch Van Swieten," in *Wiener Gespräche zur Sozialgeschichte der Medizin*, Vorträge des Internationalen Symposions an der Universität Wien 9–11 November 1994, eds. H. Grössing, S. Horn and T. Aigner (Erasmus, 1996), 75–96.
42 Van Swieten, "Considerazione intorno alla pretesa magia postuma," 10–11.
43 Nick Groom, *The Vampire: A New History* (University Press, 2018), 70. See also N. Ristović, "Latin and Vernacular Relations in the Eighteenth and Nineteenth Centuries: The Serbian Case," in *Latin at the Crossroads of Identity: The Evolution of Linguistic Nationalism in the Kingdom of Hungary*, eds. G. Almási and L. Šubarić (Brill, 2015), 256–77.
44 Van Swieten, "Considerazione intorno," 17.
45 Van Swieten, "Considerazione intorno," 15.
46 M. Slezáková, "Charakteristika a historická interpretace vampýrských událostí na Moravě a ve Slezsku. Na případu Marianny Saligerové ze Svobodných Heřmanic na Bruntálsku," *Vlastivědný věstník moravský* 64 (2012): 132–35.
47 Wojtucki, *Magia Posthuma*, 422–23.
48 Wojtucki, *Magia Posthuma*, 427–28; and Mézes, "Doubt and Diagnosis," 410.
49 *Sammlung aller k. k. Verordnungen u. Gesetze vom Jahre 1740 bis 1780, die unter der Regierung des Kaisers Joseph des II. theils noch ganz bestehen, theils zum Theile abgeändert sind, als ein Hilfs- und Ergänzungsbuch zu dem Handbuche aller unter der Regierung des Kaisers Joseph des II. für die k. k. Erbländer ergangenen Verordnungen und Gesetze in einer chronologischen Ordnung*, vol. 3, no. 385 (Mößle 1786), 172–73.
50 Groom, *The Vampire*, 67. Also see D. Arlaud, "Vampire, Aufklarung und Staat: Eine militarmedizinische Mission in Ungarn, 1755–1756," in *Gespenster und Politik. 16. bis 21. Jahrhundert*, eds. C. Gantet and F. D'Almeida (Wilhelm Fink, 2007).
51 Gábor Klaniczay, *The Uses of Supernatural Power: The Transformation of Popular Religion in Medieval and Early-Modern Europe* (Princeton University Press, 1992), 171–72.
52 After the Rescript of 1755, cases clearly continued to occur, but the few official documents no longer listed them as "vampiric." In 1784 Joseph II again intervened legislatively, indirectly giving evidence of the persistence of the phenomenon, at least in Greek-rite communities. F.X. Linzbauer, ed., *Codex sanitario-medicinalis Hungariae*, vol. 3 (Typis Caesareo-Regiae Scientiarum Universitatis, 1853), 122. However, there remained the entire area that did not belong to the domains of the Habsburg Monarchy. For example, Tony Faivre, *Les vampires. Essai historique, critique et littéraire* (Losfeld, 1962), 69–77; Daniela Soloviova-Horville, *Les vampires. Du folklore slave a la litterature occidentale* (L'Harmattan, 2011), 87–88; Bohn, *The Vampire*, 124–217.

Select Bibliography

Barber, Paul. *Vampires, Burial, and Death: Folklore and Reality*. Yale University Press, 1990.
Bohn, Thomas M. *The Vampire: Origins of a European Myth* (2016). Translated by Francis Ipgrave. Berghahn, 2019.

Bombera, Jan. "Posmrtná magie na Libavsku." In *Z dob prvních letů na Koštěti*, edited by Rudolph Zuber and Jan Bombera. Moravská expedice, 2000.

de Ceglia, Francesco Paolo. *Vampyr. Storia naturale della resurrezione*. Einaudi, 2023.

Groom, Nick. *The Vampire: A New History*. Yale University Press, 2018.

Hamberger, Klaus, ed. *Mortuus non mordet. Dokumente zum Vampirismus 1869–1791*. Turia & Kant, 1992.

Fikret Kirgi, Salim. "An Early Modern Horror Story: The Folk Beliefs in Vampire-like Supernatural Beings in the Ottoman Empire and the Consequent Responses in the Sixteenth and Seventeenth Centuries." M.A. thesis, Central European University, Budapest, 2017.

Louis, Stella. *Croire aux vampires au siecle des Lumieres. Entre savoir et fiction*. Garnier, 2022.

Mézes, Ádám. "Doubt and Diagnosis: Medical Experts and the Returning Dead of the Southern Habsburg Borderland (1718–1766)." Ph.D. dissertation, Central European University, Budapest, 2020.

Nowosadtko, Jutta. "Der 'Vampyrus Serviensis' und sein Habitat: Impressionen von der österreichischen Militärgrenze." *Militär und Gesellschaft in der Frühen Neuzeit* 8 (2004).

Ranfft, M.M. *Tractat von dem Kauen und Schmatzen der Todten in Gräbern, worin die wahre Beschaffenheit derer Hungarischen Vampyrs und Blut-Sauger gezeigt, auch alle von dieser Materie bißher zum Vorschein gekommene Schrifften recensiret werden*. Teubner, 1734.

Schertz, Karl Ferdinand. *Magia posthuma*. . . . Olomouc, Rosenburg, 1704 or 1706.

Schürmann, Thomas. *Nachzehrerglauben in Mitteleuropa*. Elwert, 1990.

Soloviova-Horville, Daniela. *Les vampires. Du folklore slave a la litterature occidentale*. L'Harmattan, 2011.

Wojtucki, Daniel. *Magia posthuma. Procesy i egzekucje zmarłych na Śląsku i Morawach w XVI-XVIII wieku*. Wrocław, 2022.

INDEX

Note: Page locators in *italic* indicate a figure, and page locators in **bold** indicate a table on the corresponding page.

FSC
www.fsc.org
MIX
Papier | Fördert gute Waldnutzung
FSC® C083411

Kolibri 360 GmbH
Ferdinand-Jühlke-Straße 7
99095 Erfurt, Deutschland
produktsicherheit@kolibri360.de